SAVAGE SAND AND SURF

The Hurricane Sandy Disaster

Edited by
Lisa A. Eargle and Ashraf Esmail

University Press of America,® Inc.
Lanham · Boulder · New York · Toronto · Plymouth, UK

Copyright © 2015 by
University Press of America,® Inc.
4501 Forbes Boulevard
Suite 200
Lanham, Maryland 20706
UPA Acquisitions Department (301) 459-3366

Unit A, Whitacre Mews, 26-34 Stannary Street,
London SE11 4AB, United Kingdom

British Library Cataloging in Publication Information Available

Library of Congress Control Number: 2014958941
ISBN: 978-0-7618-6544-5 paperback
eISBN: 978-0-7618-6545-2

We dedicate this book to the people of the Mid-Atlantic Coast of the United States who were impacted by this disaster and who are still traveling on the long road to recovery.

CONTENTS

Contents

FIGURES

TABLES

FOREWORD

The mood was jubilant throughout the streets of the French Quarter from Canal Street to Jackson Square. An electrifying group of artists were lined up along the iron rod gate, just outside of the Saint Louis Cathedral. She stood out from the crowd. Vying for our business with her unpretentious compliments, she invited us to view her realistic handcrafted portraits. We were trapped in a cultural haze and could not resist the lure of her edgy depictions of ordinary people and life in the city. Convinced of her talents, another artful masterpiece was created.

A native of New Orleans, she made a living selling art on a bike cart, painting one-of-a-kind masterpieces and earning an extra income from local framing shops whenever she referred her customers. Life was good, until the unthinkable happen a few weeks later. She had no idea that her life would be turned upside down by Hurricane Katrina brewing in the Gulf. I often wondered about her and was she one of the lucky ones to escape the devastation of the storm.

While Hurricane Katrina had a major impact on the southern states in the gulf region of United States, it does not compare to forthcoming of the arrival of its counterpart nine years later. Super Storm Sandy's outlandish size and supernatural power encapsulated the northeastern most part of the United States from the coast of Maine to the shore of the Carolinas- extending inland as far as Michigan. Everything in her path was significantly altered or destroyed. Families, communities, and businesses endured nature's most horrific storm and are still rebuilding from the aftermath.

One can only imagine the amount of loss, hurt, and disappointment of the resulting effects of major storms, like Hurricane Katrina and Super Storm Sandy. Families were separated, homes and businesses were demolished, and food resources were scarce; thereby, creating financial hardships for many of its victims. Many families had to rely on close relatives, Red Cross, and government assistance programs to survive the harsh realities of life after the storm. Just merely existing had become the priority for those who did not escape.

Living with instant loss and abandonment overwhelmed many families who had to relocate without compromise. Communities suffered the loss of cultural ingenuity and vitality, which created a temporary shift in how members of the community responded and interacted socially, mentally, and emotionally. The human spirit was relentlessly snuffed out as families were overcome with grief over the loss of a love one, destruction of property, and limited monetary resources. As a result despair set in and forced families to face the unforgiving truths of living without the basic essentials. Because of these harsh realities, debilitating mental and physical illnesses have played a major role in storm victims' determination to rebuild and adjust to new standards of living expectations, i.e., ideals, cultures, communities, communication, and cost of living expense.

Rebuilding after loss and devastation is not an easy task. It takes a concerted effort of national, state, and local governments, communities, and families, coupled with the mind, body, and spirit to recreate favorable life conditions. Hurricane Katrina's landfall occurred almost a decade ago and the citizens of New Orleans are still experiencing slow and steady progress. Community renewal efforts are almost non-existent in some areas because of the sea level and the potential for more natural disasters. In addition, there is no sustainable economic backing to support the return of locals who once inhabited low-lying areas. Likewise, the victims of Super Storm Sandy are still experiencing slow growth due to bureaucratic setbacks. Gaining access to public funding for home restoration and replacement of possessions remains a challenge.

Recovering from nature's fiercest storms can be devastating and affect every aspect of a person's life. The research presented in this book provides readers with in depth insight regarding destructive weather events. It educates readers on how to take proactive measures to prepare for destructive unforeseen weather patterns and safeguard against potential damage. A sense of urgency is also created in effort to heighten awareness of the dangers of unpredictable weather, while raising and extending one's compassion and humility towards others.

Sonia Martin, EdD, Literacy Coach
Onslow County Schools
Jacksonville, North Carolina

PREFACE

When Hurricane Sandy slammed ashore in late October 2012, it became one of the costliest natural disasters in United States' history (CNN Library, 2013). Its impact on the mid-Atlantic coast quickly drew comparisons to Hurricane Katrina's devastation of the Gulf Coast in 2005 (Fischetti, 2012). While tropical weather systems are nothing new to the United States, a storm of Sandy's size, occurring so late in an otherwise quiet hurricane season, and hitting one of the most populous and urbanized areas of the country, makes this storm noteworthy. Unfortunately, climate scientists, government officials, and others have warned that Sandy-like scenarios may become more commonplace in the future, as a result of global warming, climate change, and population patterns (Halverson and Rabenhorst, 2013). Moreover, just when Sandy's devastation seems to be a part of the past and that life has moved onward, stories such as the recent fire at a partially destroyed motel in Point Pleasant, New Jersey (where families left homeless by Sandy were staying until the building caught fire) once again remind us that everything and everyone has not returned to normal (Rose, 2014). Although the storm has faded from the lead stories of the daily news, like many disasters, Sandy's effects will continue to be far-reaching and felt for years to come.

Savage Sand and Surf: The Hurricane Sandy Disaster explores the different features and impacts of Hurricane Sandy. The objectives of this book are multifold. First, we show how disasters like Sandy are created by both nature and society. For example, in the chapter, "An Unforgettable Foe," the meteorological origins of Sandy and the social characteristics of the mid-Atlantic region that contributed to the disaster are discussed in the context of several disaster theoretical frameworks.

Secondly, we document how disasters intersect with vulnerable populations, to further magnify impacts and worsen recovery situations. In the chapter, "No Disabled Left Behind," Anaza and Eargle explore the impacts of disasters like Sandy on disabled populations and propose a disaster preparedness plan to improve the survival and recovery of this population.

Third, we address how social institutions adapt to disaster situations. In "Mitigation for University Health Systems and Transfer Trauma," Greene examines how disasters like Sandy affect health care provision. Weeber examines the economic impacts of Sandy in "Fast and Slow Capitalism."

Fourth, this volume discusses Hurricane Sandy in the context of previous, similar disasters. In addition to the Esmail and Eargle chapter, McCamey and Murty compare Sandy and Katrina in their examination of the politics surrounding access to federal relief funds. Frailing and Harper compare Sandy to Hurricanes Katrina and Gustav in "Putting Hurricane Sandy In Context." Fifth, we examine the recovery process, which is addressed by several chapters, including Borland and Scardino's chapter, "Surviving Sandy, Rebuilding Community," and Gulliver-Garcia's chapter, "Hugs, Hands, and Hope."

Finally, we wanted to utilize a variety of perspectives to investigate this disaster, to produce a well-rounded, more holistic view of the disaster event and its implications. Disaster research from a variety of disciplines, including Sociology, Criminal Justice, Political Science, and Marketing, are presented in this volume. Moreover, academic and first person accounts of the storm are also covered in various chapters. While this volume does not address all of the issues surrounding the Hurricane Sandy disaster, we believe that by producing this volume, discussions of disaster creation, impacts, and resiliency will be facilitated. This will lead to a better understanding of natural disasters by governments, researchers, emergency management personnel, and average citizens.

Lisa A. Eargle, PhD and Ashraf M. Esmail, PhD

REFERENCES

CNN Library. 2013. Hurricane Sandy Fast Facts. July 13. http://www.cnn.com/2013/07/13/world/americas/hurricane-sandy-fast-facts/

Fischetti, M. 2012. Sandy versus Katrina, and Irene: Monster hurricanes by the numbers. *Scientific American*, October 29. http://www.scientificamerican.com/article/sandy-vs-katrina-and-irene/

Halverson, J.B. and Rabenhorst, T. 2013. Hurricane Sandy: The science and impacts of a superstorm. *Weatherwise*, March-April. http://www.weatherwise.org/Archives/Back%20Issues/2013/March-April%202013/hurricane-sandy-full.html

Rose, L. 2014. Sandy victims were living at Point Pleasant Beach motel destroyed by fire. The Star-Ledger, March 21. http://www.nj.com/ocean/index.ssf/2014/03/point_pleasant_beach_motel_destroyed_by_fire_housed_hurricane_sandy_victims_after_storm.html

ACKNOWLEDGMENTS

The editors would like to thank all of the contributors to this volume for their interest and hard work on this important topic, the Hurricane Sandy disaster.

CHAPTER ONE
AN UNFORGETTABLE FOE:
AN OVERVIEW OF THE
HURRICANE SANDY DISASTER

Lisa A. Eargle

In the sections that follow, I provide a brief timeline for the Hurricane Sandy event, from its first origins as a tropical wave to being a "super storm" to a low pressure off the Canadian coast. Next, the aspects of this storm made it a unique meteorological event to be examined. I also discuss what makes this event unique socially and economically, exploring some of the impacts that Sandy had on mid-Atlantic communities and the lessons learned from those impacts. Finally, three disaster process models are presented and applied to the Hurricane Sandy disaster, to better understand how such disasters are created, unfold, and resolved in society.

STORM TIMELINE

In October 2013, it was getting late in the Atlantic Hurricane season, which officially runs from June 1 to November 30. Although tropical systems can form as late as mid-October or November (such as the 2005 season), it is not a regular annual occurrence. Most tropical storms or hurricanes that threaten the United States emerge in late August or early September—the peak of the season (National Hurricane Center, 2013). So when a tropical wave[1] formed on October 11, 2013, off of the West African coast, it did not necessarily indicate that the Unite States would experience a hurricane. It was something to note and monitor meteorologically, but nothing to be overly concerned about at that point.

Seven days later, the entity entered into the Caribbean Sea as a weak wave. Two days later, on October 20, banding features began to appear in the satellite

1

imagery and signs of a deepening convection emerged. These were features indicative of a tropical system beginning to take shape. On the next day, the entity became a low pressure[2] system located approximately 200 miles south of Jamaica in the western Caribbean. From there, fairly rapid development began to occur. On the 22nd of October, the entity became a tropical depression,[3] with sustained winds of 38 mph, and was located further southward at approximately 305 miles southwest of Kingston, Jamaica. Later that day, it became a named tropical system, Tropical Storm[4] Sandy, with sustained winds of 45 mph.

The storm began to change direction, moving northward towards Jamaica. On October 24, Sandy became a hurricane,[5] with winds of 74 mph and a storm "eye" clearly visible in its center. This center was located about 80 miles south of Kingston, Jamaica. It later struck Jamaica as a Category 1 hurricane.[6] Despite crossing land, it continued rapid development, strengthening into a Category 3 hurricane (with sustained winds of 115) as it slammed into Cuba on October 25. As the storm crossed Cuba, the storm ran into mountainous terrain and wind shear,[7] which weakened it.

Once exiting Cuba on October 26, Sandy headed northward into the Bahamas, where it regained strength and became a hurricane once again. The storm also increased dramatically in spatial size, to having a maximum sustained wind radius of 100 nautical miles, while traveling through the Bahamas. On October 28, Sandy passed within 200 miles east of the North Carolina coast line. On October 29, the storm intensified into a Category 2 hurricane and changed direction, heading northwest towards the eastern coastline of the United States. At this point, it was approximately 220 miles southeast of Atlantic City, New Jersey. As it headed into colder waters, Sandy dropped to an extra-tropical cyclone,[8] losing its warm water core. It became instead, a storm fueled by sharp contrasts in air masses, developing a cold water core, much like a dreaded Nor'easter,[9] which can occur in the winter months along the Atlantic coast.

Sandy continued to move towards the shoreline of the United States, with its center eventually striking Brigantine, New Jersey late on October 29. Heavy rains and storm surge impacted the east coast shore line from North Carolina to Massachusetts, including the New York City metropolitan area. As the storm continued moving inland, with its eye passing through New Jersey, Delaware, and Pennsylvania, it further weakened. However the heavy rains continued inland and blizzard conditions occurred in West Virginia as the storm's moisture collided with colder air temperatures. By October 31, as the storm entered Ohio, Sandy no longer had a discernable "eye" and the storm core had become difficult to locate. It continued moving inland, eventually merging with a low pressure over Ontario, Canada, on November 2, and was eventually dragged eastward out to sea (Blake, Kimberlain, Berg, Cangialosi, and Beven, 2013).

Figure 1.1 Sandy's Path

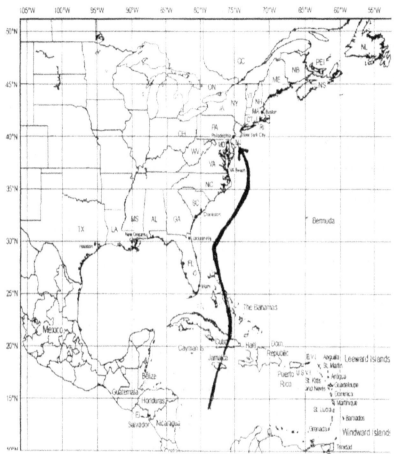

References: Halas, Darren. 2012. "Hurricane Sandy 2012: Path Is Still Not Clear." The World Electronic. http://z6mag.com/wp-content/uploads/2012/10/hurricane-Sandy-projected -path.jpg. National Hurricane Center.2014. "Blank Atlantic Hurricane Tracking chart." http:// www.nhc.noaa.gov/tracking-charts.shtml

SANDY'S UNIQUE METEOROLOGICAL FEATURES

There are several features that make Hurricane Sandy an unusual storm. It was a late season storm and although storms can and do form that late in the season, it is not an occurrence that happens every year. Although these late season storms can be very strong (such as Wilma in 2005), most of the time they tend to be weaker storms and have limited impact.

Since many of these storms tend to form in the Caribbean or around the Bahamas, they tend to get caught in the Loop Current.[10] This can inhibit their ability to affect the densely populated areas of the northeastern United States. Or, if they do continue to travel northward, paralleling the U.S. coast, they tend to strike the Canadian provinces and not the U.S. (National Hurricane Center, 2013).

This typical pattern of late season storms was altered in the case of Sandy by several other meteorological systems in place. There was a strong blocking[11] high pressure, located over southeast Canada, which would not allow the storm to continue a northward trajectory. A low pressure trough[12] in the middle of the U.S. became stronger, with part of this system breaking loose and entering the south-eastern U.S. This trough, along with very warm ocean temperatures and a decrease in wind shear, helped to fuel Sandy's re-development in the Atlantic. The combination of the trough in the middle of the U.S. and the high pressure to the north steered Sandy westward into the U.S., instead of allowing it to stay off-shore.

Sandy was also a very large storm, with its maximum sustained winds extending outward from the center for 100 nautical miles, and its rainfall extending even further outward. During its life span, the storm impacted Jamaica, Cuba, Haiti, the Bahamas, Florida, Georgia, South and North Carolina, Virginia, West Virginia, District of Columbia, Maryland, Delaware, New Jersey, New York, Pennsylvania, Ohio, Connecticut, Rhode Island, and Massachusetts. Most tropical systems (with the exception of notorious ones, such as Katrina) do not affect this much geography in their life course.

For a short period of time, Sandy was also a hybrid storm. It contained the features of a tropical system, in terms of its wind and rain patterns, but also transitioned from having a warm water core to a storm fueled by contrasts in air masses and having a cold water core. It was also, in a sense, a hybrid storm because of the great contrasts in weather impacts that it created. New Jersey and much of the Atlantic coast experienced heavy rain, high winds, and storm surge. Inland, West Virginia experienced blizzard conditions and heavy snowfall. It also shifted from having its strongest thunderstorms in the northern quadrant of the system (which is the usual pattern for tropical systems), to having its strongest thunderstorms located on the southwestern side (Blake et. al, 2013).

The coastal flooding impacts of the storm were also exacerbated by coming ashore during a full moon and high tide (Borenstein, 2012). Finally, New Jersey and its neighbor states are seldom hit by hurricanes. During the 1900 to 2010 time period, New Jersey was struck only three times by a hurricane. Areas most frequently struck by hurricanes are Florida, Louisiana, Texas, and North Carolina, and nations within or bordering the Caribbean Sea (National Hurricane Center, 2013).

Table 1.1 Saffir-Simpson Scale[6]

Hurricane Strength Category	Wind Speed, in miles per hour (mph)	Air Press. in millibars (mb)	Damage Amount	Storm Surge, in feet (ft)
1	74–95	980 & higher	Minimal–damage to vegetation and signs; coastal road flooding	4–5
2	96–110	965–979	Moderate– signifi-cant damage to mobile homes and trees; flooding of roads near coast	6–8
3	111–130	945–964	Extensive–large trees down; mobile homes destroyed; structural damage to some buildings	9–12
4	131–155	920–944	Extreme–most trees downed; structural damage to many buildings; in-land flooding	13–18
5	156 & higher	919 & lower	Catastrophic–all trees downed; complete building destruction; flooding widespread	19 & higher

References: http://www.coolgeography.co.uk/9/Risky_Earth/HurricaneWhat/Saffir_ Simpson_scale.jpg and http://www.sayville.com/news/images10/SFD_Saffir_Simpson_ Scale.jpg

PRE-STORM PREPARATIONS

A key issue in preparing for situations like Hurricane Sandy is providing current information about the unfolding event to the public, government officials, businesses, and other organizations so that they are aware of the situation and its potential impacts (Fischhoff, 2006). The National Weather Service (NWS) and weather-related media organizations (such as The Weather Channel) followed Sandy from its beginnings as a wave to a full-blown hurricane and beyond. Regular updates (such as the "Hurricane Central" segment on the Weather Channel at 0:50 past the hour) announced the development of Sandy and discussed relevant watches and warnings for areas possibly impacted by the storm, as well as possible travel paths that the storm could take several days in advance. They also discussed possible precipitation levels, wind speeds, and wave size that the storm could produce (Weather Channel, 2012). Local news outlets (such as NBC affiliate channel six in South Florida) also forecast Sandy's development and potential impacts for their area (Huffington Post, 2012a). National news organizations such as The Huffington Post, CNN, and Reuters covered the development of Sandy and its potential impacts along the East Coast (Cherry, 2012).

As it became clear that Sandy was going to impact the states along the East Coast, governors declared states of emergency to dedicate resources to addressing the storm. In press conferences, these governors also encouraged residents to gather emergency supplies and/or evacuate from flood prone areas prior to the storm (Goldberg, 2012). President Obama, speaking from the federal government response center in Washington, alongside FEMA Director Craig Fulgate, emphasized that Hurricane Sandy was a `serious and big storm' and residents should take it seriously. A press release sent from the White House emphasized the same message (Huffington Post, 2012b).

Utility companies in neighboring states mobilized their crews in preparation to assist in post-storm repairs. Consolidated Edison (an electric utility serving New York) urged customers to avoid fallen power lines and keep refrigerators closed after the storm. Residents offered ideas for storm preparation on Facebook and other social media (Goldberg, 2012). New York City closed its mass transit system and ordered residents to evacuate low lying areas such as Battery Park City, Staten Island and the Rockaways (Peltz, Dobnik, and Hajela, 2012). Emergency shelters were opened for those who evacuated to seek shelter (Bryan, 2012). New York's school system was closed in advance of the storm. National Guard troops were sent to areas potentially impacted. Entertainment districts in New York and other areas closed (Peltz, Dobnik, and Hajela, 2012). Flights into and out of the potentially impacted areas were canceled in advance of the storm (CNN Library, 2013).

SANDY'S SOCIETAL IMPACTS

Population

Most hurricanes strike the Gulf Coast states, affecting major metropolitan areas like Miami, New Orleans, or Houston. The geographic size of these urban areas may be large, such as the 1200 square miles that encompasses Miami. The population size of these metropolitan areas may be large as well, with Miami having over 5.5 million residents.

However, none of these areas of urbanization encompass as much territory as the stretch of urban development from northern Virginia to Rhode Island. Nor do they contain the populations that major metropolitan areas in this region contain. For example, New York-Newark, NY-NJ-CT encompasses 3450 square miles and a population of over 18 million residents. Philadelphia PA-NJ-DE-MD encompasses almost 2000 square miles and a population of over 5 million persons.

Washington DC-VA-MD covers 1300 square miles and has 4.5 million residents (Cox, 2012).

When Hurricane Sandy slammed into the mid-Atlantic coast of the U.S., it struck one of the most populous and densely settled areas of the country. Hence, the consequences of impact would be large in the best case scenario and catastrophic in a worst case scenario, affecting many different aspects of American society. I briefly discuss some of the impacts that Sandy had on human health and well-being, infrastructure, economics, and government. Other chapters in this volume explore these and other issues further in depth.

Health

In terms of human health, at least 117 persons lost their lives, with 53 of those deaths occurring in New York and 34 in New Jersey (CNN Library, 2013). The majority of these deaths were due to drowning. Of those who drowned, many were found in areas ordered to evacuate because of the possibility of flooding. While the number of injuries is not known, many did seek medical attention for illnesses after evacuation. In New Jersey shelters alone, over 5,000 sought medical care. Millions experienced some type of short-term psychological distress; hundreds of thousands may continue to experience long-term and more serious kinds of psychological issues such as depression or post-traumatic stress disorder (Rettner, 2013).

Infrastructure

There were numerous impacts on infrastructure. Subway and commuter train service stopped in New York, New Jersey, Pennsylvania and District of Columbia, during the storm and many lines had to be repaired or replaced before normal travel resumed. Airlines discontinued service to major northeast airports, such as LaGuardia, Kennedy, and Newark, for the duration of the storm and while repairs took place. Electric power was interrupted for almost 7.9 million businesses and households, with these outages lasting for weeks for some customers. Three nuclear reactors shut down during the storm. Bellevue Hospital in New York City was forced to evacuate its patients after sustaining major damage. Fire destroys over 100 homes in Breezy Point, NY, and approximately 40,000 others needed emergency housing in New York alone. Residents in New York and New Jersey also experience gas shortages and rationing for weeks. Over 100 million miles of shore line is lost through erosion during the storm.

Economy

For first time since 1888, because of the weather, the New York Stock Exchange was closed. Broadway performances in New York City were canceled for several days. The New York Marathon was canceled, but many runners ran anyway to raise money for Sandy's victims. Casinos in New Jersey were ordered closed by the governor before the storm hit. Total losses due to Sandy reached the hundreds of billions of dollars. New York City's mayor estimated losses of $19 billion; New York State's governor estimated losses of $42 billion across New York. New Jersey losses were estimated to be around $37 billion.

Government

A State of Emergency was declared by governors of several states, including New York, New Jersey and West Virginia. Nearly 6700 National Guard troops were sent to the affected areas by other states, including Maine. Federal offices in the District of Columbia and elsewhere closed during the storm. The United Nations closed its offices in New York City in advance of the storm. Public schools in New York, New Jersey, and other affected areas closed. For those voters whose normal polling place was closed or who had been dislocated by the storm, ballot casting via email, fax or the nearest polling location were allowed for the 2012 presidential election. Over 350,000 persons applied for FEMA assistance, totaling over $403 million (CNN Library, 2013).

Lessons Learned

The National Weather Service did not classify Sandy as a hurricane as it came ashore, but used the term "post-tropical cyclone." The mayor of New York and others did not seem to understand that this type of storm could be just as dangerous and deadly as something called a "hurricane." Hence, the public and officials were surprised by the magnitude of damage and havoc created by the storm.

Since Sandy's strike, the National Weather Service has agreed to expand the definition of hurricane and tropical storm to include those storms that later transition to other forms. This will allow the NWS to issue hurricane watches and warnings (or tropical storm watches and warnings) to the public after these storms transition. Continuing to use the term "hurricane warning" will alert the public to the seriousness of the situation, because the public understands the concept of "hurricane" much better than "post-tropical cyclone" (Rice, 2013).

Another lesson learned was despite the presence of seawalls and sand dunes, many coastal communities do not have adequate protection from the storm surge of storms like Sandy. Because of rising sea levels from global warming, building structures will need to be built higher to withstand the onslaught of flood waters. Also proposals to build sea gates across New York Harbor, which can be closed during a storm to keep sea water out of the city, have been revived once again. Major cities in Europe have this type of structure in place.

Moreover, the flood maps that the Flood Insurance Program and other government agencies use are out dated. They do not reflect the impact that rising sea levels will have on current coastal storm flooding. Hence, not all homeowners are eligible to have the kind of insurance protection that they need to recover from such storms. Members of Congress also continue to question the desirability of asking tax payers to fund rebuilding in risk prone areas (Montgomery and Murray, 2012).

Understanding Disasters Like Sandy

Our understanding of disasters like Hurricane Sandy can be further enhanced by applying theoretical models to these events. Theoretical models are explanations for why and how a particular phenomenon occurs in society. They highlight for us the important contributors and outcomes of an event, as well as reveal the relationships between these factors and the processes through which something like a disaster unfolds (Neuman, 2003). By applying theoretical models to different disaster events (i.e., Hurricane Sandy, Hurricane Katrina, 2004 Indian Tsunami), we can see the commonalities between events as well as the features unique to each event (Sheoin and Zavestoki, 2012). This can help us better anticipate, prepare and prevent future disasters, or at least ameliorate some of the disaster's impacts (Erikson, 2010).

One theoretical model used in understanding disasters is the Pressure and Release (PAR) model, developed by Blaikie et. al in 1994. This particular disaster model focuses on the conditions that make a disaster possible in a society, the conditions of a society prior to disaster's impact. While this model has been applied primarily to disaster events in developing nations, such as droughts in Kenya (Schilderinck, 2009), floods in Mozambique (Anderskov, 2004), and landslides in Bolivia (Nathan, 2005), there are elements of the PAR model that are applicable to the United States and Hurricane Sandy too.

The PAR model argues that within societies, there are Root Causes of disaster. The Root Causes are identified as the political and economic system ideologies that influence how resources are distributed in society. Societies where resources are unequally distributed, where segments of the population have limited involvement in the decision making in society, are more prone to possessing these Root Causes (Zakour and Gillespie, 2013). These Causes are long-standing, historical conditions in the society.

The presence of these Root Causes creates a fertile ground from which present-day Dynamic Pressures exist (Rauken and Kelman, 2010). These Dynamic Pressures appear as types of under- and over-development in society. Under-development is exemplified by the absence or weakness of local institutions, investments, and markets, as well as limited freedom of the press and ethical standards in public life. Over-development appears in the form of rapid population growth, hyper-urbanization, environmental degradation, large expenditures on military, and escalating national debts (Anderskov, 2004).

These Dynamic Pressures create Unsafe Conditions in society, as exemplified by a fragile physical environment, a fragile local economy, vulnerable social groups, and a lack of disaster preparedness plans or operations. At some time, a Hazard (earthquake, hurricane, floods, tornado, and so forth) impacts the society. Whether or not a Disaster subsequently occurs is dependent on the society's Risk for disaster, which is determined by the type of Hazard facing the society and the society's Vulnerability (resulting from the progression in societal phases from Root Causes to Dynamic Pressures to Unsafe Conditions). To reduce the Risk of disaster, society needs to address the Root Causes and Dynamic Pressures that contribute to Vulnerability. Otherwise, the Pressures created by the increasing Vulnerability of society are released by the resulting impacts of the Hazard on society (Anderskov, 2004; Schilderinck, 2009).

Figure 1.2 Pressure and Release (PAR) Model

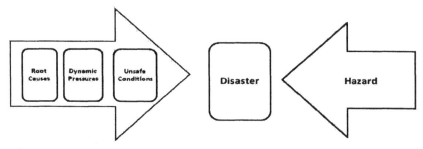

Reference: Androskov, 2004

Now that the components of the PAR model have been identified and defined, let us examine how this model applies to the United States, with an emphasis on the New York-New Jersey Area, and the Hurricane Sandy event. I will discuss how each of the PAR model's components is present within American society, particularly the New York-New Jersey region, and how they helped to contribute to the disaster that Hurricane Sandy created in that region.

Root Causes

The PAR model proposes that there are two broad Root Causes that contribute to a disaster occurring in a society. These Root Causes are Economic and Political Inequality. These inequalities express themselves in many different ways in American society; however, in the discussion below, I focus on a few of the ways that these Inequalities are found in America. In my discussion, I examine the U.S. as a whole and then I narrow my examination to the New York-New Jersey area—the area where Hurricane Sandy came ashore.

Economic Inequality

The United States is primarily a capitalist-based economy, where there is competition in the market for the buying and selling of goods and services. This includes human labor and other resources. With that said, however, some people have advantages over others in this competition. Differences in income by race, sex, education, occupation and so forth exist in the U.S. (Carl, 2013).

The Gini coefficient is a measure of economic inequality that compares the incomes of all persons living within an area, to see how equal are the distribution of those incomes. The values for the Gini coefficient range between 0, where there is perfect equality and everyone has the same income, and 1, where there is total inequality, where 1 person has all of the income and the others have zero income. In the United States, there is both great wealth and great impoverishment. The Gini coefficient for the U.S. is 0.467 (Bee, 2012); by comparison, the Gini coefficient for Sweden is 0.230 and 0.700 for Namibia. The U.S. Gini is much higher than many developed nations, but much lower than most developing nations (Carl, 2013).

If we look within the United States, there is great variation amongst counties in inequality levels, with some places having Gini coefficients as low as 0.207 and other places having Gini coefficients as high as 0.645. While many of the counties with the highest coefficients are located in the southern states, some counties within the northeast and Mid-Atlantic states also have relatively high coefficients. For example, New York City has a Gini coefficient of 0.607; Kings, New York has a Gini coefficient of 0.499. Some of the counties in neighboring New Jersey also have above average coefficients (Bee, 2012). Moreover, these levels of inequality have been increasing over time (U.S. Census Bureau, 2010).

Another way of looking at the issue of economic inequality is to examine the poverty rates for places, in comparison to the percentage of extremely wealthy in society. The poverty rate for the United States is 14.3 percent. Like the Gini coefficients, there is great variation within the U.S. poverty rates for places. While many of the highest poverty rates occur in the Southern states, New York has a poverty rate above the average (U.S. Census Bureau, 2012a). If we examine major metropolitan areas of the U.S., the cities of New York, NY and Newark, NJ have poverty rates well above the average at 18.7 and 23.9 percent, respectively (U.S. Census Bureau, 2012b). On the other hand, New York state has one the highest number of wealthy, with 168 thousand residents with assets of $1.5 million or more); New Jersey has a relatively large number of wealthy residents as well, with 79 thousand residents with assets of $1.5 million or more (U.S. Census Bureau, 2012c).

Political Inequality

The U.S. political system is a representative democracy, where power is divided into three branches at the federal and state levels, and further divided amongst various organizations at the local level (city mayor, city council, school boards, zoning boards, and so forth). With a few exceptions (felons, non-citizens, and those under age 18), most residents can register to vote in an election to select who will serve in government, from the local boards to President of the U.S.. Likewise, most citizens are free to seek political office if they are interested. However, successfully winning an election to political office is another matter. Running a successful political campaign is an expensive undertaking (Carl, 2013).

To be successfully elected to the U.S. Senate cost campaigns an average of $10.5 million. To be elected to the House of Representatives costs $1.7 million. The costs associated with campaigning have increased dramatically over time, between $300,000 and $800,000, in the last few years. Even mayoral races are expensive. Michael Bloomberg reportedly spent $268 million of his own $27 billion wealth to be successfully elected mayor of New York City for three terms (Huffington Post, 2013). However, most politicians are not Michael Bloomberg, so they must obtain most of their campaign funds from contributors. There are limits of how much money individuals can contribute directly to a campaign[13]; however, with the "Citizens United" Supreme Court ruling in 2008, restrictions on other donating entities have been removed[14] (Knowles, 2013). Therefore, many wealthy individuals such as the Koch Brothers (Koch Industries) and Sheldon Adelson (casino and resort magnate) donate to Super PAC[15] and 501(c) organizations[16] who then try to influence public policy (Toner, 2012).

Many of the major campaign contributors also are multi-national corporations. Some of the top contributors to recent national campaigns are Lockheed Martin (aerospace), Bank of America (finance), AT&T and Comcast (telecommunications), and Microsoft (computer software)(McIntyre and Hess, 2012). Moreover many corporations and political interest groups have lobbyists that regularly meet with politicians, to convince them to casts votes in favor of their organization. Lobbyists on average have a 40 percent success rate in having politicians change public policies within a four year period (Pinkham, 2010). With the costs associated with successful campaigns, the influx of money from all kinds of organizations, and with the regular contact of lobbyists, the average American citizen actually has little choice of who runs for elected office and the decisions made.

This may also be reflected in voter registration and election turnout rates. For the 2010 elections, approximately 60 percent of all U.S. residents eligible to register to vote actually registered. Approximately 42 percent actually voted. These registration and voting rates vary widely by place and race. Hawaii had the lowest (48 percent) and Maine had the highest (75 percent) registration rates. New York had a registration rate of 56 percent and New Jersey had a registration rate of 56 percent. Utah had the lowest voting rate (31 percent) and Maine had the highest voting rate (58 percent); New York had a voting rate of 38 percent and New Jersey had a voting rate of 35 percent (U.S. Census Bureau, 2012d). By race, whites and blacks had the highest rates of 46 and 43 percent; only 31 percent of Hispanics and Asians voted (U.S. Census Bureau, 2012e).

Dynamic Pressures

Dynamic Pressures—Underdevelopment

One dynamic pressure coming from a lack of investment is high unemployment rates. The unemployment rate for the U.S. at the end of 2012 was 7.6 percent. The unemployment rates ranged from a low of 4.3 percent in South Dakota to a high of

9.9 percent in Rhode Island. Both New York and New Jersey were experiencing above-average unemployment rates of 8.2 and 9.5 percent respectively (Bureau of Labor Statistics, 2014a). The situation was even worse when examining some metropolitan areas, with NY-Northern NJ-Long Island having an 8.5 percent, Atlantic City-Hammonton, NJ having a 14.9 percent, and Ocean City having a 17 percent unemployment rate (Bureau of Labor Statistics, 2014b). Many of these unemployed individuals were already experiencing financial difficulties; having a disaster damage their property could only worsen the situation.

Hence, another type of dynamic pressure is the location of housing and other buildings in low lying areas (Zakour and Gillespie, 2013). In the United States, those living in flood-prone areas must purchase flood insurance or risk total loss of material items value after a flood. Some jurisdictions prohibit development in areas with an excessive flood probability (Levin, accessed 2014), but many do not. Having inadequate rules about where building construction should take place can be viewed as a form of underdevelopment (Zakour and Gillespie, 2013).

After revised flood maps from FEMA were issued, over 33 thousand additional New Jersey homes were designated as being located in a flood zone that previously were not considered in a flood area. Owners would either have to elevate homes at least 4 feet or face higher insurance premiums. Thirty-seven thousand homes and 9300 rental units received major damage from Sandy from flooding. Forty thousand others received minor damage (Bates, 2013). In New York City, 35 thousand additional buildings were designated as being in a flood-zone (WABC-TV New York, 2013). In 2012, the U.S. government passed legislation that reduced the subsidizing of home owners flood insurance premiums, resulting in a large insurance price hike for many owners (Texas Association of Counties, 2014).

Dynamic Pressures—Overdevelopment

Two types of over-development are rapid population growth and hyper-urbanization. Certain areas of the U.S. have experienced both in recent decades. Between 1970 and 2010, the coastal population increased 39 percent. The average population density (persons per square mile) for coastal counties is 446, compared to 105 for the U.S. as a whole. Counties experiencing the largest increases in population since 1980 tend to be located along the Atlantic coast, including Kings, Queens, and Suffolk, NY, and Ocean, NJ (NOAA, 2013). Approximately 81 percent of the U.S. population now resides in urban areas, with the New York, NY-Newark, NJ comprising the most populated urban area with over 18 million residents (Huntington News, 2012). Coinciding with this rapid population growth and urbanization are the locating of buildings in flood prone areas (such as coastlines) due to real estate demand by consumers, or the creation of flood prone areas by the removal of vegetation and other natural flood control mechanisms, or the construction of elevated roadways that produce runoff to surrounding areas during storms (Konrad, 2014). These can be viewed as types of overdevelopment as well.

Unsafe Conditions

Unsafe Conditions can manifest in many ways within a society. One form of unsafe conditions is the creation of vulnerable groups, through the Dynamic Pressures in society. Lower income families are often put in danger because they live in areas where toxic materials are stored (Zakour and Gillespie, 2013). In the New York City area, many industrial sites with toxic materials are located in low-lying and waterfront sites. During coastal storms, such as Hurricane Sandy, these sites can be compromised and the toxic materials will drift into nearby residential areas. Residents will then come into unprotected contact with these materials during and after the storm, and these toxins may linger in the soil for decades after the storm (Byron and Braden, 2013).

Another group vulnerable to unsafe conditions is the disabled, who may have limited finances and may be dependent on the services of others to meet their daily needs (Feeney, 2012). The inability of the disabled to evacuate to safer facilities during Hurricane Sandy was a major issue in New York City. Even though New York City had an evacuation plan in place, many disabled faced desperate conditions after being trapped in flooded buildings or buildings without electricity. After filing law suits, a New York Court judge ruled in favor of the disabled plaintiffs (Beekman, 2013).

Also, the presence of sand dunes, coastal walls, and levees can lure residents into a false sense of security, assuming that these structures will hold back water from the ocean, rivers or lakes during a storm. However, as illustrated by Hurricane Katrina, these seemly impermeable structures can fail, putting thousands in danger (Handwerk, 2005). Similarly, some of the coastal protective structures during Hurricane Sandy were swept away, allowing storm surge to rip apart buildings and flood city streets (Richard Stockton College of New Jersey, 2012).

A third type of unsafe condition created during Hurricane Sandy was the misinterpretation of weather information. When the National Weather Service stopped referring to Sandy as a "hurricane," but instead called it a "post-tropical storm," many including the then mayor of New York City interpreted the information as meaning the storm was weakening or becoming less dangerous. Quite the contrary was occurring; instead the changing structure of Sandy prompted the name change, not the lessening severity of the situation (Rice, 2013).

Hazard Presence

Just simply being coastal states makes it possible for hurricanes to impact New York and New Jersey. Even though the probability of such a hazard hitting the region is relatively small from a historical viewpoint (only three storms in the 1900-2010 time period), it is still possible to have a hurricane. This was illustrated in the previous year by the movement of Hurricane Irene northward along the Atlantic Seaboard, negatively impacting the northeastern United States. Moreover some scientists have speculated that with global warming and the rise of sea levels that the intensity of hurricanes may increase over time (Geophysical Fluid Dynamics Laboratory, 2013), potentially inflicting more costly damage on societies (Accuweather.Com, 2012), and that current preventative measures are inadequate to address future conditions (Montgomery and Murray, 2012). Even areas frequently by hurricanes may not have adequate preparation and protection, as evidenced by Hurricane Katrina in New Orleans (2005) or Hurricane Andrew in Florida (1992).

Disaster

Hence, when a hazard is present (i.e., a major hurricane) in unsafe conditions (i.e., vulnerable populations in the hazards path), then some degree of disaster will occur. The extent of the disaster will be determined by the extent of unsafe conditions (i.e., number of unsafe conditions and people subject to them) and the magnitude of the hazard (in the case of a hurricane, how strong are the winds, large is the storm surge, amount of rainfall, and geographical size of the storm). Sandy was a large and powerful storm, entering into an area of the country not used to those conditions, where large urban populations and built infrastructure were located. It is not surprising then, that the hurricane had major impacts.

Disaster Resilience of Place (DROP) Model

A second disaster model that can be applied to the Hurricane Sandy disaster is the Disaster Resilience of Place (DROP) model, developed by Cutter and associates in 2008. The DROP model argues there are Precursor Conditions existing in society's natural, built, and social environments. It is within these environments that some potential disaster event occurs. The Conditions of this Event, along with the Coping Responses of the society, determine the extent and nature of the Disaster's Impact on society. If the impact of the disaster does not exceed the Absorptive Capacity of the society, then the Degree of Recovery the society experiences will be high. If the impact of the event exceeds the absorptive capacity of the society, then the degree of recovery can vary according to the ability of the society to engage in improvising and social learning. If the improvising and social learning occur, the degree of recovery can be relatively high. However, if improvising and social learning do not occur, then recovery is severely hampered. Whether or not the degree of recovery is high or low also impacts the antecedent conditions for future events, in terms of Disaster Mitigation and Preparedness (Cutter et. al, 2008).

Now that the components of the DROP model have been identified and defined, let us examine what the commonalities between this model and the previous model discussed, the PAR model. The first three components of the PAR model (Root Causes, Dynamic Pressures, and Unsafe Conditions) could be considered as the Precursor Conditions that the DROP model refers to, as they are aspects of a society's natural, built and social environments. As discussed earlier in this chapter, there were relatively high levels of economic and political inequality in the Sandy impacted states. Many residences were located in storm vulnerable areas. These situations were exacerbated by the rapid population growth and urbanization rates in the region.

However, unlike the PAR model, the DROP model also identifies the Coping Ability of a society as an important influencer of how a hazard affects a society. While many were surprised by the extent of damage that Sandy left behind, personnel were quickly dispatched to begin repairs on the mass transit system and electrical grid in New York and New Jersey. Mass transit systems resumed operations five days after Sandy (Snider and Everett, 2012). The Wall Street Stock Exchange resumed operations a few days after Sandy as well (Craig and Protess, 2012).

Both the DROP and PAR models include a Hazard Event (in this case, a large hurricane coming ashore), which creates Impacts. Unlike the PAR model, the DROP model examines the disaster process beyond the impact phase to what occurs in society afterwards. Once Hurricane Sandy came ashore, major alterations occurred in the landscape and infrastructure, which required communities and their residents to change how they operated on a daily basis. The Adaptive Ability of different communities and social groups varied widely, depending on where they were located and what resources they had available to use. Some of hardest hit communities were those along the New Jersey and New York shorelines. Storm surge washed away protective sand dunes, knocking some buildings off of their foundations and flooding others, and wiping out transportation, electrical and communications infrastructures. Other communities were devastated by fires. During and after the storm, many residents were forced to take shelter in emergency shelters and hotels for months, as they lost almost everything they owned in the storm, including their homes, jobs, family members, and other sources of support. Funds from the federal government to be used for disaster recovery were delayed by a hostile U.S. Congress, which seemed reluctant to support actions advocated by the President. Meanwhile, other communities in the U.S. far away from Hurricane Sandy's impacts, sent funds, personnel, and other resources to the mid-Atlantic region to help those impacted begin to recover.

Figure 1.3: Disaster Resilience of Place (DROP) Model

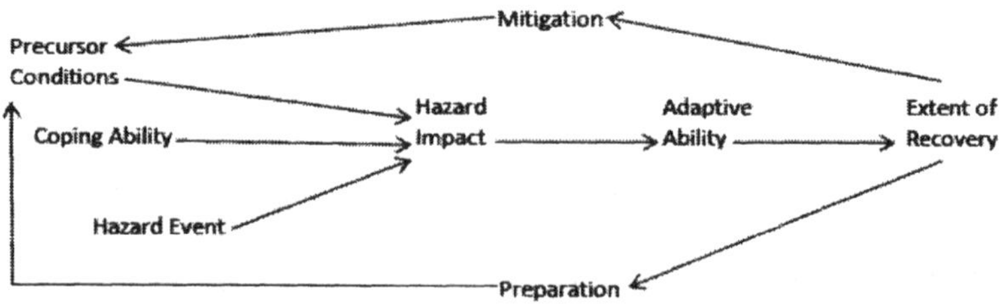

Reference: Cutter and Associates, 2008, modified.

Since the Adaptive Ability of communities varied widely, the recovery rates have varied as well. Those in shoreline areas of Nassau and Suffolk counties in New York and Middlesex, Monmouth and Ocean counties have the lowest rates of recovery. These communities tend to be lower income neighborhoods, where a lack of trust amongst people and property crimes are an issue (Tompson et. al, 2013). As indicated by the DROP model, the degree to which communities can recover from disaster affects their ability to prepare and mitigate for future disasters, either preventing a potential disaster all together or to lessen the impacts of a future disaster. One example of a mitigation effort that communities have undertaken since Hurricane Sandy is paying property owners to relocate their residences in safer locations, instead of the damage-prone shoreline. Property owners who wish to remain in flood prone, coastal areas must adhere to new building codes which require homes' elevations to be ten feet higher than before Hurricane Sandy hit (Montgomery and Murray, 2012). Another mitigation effort undertaken by the National Weather Service to emphasize the power and life-threatening impacts of post-tropical and extra-tropical storms, which Sandy became, is to issue storm warnings as if these storms are still hurricanes (Rice, 2013). These are two examples of lessons learned from Hurricane Sandy, as discussed earlier in this chapter.

Stages of A Natural Disaster Model

A third disaster model that can be applied to the Hurricane Sandy Disaster is the Stages of Natural Disaster, as developed by Picou and Marshall. A Natural disaster involves acts of God or Nature, such as hurricanes, tornadoes, and earthquakes. According to Picou and Marshall (2007), there are eight phases that occur in a natural disaster. These phases are shown in Figure 1.4. The first phase, Warning, occurs when the possibility of a natural disaster event exists in the near future. The second phase, Threat, occurs when it is evident that the disaster event will occur. The third phase, Impact, occurs when the event happens. After the event, the Rescue phase occurs as people and property caught in harm's way are removed from the strike area. Next, the Inventory phase occurs as assessment of the extent and nature of the damage and needed recovery/reconstruction efforts take place. The sixth phase, Restoration occurs when damaged facilities that can be repaired are repaired. The seventh phase, Reconstruction, occurs when those facilities that were destroyed are replaced. Finally, the last phase, Recovery, occurs when a new community or one similar to the pre-disaster community exists (Picou and Marshall, 2007).

Figure 1.4. Stages of a Natural Disaster Model

WARNING➜THREAT➜IMPACT➜RESCUE➜INVENTORY➜ RESTORATION➜RECOVERY

Reference: Picou and Marshall, 2007

This model adds to our understanding of the Hurricane Sandy disaster by eluci-
dating the aspects of a disaster that occur between the existence of Precursor
Conditions and the Impact of a Hazard on a society (in which the PAR and DROP
models do not show). Prior to the strike of hurricane, Warnings are issued by the
National Weather Service and other weather reporting media entities. These
warnings indicate the likely size, strength, and path of the storm, in the immediate
future as well as five days into the future. These warnings are updated regularly
throughout the course of the day. Communities in which the storm is likely to
become a Threat are informed well in advance of the storm, so that timely
evacuations of persons and property in harm's way can occur (Weather Channel,
2012).

This model also identifies stages of the disaster that occur between Impact and
Recovery, that can be considered as part of the Adaptation stage (as shown in the
DROP model) that takes place after Impact. During and after Hurricane Sandy,
there were people and possessions that had to be rescued from flood waters and/or
fires, to prevent death or further injury and destruction (Hamill, 2013). Once the
winds and waters of Hurricane Sandy had subsided, communities began taking
Inventory of what kind and amount of damage had occurred, and how much
expense and effort would be required to restore electrical, communication, and
transportation systems and buildings back to their original state. In many cases,
Restoration actually meant total Reconstruction of facilities that were swept away
or too severely damaged in the storm (Byron and Conte, n.d.). How quickly
Restoration and Reconstruction would take place depended on many factors,
including ready access to funding from governments and other financial entities, the
degree of damage incurred, and the ability of residents and business owners to
return to storm impacted areas. The progression of these stages has been uneven
across communities in New York and New Jersey, with some areas recovering
within a few weeks and other areas still lacking full recovery today (Tompson et.
al, 2013).

Conclusion

Every year, starting in June, many eyes turn to the tropics to see what is brewing
in the Atlantic Ocean. After several major damaging hurricanes in the last decade
left their marks on the American landscape and psyche (i.e., Katrina, Rita, Wilma,
Gustav, and Irene), no one seems really immune to their effects and the effects can
be wide-ranging. This was made clear especially after Hurricane Sandy hit the mid-
Atlantic region in October 2012, devastating parts of the Jersey Shore and New
York City, and burying parts of the Appalachians with snow. Whether or not these
types of disaster events will be more common in the future remains to be seen; yet
it is certain that another hurricane event will eventually occur, affecting everyone
in its path.

However, after each of these events, there are renewed efforts to better understand, prepare and mitigate for such events. Lessons learned from previous disasters
are re-emphasized, as well as new lessons learned, for scientists, policy analysts,

emergency personnel, government officials and residents. This chapter has provided a brief overview of the Hurricane Sandy disaster, from its initial origins as a tropical wave in the Atlantic, to its unique features as a storm, to its impacts on society and lessons learned, and to the utility of theoretical models to better understand Sandy as a disaster phenomenon. In the chapters that follow, additional aspects of the disaster are examined further in depth.

Notes

1. A tropical wave is an unorganized group of thunderstorms, clustered together, without a wind circulating amongst them (Landsea, 2006). Their length covers about 1200 to 1500 miles and they can last for three or four days, without dissipating or experiencing further development (Oblack, n.d.).
2. A low pressure is an area where the air pressure in the atmosphere is lower than in surrounding areas. Low pressures are typically associated with high winds, warm air, and inclement weather. By contrast, a high pressure is an area where the air pressure is higher than in the surrounding areas. High pressures are typically associated with clear skies and good weather, and their sinking air can act as an impediment to storm production (Briney, n.d.).
3. A tropical depression forms when a group of thunderstorms develops into an organized circulation around a center and the winds in the center of the system range between 23 and 39 miles per hour (Wihelmson and Ramamurthy, n.d.).
4. A tropical storm forms when the maximum sustained winds in a thunderstorm cluster range between 39 and 73 miles per hour. It is a more organized weather system than a tropical depression, and takes on a circular shape. It is at this stage of development that a tropical system gets assigned a name. Heavy rainfall is the major issue associated with this type of system (Wihelmson and Ramamurthy, n.d.).
5. A hurricane forms when the maximum sustained winds in a tropical system reach 74 miles per hour or higher. There is a rotation of thunderstorms around a well-defined core or "eye," with bands of rain and wind emanating from the core in a spiral fashion. Hurricanes can last a few weeks if they do not encounter land, colder waters, or strong winds that disrupt their rotation, which can tear them apart (Wihelmson and Ramamurthy, n.d.).
6. The Saffir-Simpson Scale is used to rate the strength of hurricanes, by wind speed and barometric pressure. The strength category also provides us with the degree of damage we can expect from the storm and how much storm surge (water rushing inward from the ocean onto the coast) is likely (See also Table 1.1).
7. Wind shear occurs when a rapid change in the speed, direction, and height of the air in the atmosphere occurs (Weather Street.com, 2013).
8. An extra-tropical storm or post-tropical cyclone receives its energy from dramatic changes in horizontal air temperatures, typically associated with cold fronts, and can retain the wind speeds that they had as tropical storms or hurricanes. Tropical cyclones (i.e., tropical storms or hurricanes) have no differences in air temperatures within them and receive their energy from warm and moist air (Hurricane Research Division, 2004).
9. A Nor' Easter is a storm that forms in the Gulf of Mexico or off the East Coast of the U.S. in the winter season, then moves northward up the Atlantic Coast. It is called a Nor'Easter because of the strong northeasterly winds associated with it. It can even have an "eye" like a hurricane and typically produces large amounts of precipitation along its path (Weather Channel, 2012).

10. The Loop Current is an area of warm water that travels up the eastern side of the Mexican coast, off the shores of the Gulf Coast States of the U.S., around the Florida peninsula, and northward along the Eastern U.S. coast to Virginia, where it exits eastward out into the open Atlantic Ocean (National Ocean Service, 2013).
11. Blocking refers to the stagnating weather patterns that can last for days or weeks. It is commonly associated with high pressures that get locked into place because their wind speeds and movement are much slower than low pressures' are (Haby, n.d.).
12. A trough is an elongated area of low pressure that is not associated with any kind of closed air circulation system (National Weather Service, 2009).
13. This applies only to campaigns for federal office (Knowles, 2013).
14. The exception is campaigns for federal office (Knowles, 2013).
15. A Super PAC is a Political Action Committee (PAC) that can receive unlimited funds to support or oppose an issue, but is not allowed to coordinate its activities with a political candidate. However, the dividing line between supporting issues and coordinating political candidate activities is not always clear-cut (Krieg, 2012).
16. A 501(c) organization is a nonprofit, tax-exempt organization. To maintain its tax-exempt status, the organization is not allowed to make influencing political legislation a major part of its' activities, not participate in any political activity supporting or opposing political candidates (Internal Revenue Service, 2014).

The author would like to thank Dr. Nwamaka Anaza for her comments on previous drafts of this chapter.

REFERENCES

Accuweather.com. (2012). Will climate change increase hurricane damage costs? http://www.accuweather.com/en/weather-news/hurricane-cost-rising-climate-change/63881

Anderskov, C. (2004). Anthropology and disaster. Thesis for Aarhus University. http://www. anthrobase.com/Txt/A/Anderskov_C_03.htm.

Bates, T. B. (2013). 33K more homes in NJ added to new flood zone. Asbury Park Press, March 14. http://www.app.com/article/20130313/NJNEWS/303130085/NJ-Sandy-flood-zone

Bee, A. (2012). Household inequality within U.S. counties: 2006-2010. United States Census Bureau, American Community Survey Briefs, February. http://www.census.gov/prod/2012pubs/acsbr10-18.pdf

Beekman, D. (2013). NYC discriminated against people with disabilities during Sandy, judge rules. New York Daily News, November 7.

Blake, E. S., Kimberlain, T.B., Berg, R. J., Cangialosi, J.P., and Beven, J.L. II. (2013). Tropical cyclone report: Hurricane Sandy. National Hurricane Center. http://www.nhc.noaa.gov/data/tcr/AL182012_Sandy.pdf

Borenstein, S. (2012). Hurricane Sandy, winter storm hybrid threatens New York, Delaware, Maine with Bad Weather. Huffington Post, October 25. http://www.huffingtonpost.com/2012/10/25/hurricane-Sandy-newyork-delaware_n_201378

Briney, A. (n.d.). Low and high pressure. About.com Education. Accessed 2014. http://geography.about.com/od/climate/a/highlowpressure.htm

Bureau of Labor Statistics. (2014a). Over-the-year change in unemployment rates for states. January 28 report. http://www.bls.gov/web/laus/laumstch.html

Bureau of Labor Statistics. (2014b). Over-the-year change in unemployment rates for metropolitan areas." February 5 report. http://www.bls.gov/web/metro/laummtch.htm

Bryan, A. (2012). Full list: Local shelters open for safety during Sandy. WTVR.com,

October 29. http://www.wtvr.com/2012/10/29/full-list-local-shelters-open-for-safety-during-sandy

Byron, J. and Braden, J. (2013). Toward an informed rebuilding: documenting Sandy's impacts. Pratt Center for Community Development, June 4. http://www.pratt center.net/research/toward-informed-rebuilding-documenting-Sandys-impacts

Byron, J. and Conte, E. (n.d.). In the aftermath of Hurricane Sandy, Pratt Center is working to develop community-driven long-term resiliency strategy. Accessed 2014. http://prattcenter.net/projects/sustainable-community-development/post-sandy-resiliency-planning

Carl, J. D. (2013). THINK Social Problems 2013. Boston: Pearson Education.

Cherry, G. (2012). Hurricane Sandy threatens U.S. East Coast. Huffington Post, October 28. http://www.huffingtonpost.com/2012/10/28/hurricane-sandy-2012-east-coast_n_2032599.html

CNN Library. (2013). Hurricane Sandy Fast Facts. July 13. http://www.cnn.com/2013/07/13/world/america/hurricane-sandy-fast-facts/index.html

Cox, W. (2012). New U.S. urban data released. *New Geography*, March 26. http://www.newgeography.com/002747-new-us-urban-area-data-released.

Craig, S. and Protess, B. (2012). After Hurricane Sandy, stock exchanges prepare to open. DealB%k, October 30. http://dealbook.nytimes.com/2012/10/30/after-hurricane-sandy-stock-exchanges-prepare-to-open/?_php=true&_type=blogs&_r=0

Cutter, S. L., Barnes, L., Berry, M., Burton, C., Evans, E., Tate, E. and Webb, J. (2008). A place-based model for understanding community resilience to natural disasters. Global Environmental Change, 18: 598–606.

Erikson, K. (2010). Foreword. Pp. XVII to XXII in David L. Brunsma, David Overfelt, and J. Steven Picou (Eds.), The Sociology of Katrina: Perspectives on a Modern Catastrophe, Second Edition. Lanham, MD: Rowman and Littlefield.

Feeney, S. A. (2012). Disabled people especially vulnerable in calamities such as Sandy. Am New York, November 19. http://www.amny.com/urbanite-1.812039/disabled-people-expecially-vulnerable-in-calamities-such-as-sandy

Fischhoff, B. (2006). Communicating with the public about hazards. Carnegie Mellon Conference on Crisis Readiness. February 28. http://www.epp.cmu:49157/domestic security/BaruchFischhoff.pdf

Geophysical Fluid Dynamics Laboratory. (2013). Global warming and hurricanes: An overview of current research results. http://www.gfdl.noaa.gov/globa-warming-and-hurricanes

Goldberg, B. (2012). Hurricane Sandy: State of emergency declared in Virginia. Huffington Post, October 26. http://www.huffingtonpost.com/2012/10/26/hurricane-sandy-state-of-emergency_n_20247

Haby, J. (n.d.). Blocking. Weather prediction.com. Accessed 2014. http://www.Weatherprediction.com/blocking

Halas, D. (2012). Hurricane Sandy 2012: Path is still not clear. The World Electronic. http://z6mag.com/wp-content/uploads/2012/10/hurricane-Sandy-projected-path.jpg

Hamill, D. (2013). Hurricane Sandy hero who rescued 200 people is now homeless. *New York Daily News*, July 31. http://www.nydailynews.com/new-york/hamill-sandy-hero-rescued-200-homeless-article-1.1414171

Handwerk, B. (2005). New Orleans levees not built for worst case events. *National Geographic News*, September 2. http://news.nationalgeographic.com/news/pf/14919 583.html

Huffington Post. (2012a). Hurricane Sandy: What it means for Miami. Huffington Post, October 25. http://www.huffingtonpost.com/2012/10/24/hurricane-sandy-miami-forecast-cone_n_2012

Huffington Post. (2012b). Obama: Hurricane Sandy is a serious and big storm. Huffington Post, October 28. http://www.huffingtonpost.com/2012/10/28/obama-hurricane-sandy_ n_203516.html

Huffington Post. (2013). Bloomberg spent $650 million of his own money as mayor of New York City. Huffington Post, December 30. http://www.huffingtonpost.com/2013/ 12/30/boomberg-mayor-billionaire-_n4519265.htm

Hurricane Research Division. (2004). Extratropical storm. http://www.aoml.noaa. gov/hrd/tcfaq/A7.html

Huntington News. (2012). Census Bureau: Increase in urban population outpaces nation's overall growth rate." Huntington News, March 26. http://www.huntingtonnews. net/27317

Internal Revenue Service. (2014). Exemption requirements—Section 501 (c) (3) Organizations. IRS, January 22. http://www.irs.gov/Charities-&-Non-profits/ Charit-able-Organizations/Exemption-Requirements

Knowles, D. (2013). U.S. Senate seat now costs $10.5 million to win, on average, while U.S. House seat costs, $1.7 million, new analysis of FEC data shows. *New York Daily News*, March 11. http://www.nydailynews.com/news/politics/cost-u-s-senate-seat-10-5-mil lion-article-1.1285491#ixzz2thtQKR6w

Konrad, C. P. (2014). Effects of urban development on floods. U.S. Geological Survey Fact Sheet 076-03. http://pubs.usgs.gov/fs/fs07603/

Krieg, G. (2012). What is a Super PAC? A short history. ABC News, August 9. http://abcnews.go.com/Politics/OTUS/super-pac-short-history/story?id=16960267

Landsea, C. (2006). What is an easterly wave? Hurricane Research Division. www.aoml. noaa.gov/hrd/tcfaq/A4.html

Levin, David M. (n.d.). Coastal construction. Accessed 2014. http://www.flwaterfront. com/coastalconstruction.htm

McIntyre, D. A. and Hess, A. E. M. (2012). 10 Companies making the biggest political donations. Huffington Post, July 2. http://www.huffingtonpost.com/2012/7/02/ corp orate-political-donations_n_1644375.html

Montgomery, J. and Murray, M. (2012). Lessons learned from Sandy: What heartbreak in New Jersey should mean for Delaware. *The News Journal*, November 18. http://www.delawareonline.com/article/20121118/NEWS08/Lessons-learned-from-sandy

Nathan, F. (2005). Vulnerabilities to natural hazards: an example of landslide risk in La Paz, Bolivia. http://www.afes-press-books.de/pdf/Bonn/Nathan_present.pdf

National Hurricane Center. (2013). Tropical cyclone climatology. http://www.nhc. noaa.gov/climo

National Hurricane Center. (2014). Blank Atlantic hurricane tracking chart. http:// www.nhc.noaa.gov/tracking-charts.shtml

National Ocean Service. (2013). Loop current. http://ocean.service.noaa.gov/facts/ loopcurrent.html

National Weather Service. (2009). Trough. http://www.weather.gov/Glossary

Neuman, W. L. (2003). Social Research Methods: Qualitative and Quantitative Approaches, Fifth edition. Boston: Allyn and Bacon

NOAA. (2013). State of the Coast. http://stateofthecoast.noaa.gov/population/welcome.html

Oblack, R. (n.d.). Tropical wave. About.com Weather. http://weather.about.com/od/t/g/ tropical_wave.html

Peltz, J., Dobnik, V. and Hajela, D. (2012). New York public schools close. Huffington Post, October 28. http://www.huffingtonpost.com/2012/10/28/nyc-evacuations-hurri cane-sandy-public-schools

Picou, J. S. and Marshall, B. K. (2007). Katrina as paradigm shift, pp. 1–22 in *The Sociology of Katrina*. First Edition. Edited by David L. Brunsma, David Overfelt, and J. Steven Picou. Lanham: Rowman and Littlefield Publishers.

Pinkham, D. (2010). Do lobbyists have influence? Public Affairs Council, August 25. http://pac.org/blog/do-lobbyists-have-influence

Rettner, R. (2013). Hurricane Sandy's toll on health. Live Science, October 28. http://www.livescience.com/40754-hurricane-sandy-health-impact.html

Rice, D. (2013). Weather Service changes warning system after Sandy. USA Today, April 4. http://www.usatoday.com/story/weather/2013/04/04/hurricane-sandy-warnings/2052773

Richard Stockton College of New Jersey. (2012). Hurricane Sandy dune performance assessment of New Jersey Beach profile network. December 12. http://intraweb.stockton.edu/eyos/coastal/content/docs/sandy/northernmonmouth.pdf

Schilderinck, G. (2009). Drought Cycle Management in arid and semi-arid Kenya: A relevant disaster risk reduction model? An empirical study of Garissa, Marsabit, Samburu and Wajir. The Hague: Catholic Organisation for Relief and Development Aid

Sheoin, T. M. and Zavestoki, S. (2012). Corporate catastrophes from UC Bhopal to BP Deepwater Horizon: Continuities in causation, corporate negligence, and crisis management." pp. 53–93 in Lisa A. Eargle and Ashraf Esmail (Eds.), Black Beaches And Bayous: The BP Deepwater Horizon Oil Spill Disaster. Lanham: University Press of America.

Snider, A. and Everett, B. (2012). New York transit, commuter lines turning the corner post-Sandy. Politico, November 1. http://www.politico.com/news/stories/ 1112/83193. html#ixzz2B1QgUMBo

Texas Association of Counties. (2014). Changes to the national flood insurance program begin Jan. 1. http://www.county.org/member-services/legislative-updates/news/Pages/Changes-to-the-national-flood-insurance-program

Tompson, T., Benz, J., Agiesta, J., Cagney, K. and Meit, M. (2013). Resilience in the wake of Superstorm Sandy. The Associated Press-NORC Center for Public Affairs. http://www.apnorc.org/PDFs/Resilience%20in%20Superstorm%20Sandy/AP_NOR C_Resilience%20in%20the%20Wake%20of%20Superstorm%20Sandy-FINAL.pdf

Toner, M. (2012). American Crossroads, Crossroads Gps and the growing importance of outside groups in American politics. Sabato's Crystal Ball, University of Virginia Center for Politics. September 27. http://www.centerforpolitics.org/crystalball/ articles/american-crossroads-crossroads-gps-and-the-growing-importance-of-outside-groups-in-american-politics

U.S. Census Bureau. (2010). Table S4. Gini ratios by state: 1969, 1979, 1989, 1999." http://www.census.gov/hhes/www/income/data/historical/state/state4.html

U.S. Census Bureau. (2012a). Table 709. Individuals and families below poverty level – Number and rate by state: 2000 and 2009. Statistical Abstract of the United States: 2012. http://www.census.gov/compendia/statab/2012/tables/12s0709.pdf

U.S. Census Bureau. (2012b). Table 708. Household, family and per capita income and individuals, and families below poverty level by city: 2009. Statistical Abstract of the United States: 2012. http://www.census.gov/compendia/statab/2012/tables/12s0708.pdf

U.S. Census Bureau. (2012c). Table 719. Top wealth holders with net worth of $1.5 Million or more —Number and Net Worth by State: 2004." Statistical Abstract of the United States: 2012. http://www.census.gov/compendia/statab/2012/tables/12s0719.pdf

U.S. Census Bureau. (2012d). "Table 400. Persons Reported Registered and voted by State: 2010." Statistical Abstract of the United States: 2012. http://www.census.gov/compendia/statab/2012/tables/12s0400.pdf

U.S. Census Bureau. (2012e). "Table 401. Reported Voting and Registration Among Native and Naturalized Citizens by Race and Hispanic Origin: 2010." Statistical Abstract of the United States: 2012. http://www.census.gov/compendia/statab/2012/tables/12s0401.pdf

WABC-TV. (2013). "35,000 More Buildings in Flood Zone." WABC-TV New York, January 28. http://abclocal.go.com/wabc/story?section=news/local/new-york&id=8971093

Weather Channel.com (2012). "Nor' Easter." http://www.weather.com/encyclopedia/winter/noreast.html

———. (2014). "Hurricane Central." http://www.weather.com/newscentral/hurricane central/

———. (2013). "Wind Shear." http://www.weatherquestions.com/What_is_wind_shear.htm

Wihelmson, B. and Ramamurthy, M. (n.d.). "WW2010." Department of Atmospheric Sciences, University of Illinois Champaign-Urbana. Accessed 2014. http://www.2010.atmos.uiuc.edu/(Gh)/guides/mtr/hurr/stages/td.rxml

Zakour, M. J. and Gillespie, D. F. (2013). "The Development Perspective on Vulnerability." Chapter 3 in Michael J. Zakour and David F. Gillespie (Eds.), Community Disaster Vulnerability: Theory Research and Practice. New York: Springer Science and Business Media.

———. (n.d.). "Saffir-Simpson Scale." Accessed 2014. http://www.coolgeography.co.uk/9/Risky_Earth/HurricaneWhat/Saffir_Simpson_scale.jpg

———. (n.d.). "Saffir-Simpson Scale." Accessed 2014. http://www.sayville.com/news/images10/SFD_Saffir_Simpson_Scale.jpg

CHAPTER TWO
SURVIVING SANDY, REBUILDING COMMUNITY: UNDERSTANDING POST-SANDY IMAGES FROM THE JERSEY SHORE

Elizabeth Borland and Jessica M. Scardino

INTRODUCTION

If you read New Jersey shore newspapers in the weeks after Hurricane Sandy, you would have encountered hundreds of photographs of ravaged boardwalks, collapsed homes, downed power lines, and bereft homeowners. However, if you were living in the devastated seaside town of Belmar, you also would have seen new vibrant murals painted on cement barriers by local artists, paintings that depicted beach scenes and peace flags, mermaids and uplifting messages. Folks on the shore and elsewhere in New Jersey also got used to seeing state-shaped bumper stickers with an image of the collapsed Jet Star roller coaster in Seaside Heights superimposed with the motto "Restore the Shore." These images document the effects of Sandy, but also hint that restoring the shore is about not only physical structures but also cultural identity. Our project turns to visual sociology to study images that emerged during the destruction and rebuilding of the Jersey Shore in order to understand how community identity is depicted and deployed and how art became a resource for the creation and assertion of collective identity in the wake of Sandy.

Why focus on community identity? We came to this project with an interest in community development and response to disaster, as well as an eye for the visual elements of community. Sociologists have long been interested in community: from classical sociology's concerns about the effects of changing ties (what Tonnies and Weber referred to as the shift from gemeinschaft to gesellschaft) to more recent work on how race, gender, and class segregation have an impact interaction in communities (Massey and Denton 1993, Duneier 1999, Spain 1992). Communities are important for meeting our need for belonging and for feelings of unity, social support, and trust that are essential for our well-being (Keller 2003, 3-11). Though the term community is notoriously difficult to define (see Crow 2007, Goe and Noonan 2007 for useful reviews), it often refers to both geographic space and what Hillery (1955) terms "consciousness of kind" (119)—a sense of common lifestyles, beliefs, work, goals, or institutions that bring groups together. Visual symbols are part of this common fabric, for they reference shared experiences and memories and have common interpretations that act as markers of belonging to a group or community.

Alongside community, we also turn to the related notion of collective identity, a sociological concept that arises from the literature on social movements. Social groups actively construct collective identity (Hunt and Benford 1994; Klandermans 1994; Melucci 1989); this is true of communities, too (Gusfield 1975). Polletta and Jasper (2001) point out that collective identity is relational and about "us" as much as "them." By sharing stories about "we" and "they," people bring groups into being (Polletta 1998). Collective identity is the result of a process of negotiation (Johnston, Laraña, and Gusfield 1994); it is a form of what Einwohner, Reger, and Myers (2008) and others term "identity work"—the active process of creating and sustaining identity. As we consider the collective identity that was deployed by groups during Sandy reconstruction, we consider what images say about their creators (for example, as members of a group or community, as residents of a particular shore town or of New Jersey) as well as what they might say about others outside of the group being referenced. Doing so enables us to understand the images and their creators in order to gauge their importance as resources for the creation of cultural identity in the face of Sandy.

Despite an emphasis on shared culture in definitions of community, scholars have not considered images of community or identity after disaster. After Hurricane Katrina, many studied the disparate effects on communities in New Orleans and the Gulf Coast (Jones-Deweever and Hartmann, Potter 2007, David and Enarson 2012, Wailoo 2010, Waterhouse 2009), and some visual analysis was done on media and housing patterns before and after the storm (Stevenson 2010, Warren 2009). However, none of this visual sociology considers community response. To address this gap we draw on work by Barton (1970) and Freudenberg (1997), who presented the notion of "therapeutic community" to describe the reaction of people to respond to a disaster by offering help, since one way that this happens is through the arts and other visual displays. We employ tools from the growing subfield of visual sociology that is part of the larger field of visual studies (Adams 2012, Harper 2012, Manghani 2013, McDonnell 2010, Spencer 2011) to assess Sandy's impact on the cultural identity of the Jersey Shore.

In this chapter, we first present the results of our visual analysis of images of shore communities that appeared in local newspapers, followed by our research on public art images created by people in these communities as part of the rebuilding effort. We analyze patterns in these depictions based on town demographics and supplement this with data gathered during interviews with those involved in the creation and display of public art. We argue that the news photographs focus on happenings during and after the storm, while the public art emphasizes the social meanings of Sandy and who "we" are in her wake—in other words, collective identity and interpretation of Sandy and its effects. Rather than seeking to establish a new cultural identity, artists and others involved in the creation and display of public art images sought to re-assert Jersey shore identity, to "restore the shore" as a vibrant and resilient community.

COMMUNITY IN THE NEWS: PHOTOGRAPHS OF SANDY DAMAGE AND RESPONSE

As French theorist Roland Barthes stated, "Photography presents to us the scene itself, the literal reality" (Barthes 1977). News photographs of Sandy presented the viewer with images of what happened in and after the storm. Of course, there were an infinite number of photographs that might have appeared in the press, but only some were published. What patterns in news photo coverage emerged after Sandy? Because most newspapers publish a wide array of photographs daily, it makes it possible to measure the most common themes and symbols that are circulating after an event like Sandy. This can help us gauge the community's understanding of the events, or at least the local media construction of what happened.

We were especially interested in local newspapers produced for local audiences, so we created a newspaper database of photographs published during the month of November 2012 from the two major New Jersey daily newspapers based at the shore, the Asbury Park Press and the Atlantic City Press. We chose these newspapers because of their high circulation frequencies and the geographic location of their target audiences. The Asbury Park Press (daily weekday circulation 91,098) circulates along the northern coast of New Jersey, while the Atlantic City Press (circulation 72,846) reaches the southern coast target audience. Only photographs that represented Sandy's effect on the state of New Jersey and its residents were included in the database. We omitted photographs that depicted Sandy's effect on the state of New York as well as photographs associated with the nor'easter that followed Hurricane Sandy. We also omitted "before" photographs taken pre-Sandy and neutral studio-type headshots that sometimes accompanied articles to illustrate the people referenced. Most of the photographs appeared in black and white, although both presses published books full of striking color photographs from Sandy coverage after the storm in which some of the database photographs were reproduced in color (see Donovan 2013 and Liebman and Siditsky 2013). Our database catalogued the newspaper, issue date, page, section title, article title, author, photographer, caption, location, and image description for each photograph. We coded the database images according to the following three main themes: physical destruction (to amusements, businesses, homes, roadways, etc.), human devastation, and human response (both collective and individual). We also included a category to code businesses back in operation ("Open for Business") and a residual category. The categories are not mutually exclusive, as some of the photographs satisfied more than one category (i.e., physical destruction and human devastation). We then analyzed the images to determine major patterns and trends within these themes and compared these with demographics for the towns depicted using 2010 U.S. census data.

Table 2.1. Images in All Photographs of Sandy's Effects in New Jersey from the *Asbury Park Press* and the *Atlantic City Press*, November 2012 (n=890)[1]

Coding Category	Frequency	% of All Photographs
Physical Destruction	476	52.5
Home	211	23.7
Flooding	109	12.2
Business	61	6.9
Utilities	47	5.3
Boardwalk	43	4.8
Amusements	24	2.7
Other Destruction	62	7.0
Human Devastation	306	34.4
Physical Destruction and Human Devastation	176	19.8
Human Response	299	33.6
Individual Response	98	11.0
Politicians	70	7.9
Sports Figures	18	2.0
Other Individuals	10	1.1
Collective Response	201	22.6
Food and Clothing Drives	71	8.0
Shelter	37	4.2
Cleaning Debris	32	3.6
Fundraisers	23	2.6
Emergency Response	10	1.1
Other Collective Response	28	3.1
Open for Business	36	4.0
Other	52	5.8

When we coded the 890 photographs depicting the effects of Sandy in New Jersey to determine what images prevailed, the most common category was physical destruction (52.5 percent of all photographs), which included destruction to the natural and/or built environment. The next most prevalent category was human devastation (34.4 percent of all photographs), a set of photographs that depicted victims of the storm individually or in groups. Many of these photographs included victims interacting with physical destruction or damaged or abandoned objects that represented their lives prior to Sandy—these are coded for both physical destruction and human devastation (19.8 percent of all photographs). The third major category of photographs was human response (33.6 percent of all photographs), a category dominated by collective response (22.6 percent), while smaller sets of photographs depicted the individual response of politicians, sports figures, and other individuals. The final and much smaller category, "Open for Business," included images depicting restaurants and other businesses that were back in operation after the storm (4 percent of all photographs).

Photographs depicting physical destruction to the natural and/or built environment recorded the historical impact and drama of the hurricane by depicting large-scale damage, such as collided houses, demolished boardwalks, and severely flooded roadways. While these images possessed a "shock-factor," much of their emotional impact came from the destruction of recognizable symbols of identity and everyday life. The images included destroyed elementary school classrooms, smashed family cars, trees crashing through bedroom windows, homes buried in the sand, and ravaged domestic belongings, such as furniture and toys. For instance, one *Asbury Park Press* image showed a family's kitchen with their refrigerator turned on its side, with framed family pictures still hanging on the walls. While the ability of the storm to turn a refrigerator on its side is astonishing, the presence of family photographs demonstrates to the viewer that Sandy's destruction reached far beyond the walls of a home; it rattled the family identity.

In addition to the devastation of personal symbols of identity, the newspapers' images depicted the devastation of recognizable symbols of Jersey Shore collective identity. One such symbol, the Jet Star roller coaster, which Hurricane Sandy wiped from the Seaside Heights boardwalk and left standing in the ocean, was the subject of approximately half of the photographs that depicted destruction to amusements. The frequency of images of the Jet Star and other rides demonstrates how integral the amusement park experience is to the Jersey Shore identity. Another ubiquitous symbol of Jersey Shore life is the boardwalk. Images of destroyed boardwalks were present in 43 photographs, while amusements appeared in 24. Like the destruction of a family's kitchen, images of the destruction of Jersey Shore amusement piers and boardwalks demonstrated to the viewer that Hurricane Sandy shook the community identity.

Photographs that depicted human devastation featured victims of the storm interacting with objects that represented their life prior to Sandy. This category also contains headshots of storm victims with looks of sadness or distress on their faces. The people featured in photographs of human devastation included homeowners standing in debris, newly homeless children sitting on cots at emergency shelters, business owners cleaning their flooded storefronts, and schoolteachers throwing away destroyed books. One *Asbury Park Press* cover story about a Union Beach homeowner named Anna Yurgelonis included several photographs of her destroyed house and forlorn grandchildren. The photographs showed the grandmother standing in a pile of debris behind a wooden fence that read "Yurgelonis angels gather here"—evoking happy times when the grandmother and her angelic grandchildren spent time at the beach together. Another photograph featured one of those "angels"—a little girl crying beneath her hooded jacket. This heart wrenching photograph demonstrated the sadness and loss experienced by so many.

Unlike the despondency evoked in pictures of devastated homeowners like Anna Yurgelonis, pictures of business owners emphasized industry and hard work. Business owners were often photographed cleaning or repairing their damaged stores. For example, restaurant owners were shown removing water-damaged equipment or sweeping flooded areas. In contrast, residents often appeared standing motionless in the storm debris, as if they were mourning the loss of their items but did not know how to move forward.[2] While there were some images of home-owners working with debris, too, the vast majority of photographs depicted residents in a more passive role, paralyzed by the damage, waiting for help, or getting help from others. The depiction of business owners as resourceful and industrious, and shore residents as devastated and paralyzed, fits well with American ideals about business and capitalism. Rather than waiting for help (from the federal or state government, from insurance companies or charities, and so on), the business owner picks up a tool and gets to work "restoring the shore" in a race to get back to business in time for summer.

While the images of human response include individual politicians (70 photographs) and sports figures (n=18), the majority demonstrate collective response from charitable and other groups (n=201, which represents 22.6 percent of all photographs). We analyzed the content and context of the image and caption to determine whether a photograph depicted collective response. One *Asbury Park Press* caption read, "Members of the Brick American Baseball League have worked together to supply food, clothing, toys and supplies to families in need after Hurricane Sandy." In fact, "working together" was a common theme in images that were categorized as showing collective response. These photographs featured teams of people handing out clothing or food (n=71), cleaning up debris (n=32), helping at temporary shelters for humans or animals (n=37), and doing fundraisers (n=23). In these relief efforts, the newspaper photographs highlighted the teamwork demonstrated by the volunteers: photographs tended to foreground the groups of volunteers, rather than the people they were helping. For example, they showed cooperation by groups carrying goods. By displaying the values of teamwork fostered by volunteer-volunteer interaction, the newspapers demonstrated the importance of unity and cooperation in the rebuilding process. Photographs showed volunteers from near and far and may have been a way of displaying how the reader might get involved if he or she wanted to volunteer; they were also a way to show the support of others for storm victims.

Although the damage from Sandy affected each shore town in different ways, the coverage was disproportionate for some parts of the shore.[3] When we used 2010 U.S. census data to compare the most and least frequently depicted locations, we found that high coverage municipalities tended to be less racially diverse and to have a lower percentage of people living below the poverty line. After Atlantic City, the top five sites for photo coverage (each representing at least 4 percent of all coded photographs) were Brick Township, Union Beach, Long Beach Township, Seaside Heights, and Toms River Township. Of these, all except for Seaside

Heights are more than 90 percent white and have 5 percent or less of the population living below the poverty line—as compared with New Jersey as a whole, which has a population that is 68 percent white and 9.4 percent below poverty level. Atlantic City and Asbury Park are notably less white (26.7 percent and 36.5 percent, respectively) and have a lower median income (under $35,000) than the other high-coverage municipalities, but they are the headquarters of the newspapers and were bound to get more coverage. Despite what seems like disproportionate coverage for wealthier and whiter municipalities, the images themselves reflected the shore's diversity. While it is problematic to code for demographic information such as gender, sex, race, and ethnicity without speaking to the individuals in the photographs, the newspaper photographs do seem to represent diverse communities. They depict a variety of individuals in both helping and victim positions; we did not find patterns to indicate disparities in the type of coverage.

Table 2.2. Newspaper Photo Coverage of Sandy's Effects, by Town

Municipality	Popu-lation	% White	Median Income	% Below Poverty Level	No. of Photos	% Photos
Atlantic City	39,558	26.7	28,526	29.3	84	8.99
Brick Township	75,072	93.1	67,296	5.1	44	4.71
Union Beach	6,245	91.0	65,654	4.9	44	4.71
Long Beach Township	3,051	97.0	86,912	3.8	40	4.28
Seaside Heights**	2,887	80.7	32,333	20.8	38	4.07
Toms River Township	91,239	89.9	73,313	6.2	36	3.85
Ocean City	11,701	92.1	57,226	7.4	29	3.10
Belmar**	5,794	87.1	60,509	11.6	28	3.00
Asbury Park**	16,116	36.5	33,663	31.5	26	2.78
Highlands Borough	5,005	93.0	78,860	14.1	25	2.68
Point Pleasant Beach Borough**	4,665	92.3	61,476	11.0	24	2.57
Brigantine	9,450	87.3	63,883	8.4	21	2.25
Ortley Beach	1,209	95.9	57,614	7.3	18	1.93
Middletown	66,522	93.9	99,037	3.1	16	1.71
Beach Haven Borough	1,170	92.6	72,031	6.0	15	1.61
Long Branch	30,719	65.3	52,266	14.4	13	1.39
Oceanport	5,832	93.4	88,080	7.4	12	1.28
Eatontown	12,709	71.3	62,184	8.3	11	1.18
Spring Lake	4,713	96.6	73,389	6.0	11	1.18
Keyport**	7,240	80.0	59,358	8.5	10	1.07
Manasquan	5,897	96.1	89,074	3.6	10	1.07
Margate City	6,354	96.4	73,290	10.2	10	1.07
Stafford Township	26,535	94.5	68,132	5.2	10	1.07
Wildwood City**	5,325	68.0	32,222	25.1	10	1.07

** Indicates municipalities where there were public art displays involving Sandy.

In sum, our analysis of newspaper photographs on the effects of Sandy in New Jersey highlights the local media's coverage of physical destruction, and to a lesser degree human devastation and collective response. In their depiction of what happened after Sandy, news photographs showed shore communities and spaces as broken apart by the storm, with homeowners in a passive role and business owners in a more active one. Patterns in the shore coverage also point to a consensus in some of the key symbols of the storm. While many more homes and business were damaged, in comparison with amusement parks and boardwalks, the repeated theme of amusement park and boardwalk damage signals the importance of these symbols of collective identity. We found this theme to be even more pronounced in the examples of public art we studied, and explore it further in the next section.

GIVING VOICE TO COMMUNITY: PUBLIC ART AND OTHER IMAGES AFTER SANDY

To assess the creation and display of images produced in the wake of Sandy, we conducted qualitative research on public art and other images created and displayed in shore towns in the period from November 2012 to August 2013. We collected photographs of these images and conducted interviews with those involved in their creation and display. To find cases, we relied on targeted sampling of shore towns that dominated the newspaper database. We also sought out information about local arts groups and councils or other entities that might have been involved in the creation and display of images. Then, we expanded our research to include other shore towns that might have similar examples, using general Internet searches for such topics as "Sandy" and "art." We traced those involved in their creation and display to invite them to participate as interview subjects and utilized snowball sampling methods by asking those we interviewed to recommend other examples of images, artists, or projects that we might study. We took our own photographs of images that were currently on display and solicited copies of photographs of objects no longer on display (e.g., ephemeral objects like sand castles, large paintings that had since been divided, items that had been created and then and sold to raise money for Sandy-related charities). We then conducted ten tape-recorded interviews with adults involved in the creation or display of these images (e.g., artists, gallery owners, art council staff—or people who occupy more than one of these roles). Of these interviews, we conducted six in person and four via telephone. Interviews lasted under 30 minutes and included questions about the images, their creation and display, and their meaning to those involved. Each interview was transcribed. We used Atlas.TI to code images and transcripts and to determine patterns for the types of images, themes, sense of purpose, language of collective identity (us/we and them/they), and aspects of the process of creation and display.

We collected 65 examples of static images related to Sandy[4] that were on display in shore communities in the post-storm period. These include an array of visual (but not audiovisual) media: murals painted on road barriers (all 24 murals that were part of the Belmar Barriers Project), murals on buildings, traveling and ephemeral sculptures (the Arts Society of Keyport's "Butterfly Renaissance" Project, the Sandy Castle), paintings and other art displayed in public shows and galleries, and images on bumper stickers and T-shirts. While there are likely many other images related to Sandy that were produced or shown in the shore area, all of these were publicly displayed in open locations or circulated freely and widely (as in the case of T-shirts and bumper stickers). Our exhaustive search and snowball sample leads us to surmise that these images are representative of the imagery from art and other non-audiovisual and non-virtual media[5] in the nine-month period after the storm. A large proportion of the images that we studied came from the Belmar Barriers Project, a series of murals by artists who volunteered to paint assigned road barriers restricting traffic in Belmar by the local arts council. Most of the themes in this diverse set of murals echoed the images in other examples from the sample, a subject also explored in our interviews. Another numerous set came from a series of 28 collages created from Sandy debris by Toms River-based professional illustrator and painter Gregg Hinlicky and sold to raise money for the Hurricane Sandy New Jersey Relief Fund. Most of Hinlicky's collages are abstract, but they incorporate an array of items reflecting shore life that we considered as part of our visual analysis.

Given Sandy's effects on New Jersey's coastal communities, it is not surprising that many of the public art examples we collected included beach imagery, from creatures like crabs and seagulls to surfers and peaceful seaside scenes. While some of the artists we interviewed sarcastically referred to "beach art" or excused the simplicity of these images, many also referred to these subjects as meaningful for people and communities at the Jersey shore. As muralist Donna D'Amico told us, "the surfers, the Adirondack chairs, that is all just life the way we know it." She explained that depicting these scenes was a way of saying, "We'll be back." High-school art teacher Kelly Fogas said that she included beach images in her mural as a reference to "memories from the shore, images that related to the shore such as beach balls, sea creatures, underwater scenes." She wanted the mural to "relate to any viewer, because it's something that all people come down the shore to do—to vacation, to swim . . . and just feel like part of the ocean." Both muralists referenced the universality of seaside images, but linked this to individual and collective identity by saying that the images depict "life as we know it." Collagist Gregg Hinlicky encapsulated this sentiment by saying, "We're beach people." Because of this, including "beach art" or other ocean-related imagery was a way to reference collective identity and to draw in the viewer. Beach imagery was also used to show what had been destroyed or disrupted by Sandy, as in the case of a haunting painting by teen artist Kyra Martyn, an untitled piece featured as cover art in a show by the Monmouth Arts Council. The painting has a foreground with broken eyeglasses on the beach that frames children in the sand and construction trucks with damaged houses in the background. While this seaside image was not as uplifting as the rest (and was one of few to show damaged houses and boardwalks), the bright colors and images of children in the sand and an American flag in the distance echoes some of the beach art themes.

Like the newspaper photographs, public art images like Kyra Martin's untitled painting included references to the typical entertainments associated with the Jersey Shore: boardwalks or amusement parks. Artist Donna D'Amico explained why her mural has the silhouette of both a roller coaster and a Ferris wheel: "I think if you are going to talk about the shore, you have to include something about the amusement park." Gregg Hinlicky, creator of collages from debris he collected after the storm, told us that he included game tokens in every collage he made to emphasize this point. One of the largest collages prominently featured a bright green plastic section of lighting from an amusement ride. He told us that—like most of the flotsam and jetsam in the collages—he did not know where these had come from, but that they were part of the conglomeration that washed up after Sandy. Yet while many included depictions or representations of amusements and boardwalks, there were few specific references to particular places. According to the artists we interviewed, this was intentional. For example, artist David Macomber told us that the photograph of a roller coaster in his large piece (later divided and sold to raise funds for the charity Waves for Water) was a general one: "I didn't want it to be a specific roller coaster," he said. "Every town has their pier and their roller coaster. I didn't want it to be a specific image or town; it was just New Jersey in general." During our interviews, artists described that their memories of the shore include riding amusement park rides and walking on the boardwalk. While the newspaper images of the Jet Star might lead viewers to mourn their loss of a symbol related to their collective identity, these images could be turned around as a way to emphasize resilience. As one artist, Sharon Murphy, told us, "The roller coaster was our strength."

In addition to the images, some of the public art contained textual messages that drew attention to concepts the artists wished to communicate to viewers. This was true of the commercial items—bumpers stickers and T-shirts—that commonly depicted maps or silhouettes of the state and such slogans as "Restore the Shore" and "Unite, Rebuild, Enjoy." Uplifting text was also evident in many of the Belmar murals and some of the other paintings in the sample. Common textual themes included strength, unity, belief, home, hope, and resilience. Because the Belmar project was "designed to bring a smile to the faces of Belmar's storm victims" (Hutchinson 2013), many of the words painted on the murals emphasized these themes, with mottos like "Believe" (artist Donna D'Amico and her students), "There's No Place Like Belmar" (a mural with a *Wizard of Oz* theme by Katie Maricic), and "Belmar Strong" (Dennis Brosonski). David Macomber, whose painting featured a sunrise image that culminated in the words "Strength in Unity," explained to us that he included that phrase because "there is a lot of unity that happens in tragedy." Through this positive language, artists portrayed the shore community as unified, strong, resilient, and hopeful. These themes emphasized a re-assertion of identity after Sandy, not so much a change in who we are, but a restoration through strength and resilience. Though most of the images in public art were easy to identify, adding text names the key elements and makes the interpretation of themes related to collective identity even clearer.

For those involved, these symbols and themes were a way to present the viewer with their take on the storm and rebuilding, a contribution that they could make as artists. Many were eager to tell us why they had engaged in this visual work, even though we did not specifically ask them to explain their participation as part of our interview instrument. As Linda Sanfilippo, a writer and artist working with the Belmar Arts Council, summarized: "Some people gave out clothes, some people fed people. This was our gift." David Macomber echoed this idea of giving as he described the large New Jersey-themed painting that he made and then divided into 30 smaller pieces to auction for charity. He said, "We all have our own gifts and talents that we can contribute. . . . I can't build a house or help someone rebuild, but I'm an artist, so this was like my contribution. . . . I felt like the painting was very symbolic of that, where you had your one section and . . . did your own little part of the helping but it was part of a larger project." For those like Macomber who donated the proceeds from their art sales to charity, the emphasis was on the art and its message first and the financial gift second. Contributing through art was an important strategy for these creators. In fact, artist Katie Maricic volunteered with home cleanouts but found it "unrewarding" because she "wanted to help somebody who really needed help." With her mural, she said, "it was something that I could kind of control and I knew that I was doing some good to people who needed it." By turning to art, people used their creative energy to respond to Sandy as well as communicate with others. Artist Gregg Hinlicky explained, "I started thinking about just giving back with my art . . . I saw all the debris and . . . it touched me because it's like all these remnants of people's lives and I wanted to just give back in some way, maybe a memento that said, 'This is a piece of what happened.'" Even though the objects, methods, and messages varied, the artists we interviewed were passionate about art as a contribution to a bigger cause.

While some of the artists involved in creating the public art in our sample were amateurs, many were art teachers or professional artists or designers. All the creators we interviewed seemed to be invested in thinking about their artwork and in their role as artists. These pieces did not just emerge spontaneously but were the result of a process of reflection and design. Through their work, the artists made images of the shore consumable symbols that communicated to the viewer something about "us."

DISCUSSION AND CONCLUSION

When we put our analyses of the newspaper database and public art images side by side, we can see the differences between how the local newspapers depicted shore communities and how community members represented themselves after Sandy. Newspaper photographs tended to highlight the destructive force of the storm on physical spaces, individuals, and communities, while artistic representations focused on imagery associated with the beach and amusements and included uplifting messages about strength, resilience, and unity. Even when artists depicted destruction, these images tended to include text or symbols that emphasized resilience and rebuilding—a re-assertion of community.

In terms of collective identity, the sense of Jersey shore inhabitants having a common lifestyle was particularly important. Even though few public art images included human figures, the pieces in our dataset referenced shore inhabitants as resilient "beach people" who were united in determination to "come back" from Sandy's destruction. In contrast, newspaper photographs often depicted residents as passive victims. In general, it was business owners who were portrayed as active, hardworking people who would rebound from the storm. Of course, photographs also showed people working together in collective response, usually in images that emphasized their teamwork. While many of the accompanying articles explained that teams helping to provide food and shelter and to clean up storm damage came from other areas (high school sports teams from North Jersey, church groups from Tennessee), some of the volunteers depicted were also from shore communities. After all, as Barton (1970) points out, victims of disaster often get more help from one another than from non-victims.

Just as there is fuzziness about who is helping whom after a storm (victims vs. helpers), the emphasis we found in public art images on shared summer memories of recreation at the shore raises questions about which group of people is referred to by symbols that emphasize collective identity. Is it a particular shore town's community or residents of the Jersey Shore in general? Might such symbols refer to New Jersey more broadly, since so much of New Jersey's shore life draws in people from across the state? Many of the artists we interviewed stressed the universality of the imagery, depicting beach scenes or non-specific roller coasters or including commonly found objects (even debris) in order to stress the shared memories that people associate with the Jersey shore and with Sandy. Artist David Macomber highlighted this when he said he wanted to include general images of the shore to represent "New Jersey in general." This breadth parallels the fact that many aspects of the response to Sandy have been state-based and/or shore-wide. For example, there was a statewide "Restore the Shore" charity campaign to raise funds for relief "From Sandy Hook to Cape May" (Restore the Shore 2013). (In)famously, Governor Chris Christie kicked off the $25 million "Stronger Than the Storm" ad campaign throughout New Jersey and the region "to raise awareness of the Jersey Shore's recovery from Superstorm Sandy in an effort to support tourism and local businesses" (Stronger Than the Storm 2013). While individual efforts in particular municipalities or counties highlight Sandy's effects and response in particular places (Belmar, Point Pleasant, Monmouth County, etc.), these efforts were often cooperative and linked with broader efforts (even if shore towns may in fact compete with one another for tourist traffic). For those we interviewed, the collective identity referenced was a shore-based identity, even if respondents lived, worked, or associated most with a particular place on the shore. Like many in the state who are fortunate to vacation "down the shore"—being at the shore, particularly in the summertime, was what made them "beach people." Even when images or text referenced a particular place or town—as in the words "There's No Place like Belmar" on one barrier mural—the sentiment and symbols were shared with other coastal communities. Katie Maricic, the artist who painted this mural, was not from Belmar but from a neighboring town. She told us: "I never lived in Belmar, I don't have any deep connection in that sense, but it's my next door [town] and it all seemed equally as affected . . . it's like we are a bunch of little towns, but we are all one big area."

Interviewing people involved in the creation and display of public art images helps us to understand more about the meaning and purpose of the images presented and the vision of community that artists embraced. While local newspaper photographs might have had the purpose of documenting and recording Sandy's effects and letting readers know about the damage they and their communities had sustained, the artistic images aimed to contribute directly to the rebuilding efforts. Artists saw their work as a way to give back, a small gift that could be part of the larger response. For this reason, many chose to depict uplifting and positive themes like unity and strength. This fits with what Barton (1970) and Freudenberg (1997) have called a "therapeutic community"—artists, like others in the community, responded to the disaster by identifying with the victims and trying to help their communities rebound. For example, Belmar Barrier Project muralists responded to the email call for artists to paint murals made by the Belmar Arts Council soon after the storm. Many did not know what this would entail; they just wanted to help and to share their talent. Other artists shared this sentiment: "I wanted to just give back in some way," as artist Gregg Hinlicky put it.

In fact, this case can help us to think about the cultural impact of disaster and response. While many recognize the therapeutic role that the arts can play in healing after disaster and other trauma (American Art Therapy Association 2012), the arts and public images more generally can be a vehicle for fostering community and expressing solidarity. Many of the people involved in the creation and display of the public art examples told us moving stories about the reactions of people who viewed these works. One muralist broke down in tears as she told us, "all of these people came by and walked by and said how much it meant to them." The owner of the gallery Idiosyncrazies in Point Pleasant, Sharon Murphy, shared her impressions of the reactions of gallery visitors to a collection of Gregg Hinlicky's collages composed of Sandy debris: "I had one woman . . . she said, 'I can't even look at this, I just want to throw up . . . that was my house, it was just in pieces.'" Such strong reactions, positive or negative, speak to the power of the arts after the storm. By paying attention to images produced in the wake of disaster, we can analyze symbols and the rich visual language that come along with community rebuilding. Some of the muralists in the Belmar Barriers Project, for example, had limited painting experience. An established painter, Gregg Hinlicky had not done much collage—the events of Sandy disrupted artists' lives and their everyday experiences, and sometimes this contributed to their creativity. To explore these patterns further, future research might consider how events like Sandy constrain artists (for example, by destroying resources like workshops and art materials), but also how they inspire artists to get involved as part of a therapeutic community.

Our work also has implications for the literature on community development and collective identity. Visual sociology is well suited to shine light on cultural identity, for it studies the messages that images contain—a visual communication system that emphasizes a "world that is seen, photographed, drawn or otherwise represented visually" and an approach that emphasizes "seeing as socially constructed" (Harper 2012: 4) and the materiality of culture (McDonnell 2010). By comparing images that appeared after the same disaster event but told different stories, we highlight the importance of lifestyle as part of collective identity, and think about the social constructions at play. For example, without the visual elements, we might miss or (especially) dismiss the importance of beach culture, or the associations people have with amusements and recreational spaces on the Jersey shore. In this way, our work adds to the growing literature in visual sociology by considering the impact of disaster on visual representation and communication. To extend these contributions, future work might compare different types of disasters (for example, natural disasters vs. industrial accidents) to see how they vary in terms of visual representation and effect.

Finally, as people take stock of the tourist season on the Jersey Shore after Sandy, it is clear that many towns did not "come back" as quickly as many had hoped. Homeowners continue to fight with insurance companies and many—especially those with rental properties—have not yet rebuilt (if, indeed, they ever will). Fewer owners, renters, and tourists at the shore means fewer dollars spent in shore economies. Despite a widespread state campaign to increase tourism, many shore businesses have reported big declines in revenue; even Governor Christie recently estimated that the 2013 season was down as much as 40 percent from the previous summer (CBS 2013). News coverage that emphasized destruction —both in local newspapers like the *Asbury Park Press* and the *Atlantic City Press* and in coverage that was likely similar in state and national papers—may indeed have had a big impact on this decline. While there is an important role for journalists (including photojournalists) to play in documenting disaster, it is clearly not the only story. Local people should have a voice in how their communities are depicted after disaster, and the arts provide one avenue for self-expression of community that should be recognized, studied, circulated, and supported.

NOTES

1. The counts in Table 2.1 represent the number of times each code appeared. Except where noted, this is a summative count of all cases where photographs were coded with these items—this implies inclusive rather than mutually exclusive categories. In all, 848 of the 890 photographs were coded with at least one of the four major categories. The remaining 52 photographs had images coded "other;" common examples in this category included aerial views of the coastline, vehicles on New Jersey roadways, or undamaged storefronts.
2. Of course, we recognize that many business owners were also homeowners affected by the storm. However, the photographs and captions emphasized their status as entrepreneurs, even if the accompanying story sometimes mentioned that they lived nearby and were also dealing with the destruction of their homes.
3. Of course, coverage likely was affected by the extent and type of damage to municipalities, as well as the population size. Some hard-hit towns were surely covered more than others that suffered less damage, but immediately following the storm, law enforcement restricted access to severely damaged areas, so this may have limited

initial coverage.

4.   *Drawings/Paintings/Murals* include Belmar Barriers (24), Keyport "Renaissance" Butterfly (1), and paintings from the Monmouth Teen Arts show (1), by David Macomber (1), and by Autumn de Forest (1). *Sculptures* include items from Monmouth Teen Arts (1), by Gregg Hinlicky (28 sculptures and 1 table), and the Point Pleasant Sandy Castle (1). *T-shirts/Bumper Stickers/Car Magnets* include works by Ergo (1 image, several items), Seven3two (1 image, several items), shoes created by a teen displayed at the Middletown Arts Center, and car magnets (3).

5.   While we did encounter a few films related to Hurricane Sandy and plenty of images that circulated online, for the purposes of even comparison and sample definition, we analyzed only static images (rather than film or other audiovisuals) and only items that were physically displayed in the shore region (rather than solely virtual). Future research might include a broader array of media in order to gauge if patterns are similar to the ones we found and if there are differences between visual and audiovisual representations, or between physical and virtual ones.

REFERENCES

Adams, J. (2012). Surviving Dictatorship: A Work of Visual Sociology. New York: Routledge.

Barthes, R. (1977). Image Music Text, translated by Stephen Heath. London: Fontana Barton.

Barton, A. (1970). Communities in Disaster: A Sociological Analysis of Collective Stress Situations. New York: Columbia University Press.

CBS. (2013, Aug 30). "Jersey Shore Revenues Down In Spite of Pricey Ad Campaign." Retrieved from http://newyork.cbslocal.com/2013/08/30/jersey-shore-revenues-down-in-spite-of-pricey-ad-campaign/

Crow, G. (2007). "Community" The Blackwell Encyclopedia of Sociology. V 2, p. 617–620.

David, E., & Enarson, E. (Eds.). (2012). The Women of Katrina: How Gender, Race, and Class Matter in an American Disaster. Nashville: Vanderbilt University Press.

Donovan, T. M. (Ed.). (2013). Sandy: Devastation and Rebirth at the Jersey Shore. Canada: Pediment Publishing.

Duneier, M. (1999). Sidewalk. New York: Farrar, Straus and Giroux.

Einwohner, R. L., Reger, J. & Myers, D.J. (2008). "Introduction: Identity Work, Sameness, and Difference in Social Movements." pp. 1–17 in Identity Work in Social Movements., edited by J. Reger, D.J. Myers and R.L. Einwohner. Minneapolis: University of Minnesota Press.

Freudenberg W. (1997). "Contamination, Corrosion, and the Social Order. *Current Sociology* 45:19–39.

Goe, W.R. & Noonan, S. (2007). "The Sociology of Community." pp. 455–465 in 21st Century Sociology: A Reference Handbook. Vol 1. Thousand Oaks: Sage.

Gusfield, J.R. (1975). Community: A Critical Response. New York: Harper Collins.

Harper, D. (2012). Visual Sociology. New York: Routledge.

Hillery, G.A. (1955). "Definitions of Community" Areas of Agreement" *Rural Sociology* 20:111–123.

Hristova, S. (2011). Offering a Helping Hand in the Aftermath of Hurricane *Katrina. Women and Language,* 34(1), 79–82.

Hunt, S.A. & Benford, R.B. (1994). "Identity Talk in the Peace and Justice Movement." *Journal of Contemporary Ethnography* 22(4):488–517.

Hutchinson, P. (2013). "The Belmar Barriers Project." Public presentation at the Monmouth

County Library, May 22.
Johnston, H., Larana, E. & Gusfield, J.R. (1994). "Identity, Grievances, and New Social Movements." Pp. 3–35 in New Social Movements: From Ideology to Identity., edited by E. Laraña, H. Johnston and J.R. Gusfield. Philadelphia: Temple University Press.
Jones-Deweever, A.A.& Hartmann, H. (2006). "Abandoned Before the Storms: The Glaring Disaster of Gender, Race, and Class Disparities in the Gulf." Chapter 5 in Hartman, Chester and Squires (Eds.). There is No Such Thing as a Natural Disaster: Race, Class and Hurricane Katrina. New York: Rutledge.
Keller, S. (2003). Community: Pursing the Dream, Living the Reality. Princeton: Princeton University Press.
Klandermans, B. (1994). "Transient Identities? Membership Patterns in the Dutch Peace Movement." pp. 168–184 in New Social Movements: From Ideology to Identity., edited by E. Laraña, H. Johnston & J.R. Gusfield. Philadelphia: Temple University Press.
Liebman, S. & Siditsky, S. (Ed.). (2013). When Sandy Hit: The Storm that Forever Changed New Jersey. Battleground, WA: Pediment Publishing.
Manghani, S. (2013). Image Studies: Theory and Practice. New York: Routledge.
Massey, D. & Denton, N. (1993) American Apartheid: Segregation and the Making of the Underclass. Cambridge, MA: Harvard University Press.
McDonnell, T. E. (2010). "Cultural Objects as Objects: Materiality, Urban Space, and the Interpretation of AIDS Campaigns in Accra, Ghana." *American Journal of Sociology* 115(6): 1800–1852.
Melucci, A. (1989). Nomads of the Present: Social Movements and Individual Needs in Contemporary Society. Philadelphia: Temple University Press.
Polletta, F. (1998). "Contending Stories: Narratives in Social Movements." *Qualitative Sociology* 21(4):419-446.
Polletta, F. & Jasper, J. (2001). "Collective Identity and Social Movements." *Annual Review of Sociology* 27:283-305.
Potter, H. (Ed.). (2007). Racing the Storm: Racial Implications and Lessons Learned from Hurricane Katrina. Lanham, MA: Rowman and Littlefield.
Restore the Shore. (2013). Retrieved from http://restoretheshore.com/
Spain, D. (1992). Gendered Spaces. Chapel Hill, NC: University of North Caroline Press.
Spencer, S. (2011). Visual Research Methods in the Social Sciences: Awakening Visions. New York: Routledge.
Stevenson, J. R. (2010). Rebuilding Coastal Mississippi Following Hurricane Katrina: A Spatial and Temporal Analysis. Retrieved from Masters Abstracts International.
Stronger than the Storm. (2013). Retrieved from http://www.strongerthanthestorm.com/
Tonnies, F. (1955). Community and Association. London: Routledge.
Wailoo, K. (2010). "Dialysis Patients, Technological Failure, and the Unfulfilled Promise of Health in America." Chapter 3 in Wailoo, K., O'Neill, K.M., Dowd, J & Anglin R. (Eds.). Katrina's Imprint: Race and Vulnerability in America. New Brunswick: Rutgers University Press.
Warren, D. M. (2009). The Social Construction of the Katrina Evacuee: Formal and Informal Responses in Houston, Texas Post-Hurricane Katrina. Retrieved from Dissertation Abstracts International, A: The Humanities and Social Sciences.
Waterhouse, C. (2009). "Failed Plans and Planned Failures: The Lower Ninth Ward, Hurricane Katrina, and the Continuing Story of Environmental Justice." Chapter 7 in Levitt, J.I. & Whitaker, M.C. (Eds.). Hurricane Katrina: America's Unnatural Disaster. Lincoln: University of Nebraska Press.

CHAPTER THREE
NO DISABLED LEFT BEHIND:
A DISASTER PREPAREDNESS MODEL
AFTER SANDY

Nwamaka A. Anaza and Lisa A. Eargle

INTRODUCTION

The aftermath of any disaster whether natural, triggered by man-made efforts or a convergence of both can be fatal to human lives, costly to societal development, and detrimental to environmental growth (Mileti, 1999). Preparedness and resilience have for years been the mantras for planning and coping with disasters. Yet some of the most at risk people are often the most neglected before, during, and after a disaster hits. Of the many vulnerable social groups living in society today, people with disabilities are some of the most neglected and unprepared individuals when disasters strike.

Despite public policy awareness about natural hazards and governmental commitment to alleviating society's exposure to such hazards, individuals with disabilities continue to face imminent social, physical, and psychological dangers during and after natural disasters (Bethel, Foreman, & Burke, 2011; Fox, White, Rooney, & Rowland, 2007). An example of this was observed during the 2004 Indian Ocean Tsunami that killed and injured close to 150,000 individuals (National Geographic News, 2005). Immediately following the Tsunami, it became apparent that many disabled individuals were left to fend for themselves during and after the disaster (National Geographic News, 2005). The 2005 Hurricane Katrina that hit the Gulf Coast region of the U.S. was no exception to the abandonment of disabled people. Reports filed subsequent to the Hurricane revealed that scores of disabled people were left homeless and stranded staying in unsanitary conditions without access to public aid during and following the Hurricane (Hoag, 2011).

Sadly, individuals with disabilities experienced similar circumstances during and after Hurricane Sandy. In New York City, for example, people with disabilities living in high-rise buildings were trapped for days without access to transportation and supplies due to power outages and a City-wide evacuation plan that ignored them (Santora & Weiser, 2013). Interestingly enough, close to 11 percent of New York City residents are disabled (Santora & Weiser, 2013), which means that about 889,219 individuals had special needs that went unmet when Hurricane Sandy hit. Other reports have also shown that individuals with disabilities rarely receive timely notices that prepare them for an evacuation (Philips & Morrow, 2007). For instance, reports released by the National Organization on Disability in collaboration with the Harris Poll showed that 61 percent of disabled people living in the U.S. today do not have any plans in place that directly address their safe and quick evacuation in the face of a disaster (National Organization on Disability, 2004). When disasters strike, it is apparent that disabled people take longer times to evacuate and in most cases are unable to take the necessary steps to successfully respond to the disaster (Bethel, Foreman, & Burke, 2011).

Added to these challenges is the discrepancy that exists between the perceptions a disabled person holds concerning his or her ability to implement a preparedness plan and the individual's actual ability to successfully execute the plan upon the impact of a disaster (McClute, Boninger, Oyster, Roach, Nagy, & Nemunitis, 2011). McClure et al. (2011) found that disabled individuals who felt prepared to evacuate in the face of a natural disaster fell short of executing the evacuation plan when the disaster actually happened. This shows that the disabled themselves are not as equipped with the knowledge needed to address their unique emergency needs when a disaster surfaces. Moreover, with the aging population increasing the number of disabled people living in the U.S. (Wiener & Tilly, 2002) and the threat for natural disasters growing (Iezzoni, 2014; Patrick, 2012), disabled individuals remain at a greater risk to be impacted by a disaster. Clearly, there is no question that disabled people require different disaster preparedness plans, however, many of the approaches used to communicate and deliver preparedness services disregard their differences (Hoffman, 2009). Hurricane Sandy was a perfect example of how plans in place to prepare people for a disaster were unsuitable and incompatible to meet the needs of the disabled.

Given the general lack of meaningful discussions about the issues concerning the disabled before, during and after Hurricane Sandy, this chapter examines the issues that the disabled face during times of disaster, and in particular, during Hurricane Sandy. In response, a theoretically informed qualitative disaster preparedness plan is proposed, to effectively address the needs of the disabled population. This plan recognizes that adequate disaster preparedness and management is a continuous process that begins long before a disaster event occurs and continues well after the event. It also recognizes that disaster preparedness for the disabled is a multi-tiered affair, involving all levels of society.

Understanding Disability

Disability can be addressed from a biological, psychological, social or integrated perspective. From a biological and psychological perspective, an individual with a disability is defined by the Americans with Disabilities Act as "a person who has a physical or mental impairment that substantially limits one or more major life activities, a person who has a history or record of such an impairment, or a person who is perceived by others as having such an impairment" (U.S. Department of Justice, 2009). Disability from a social perspective is described as "the disadvantage or restriction of activity caused by contemporary social organizations which takes little or no account of people who have physical impairments and thus excludes them from participation in the mainstream of social activity" (Davis, 1990, p. 3). Disability can finally be portrayed from a "bio-psycho-social" paradigm, wherein it is seen as resulting from "the interaction between persons with impairments and attitudinal and environmental barriers that hinder their full and effective participation in society on an equal basis with others" (World Health Organization, 2011, p. 4).

By the end of 2010, a billion people representing approximately 15 percent of the world's population lived with some form of disability (World Health Organization, 2011). In the U.S. alone, these statistics appear to be higher with 19 percent—56.7 million—of the civilian noninstitutionalized population categorized as disabled (U.S. Census Bureau, 2010). This means that one in five Americans have a disability. Shockingly, the presence of disabilities will worsen in young adults as they age, with one in every four of 20 year olds becoming disabled before reaching retirement age (67 years) (Social Security Administration, 2013).

Reedy (1993) proposes categorizing disabled consumers by their limitations. These categories are mobility, hearing, sight, and speech impaired. Other categories of disability include the cognitively impaired, those with physical size, medical and dietary conditions (National Fire Protection Association, 2007), spinal cord injuries, head injuries, psychological disorders, and invisible disabilities (Disabled World, 2014a). Disabilities can also be grouped by their level of impediment, ranging from little to severe impediment (e.g., totally blind *versus* retina pigmentosa), length of impairment, i.e., in-born, man-made, or acquired with age (e.g., blind from birth *versus* blind at 30 years old due to bad water consumption *versus* loss of eye sight due to aging), and the combination of impediments (both blind and deaf *versus* deaf and immobile).

Of the 51.5 million American adults with some form of disability, the majority of them suffer from physical, mental (cognitive), communicative (seeing/hearing/ speaking), or a combination of disabilities. Roughly 41.5, 16.8, and 15.7 million adults claim to have a physical, mental, and communicative disability, respectively (Brault, 2012). Physical or mobility disability is a physical impairment that prevents people from freely using any part of their extremities for bodily movement including walking, holding objects, running, and sitting comfortably. Individuals with physical impediments make use of mobility aids like wheelchairs, canes, crutches, walkers, and artificial limbs (Disabled World, 2014b). "Cognitive disability entails a substantial limitation in one's capacity to think, including conceptualizing, planning, and sequencing thoughts and actions, remembering, interpreting subtle social cues, and understanding numbers and symbols" (Braddock, Rizzolo, Thompson, & Bell, 2004, p. 49). Sight disabilities are impediments experienced by individuals who are blind or find it difficult to visually see words and letters in ordinary newsprint, even with the aid of glasses or contact lenses (Brault, 2012). Visual disabilities can be caused by aging, diseases (e.g., glaucoma, macular degeneration, and diabetic retinopathy), and accident. Hearing disabilities are experienced by individuals who are completely deaf, partially deaf, and generally find it difficult to hear a normal discussion, even with the use of hearing aids (Brault, 2012; Disabled World, 2014a). Speech disabilities are impediments experienced by individuals who find it difficult to speak as a result of speech disorders, speech delays, learning difficulties, and traumatic life occurrences (Brault, 2012). Despite the variation in disability types, individuals with disabilities have one thing in common—they all experience social and economic disadvantages in society that heightens their vulnerability in the event of a disaster.

Socio-Economic Issues Affecting the Disabled

Social and economic disparities faced by people with disabilities worsen their ability to respond appropriately to emergencies. Although legislative actions have tried to protect the rights of the disabled population, the lack of public inclusiveness continues to intensify the social and economic woes they face in society. The most notable legislative action in the U.S. is the Americans with Disabilities Act. The Americans with Disabilities Act makes discrimination against disabled people illegal in employment, transportation, public accommodation, communication, and governmental activities (U.S. Department of Justice, 2009). Nevertheless, a number of socio-economic factors continue to plague the ability of the disabled to respond adequately to disasters including: higher rates of poverty, poorer participation in the labor market, lower educational participation, poorer health outcomes, and environmental obstacles (Peek & Stough, 2010; World Health Organization, 2011; Yeo & Moore, 2003).

A major consensus among scholars across the world is that people with disabilities are generally poorer than people without disabilities (Filmer, 2008; World Health Organization, 2011; Yeo & Moore, 2003; Yeo, 2005). Evidence from previous research studies indicates that many people with disabilities represent the poorest of the poor in society (Yeo and Moore, 2003) because disability as an impediment has a bidirectional link to poverty (Yeo Yeo & Moore, 2003 Moore, 2003; World Health Organization, 2011). In other words, disability increases a person's risk of poverty, while poverty also increases a person's disability risk (World Health Organization, 2011). The rate of disabled people living in poverty, across the world today, is unfortunately rising as a result of worsening social and economic conditions. In the U.S. for example, about 29 percent of adults suffering from severe disabilities live in abject poverty compared to 14 percent of the population with no disability living in poverty (Brault, 2012).

According to Yeo and Moore (2003), the disabled population experiences disproportionately high rates of poverty because of the following reasons: (1) limited access to education and employment, (2) limited access to land and shelter, (3) poor sanitation, (4) exclusion from political/legal processes, (5) limited access to healthcare, (6) insufficient or unhealthy food, (7) malnutrition, poor health and physically weak individuals, (8) lack of ability to assert rights, (9) unhygienic overcrowded living conditions, and (10) hazardous working conditions. These factors subsequently lead to higher risk of impairment, which then influences discrimination against the disabled, further excluding them from equitable income accumulation. Take the U.S. as a classic example, 55.5 percent of the adult population (16 to 64 year olds) with severe disabilities are unable to hold employment mainly as a result of their disabilities (Brault, 2012). Poor labor force participation has a direct impact on the poverty level of individuals with disabilities.

The U.S. Census Bureau (2013) indicated that persons with disabilities are three times less likely to hold employment than persons without disabilities. The unemployment statistics get worse as disabled people age (Burchardt, 2005) because many employers remain wary of hiring people with disabilities due to concerns associated with poor job qualification, low productivity levels, and high costs of accommodating disabled employees (Fujiura, Yamaki, & Czechowicz, 1998; Yeo & Moore, 2003). Misconceptions about the disabled in terms of their ability to perform their responsibilities also hinder their access to employment. Such misconceptions, according to the World Health Organization (2011), arise mainly from societal prejudice against and ignorance about disabled people. Even when employed, persons with disabilities tend to earn less and experience greater workplace stigmatization than persons without disabilities (Jenkins & Rigg, 2003). According to a 2013 U.S. Census Bureau report, most disabled people work in positions that earn lower salaries such as administrative assistants, dishwashers, refuse collectors, and building cleaners. Figure 4.1 compares the earnings of individuals with disabilities and those with no disabilities from 2008 to 2010 using the U.S. Census Bureau Data. The Figure indicates that more than half of the disabled working class (52 percent) earns less than $25,000 in comparison to 38 percent of workers with no disabilities.

A key contributor for the income disparity between individuals with disabilities and those without disabilities is the diminished access disabled people have to formal education. In addition, several individuals with disabilities lack opportunities to develop skills desirable to accumulate human capital and function equitably in the labor market (Burchardt, 2005). In a recent study conducted across thirteen developing countries, Filmer (2008) found that children with disabilities were more likely to begin school later in life. These children also showed a higher likelihood of low educational outcomes such as dropping out and repeating classes than those without disabilities (Filmer, 2008). Among adults with disabilities, a similar finding of lower educational attainment was reported in comparison to adults with no disabilities. Despite universal attempts to equalize primary and secondary education for all, children and youths with disabilities are still less likely to get an education, which has a direct significant impact on poverty in their adult years (World Health Organization, 2011).

Figure 3.1 Earnings of Employed U.S. Population, By Disability Status

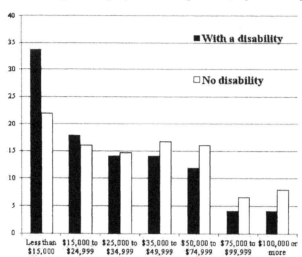

Reference used: U.S. Census Bureau (2013). Numbers are provided in percentages.

Another economic issue that affects the lives of people with disabilities is environmental barriers that restrict their full involvement in society on an equal basis with people without disabilities (World Health Organization, 2011). From an environmental standpoint, inaccessible surroundings contribute to the further alienation of disabled people in the society (World Health Organization, 2011). The United Nations *Convention on the Rights of Persons with Disabilities* (CRPD) declares that accommodations must be made to ensure that individuals with disabilities have equal access to the physical and information environments as well as public facilities and services (United Nations, 2006). Due to their lack of equal access to environmental resources, disabled people are more likely to live in areas at risk of disasters due to their low economic status (Wisner, Blakie, Cannon, & Davis, 2004). The impact from such disasters put disabled people in more harm's way by exposing them to greater personal and material damage. The impacts of these damages are not short lived, but instead have long-term disruptions for families with disabled people (Van Willigen, Edwards, Edwards, & Hessee, 2002).

We next discuss the experiences of the disabled during Hurricane Sandy by identifying how their socio-economic status hindered their ability to successfully prepare and respond to the disaster. These experiences are stories recounted by living survivors of the Hurricane.

EXPERIENCES OF THE DISABLED DURING SANDY

The disabled population in the mid-Atlantic region experienced a variety of difficulties immediately before, during and after Hurricane Sandy. As one disabled person remarked in an interview, "Our community is frequently marginalized. That becomes amplified in a disaster," (Livio, 2014) where everything is already chaotic and the needs of the disabled are not the top priority. Moreover, some independently living individuals are not fully aware of what their needs would be in a disaster, so they have not adequately planned and prepared for the situations that they will experience in a disaster (Livio, 2014). Others feel that it is the government's responsibility to protect the disabled from harm, but even amongst the disabled, views on what those efforts should entail differ widely (Feeney, 2012).

Stories emerged after Sandy of the disabled dying during the storm. These stories sounded eerily similar to stories that emerged out of New Orleans after Hurricane Katrina, where a majority of the fatalities were the disabled and the elderly, even though they constituted a relatively small segment of the population. Like during Hurricane Katrina, in Hurricane Sandy, some individuals drowned in flood waters, while others died when the loss of electrical service stopped the functioning of vital equipment. Still others almost became fatalities, until they were rescued by neighbors from dire situations when their cries for help were heard (Feeney, 2012).

For some disabled, they were personally safe but lost access to possessions like vehicles and wheelchairs that were critical to their mobility (AmeriCares, 2013). Those residing in nursing and adult care homes were quickly evacuated as flood waters intruded facilities, which left many with only the clothes on their bodies. Additional clothing and other possessions were left behind and lost in the storm (Associated Press, 2012). Some of the disabled decided to shelter in place, even though they were residing in a dangerous flood zone, because needed equipment like electric lifts, cough machines, and hospital beds could not be easily moved to other locations. Once flood water shut off the electricity, they were stuck in place without the functioning of their equipment. Emergency workers had to remove them to other facilities, such as hospitals, to protect their wellbeing (Richardson, 2012).

Other disabled individuals sheltering in place had difficulty obtaining food, batteries, and gasoline for power generators after the storm because businesses were closed and/or damaged by the storm. Many residents also worried about theft of equipment left behind or generators placed outdoors after the storm. Those with psychological and substance abuse counseling needs had difficulty receiving the assistance they needed, due to reduced hours of operation of organizations (Westcott, 2013a).

Some individuals with cerebral palsy were relocated to higher level apartments when flooding began, but equipment that allowed them to get around (electric wheelchairs) and communicate (DynaVox machine) with others had been lost. This impaired their ability to attend classes or perform their jobs after the storm. Medicaid regulations restrict how often recipients can apply for funds to purchase equipment. For some, they have turned to the Federal Emergency Management Agency (FEMA) for funding. Charitable organizations such as Family Support Services for United Cerebral Palsy have assisted families with funds and donations of equipment (Mays, 2012).

Another organization, Portlight Strategies of South Carolina opened offices in

New Jersey immediately after Sandy, so they could assist the disabled. For one family with multiple disabled family members, the organization assisted them by providing a wheelchair lift into their newly reconstructed, higher elevation home. For another family, the organization purchased an iPad for an autistic child. Portlight also provided financing for other charitable organizations and is encouraging the disabled to make plans and preparations well before a disaster event occurs (Livio, 2014).

Legislators have also once again taken up the cause of the disabled. Two New York state law makers, Assemblyman Michael Cusick and Senator Diane Savino, have reintroduced legislation that would mandate that counties keep a confidential registry of disabled persons, so local governments can better assist them during emergencies. This action was taken in response to a federal court ruling in a class-action lawsuit that New York City had violated The Americans With Disabilities Act. Many disabled residents were left stranded for days after Hurricanes Irene and Sandy in unsafe conditions without the ability to seek emergency assistance (Randall, 2013). The City's pre-existing emergency plans had relied on public transportation for the evacuation of disabled individuals, even though those transportation systems could be damaged during the disaster. Evacuation orders from authorities often came too late for the disabled to make alternative trans-portation arrangements. Also, plaintiffs in the case argued that access to some shelter facilities were blocked (i.e., locked gates around wheelchair ramps) and there were not enough beds in shelter facilities (Beekman, 2013).

In addition to remedying these issues, the state-wide legislation would also require owners of high-rise apartments to produce emergency evacuation plans for the disabled and for police, fire, and emergency management officials to provide accessible shelters for the disabled. New York City Council had already passed legislation to improve preparedness for special medical needs in emergency shelters and to produce a recovery plan to assist homebound disabled individuals (Randall, 2013).

Moreover, recognizing that the disaster-preparedness and safety of the disabled is a universal concern, the United Nations Office for Disaster Risk Reduction (UNISDR) is administering surveys world-wide to those disabled individuals who have experienced a disaster. The objective is to produce global data on disaster risks and needs, so that governments can better prepare their citizens and respond to disaster needs (Westcott, 2013a). By gathering information from the disabled themselves about their experiences and needs, governments will have a better understanding of how they can serve this population, thus allowing the disabled to play an important role in seeing that their needs are met. To the non-disabled population, unless they have a loved one with special needs, often the disabled are invisible (Westcott, 2013b).

THEORETICAL UNDERPINNINGS OF A DISASTER PLAN

Disaster preparedness and management planning can be informed by different perspectives. One possible perspective is the Community-Based Disaster Prepared-ness Approach (CBDP). CBDP involves investing in communities' knowledge, assets, and capacities that will help them to effectively *respond* to a disaster event once it occurs (Centers for Disease Control, 2012). Examples of the CBDP Approach are the creation of a database that keeps track of equipment, facilities, and specialized skills of personnel that can be called upon during a disaster (Troy, Carson, Vanderbeek, & Hutton, 2008), creation of evacuation routes and shelters, and disaster notification systems (Griffith, Jeffers, & Gardner, 2012).

A second perspective is the Community Resilience Approach (CRA). CRA advocates that communities develop characteristics and resources to *reduce the risk* of a disaster. In cases where a disaster event does occur, CRA allows for a response that is quick and effective, which will minimize the time and effort needed for community recovery (Centers for Disease Control, 2012). Examples of the CRA approach are to diversify the source of community members' livelihoods beyond one industry, locate buildings and infrastructure above flood levels, and create safety awareness programs (Department for International Development, 2011). With this approach, efforts are made to reduce vulnerabilities of people and places, and to reduce potential precursors to disaster.

There is some overlap in the CBDP and CRA perspectives in terms of concrete actions that communities can take. Some CBDP actions can also lead to improved Community Resilience (Centers for Disease Control, 2012). For example, creating a database of existing community resources can highlight for planners which types of resources are currently lacking in the community or parts of the community that are underserved. Having this awareness in advance of a disaster allows the community to take action to improve the situation.

One theoretical model that serves as a useful guide in thinking about disaster preparedness and management from the CRA perspective is the Disaster Resilience of Place (DROP) model. This model shows the links between precursor conditions in a community's social, natural and built characteristics, a disaster event, adaptive ability of the community, and the community's level of recovery. It also indicates that communities can learn from their disaster experiences how to better prepare for the next disaster or even possibly how to avert future disasters. Communities are able to alter their characteristics to lessen future disaster impacts and improve their adaptive abilities to disaster, which will also improve their recovery efforts (Cutter, Barnes, Berry, Burton, Evans, Tate, & Webb, 2008).

A fourth perspective, which can be seen as part of CBDP and CRA, is Risk Communication. Risk Communication is "communication intended to supply laypeople with the information they need to make informed, independent judgments about risks to health, safety, and the environment" (Morgan, Fischhoff, Bostrom, & Atman, 2002, p. 4). It can also be defined as a bi-directional dialogue of issues relating to risk between individuals, groups, and institutions rather than a one-way information flow of risk from experts to laypeople. According to the National Research Council (1989), risk communication "is an interactive process of exchange of information and opinion among individuals, groups, and institutions. It involves multiple messages about the nature of risk and other messages, not strictly about risk, that express concerns, opinions, or reactions to risk messages or to legal and institutional arrangements for risk management" (p. 21).

The success of risk communication is dependent on its ability to provide people with the most critical knowledge needed to understand the nature, severity and consequences of a risk, including pertinent information valuable to avoiding such risk in order to ensure public safety. The content of the information must be relevant to the risk at hand and transmitted to the intended audience in a fashion which results in the clearest and maximum comprehension of information by the recipient. The source of the information must be credible and trustworthy to increase the success of the message's acceptance. The source of the message must be reputable in the sense that the information being communicated must be aligned with the sources' mission and reputation (National Research Council, 1989). This component of disaster preparedness and management is considered so vital that the Centers for Disease Control have published a volume on it (Centers for Disease Control, 2012).

In the past, discussion about disaster preparedness and management planning was an activity that experts in government agencies performed, but the effectiveness of this top-down hierarchical approach was very limited. Disasters happen in local communities, directly affecting the residents located there. It is also those same local residents who are most familiar with resources and vulnerabilities of the community, more so than outsiders. In response, disaster preparedness and management has shifted towards the Whole Community Approach. The Whole Community Approach advocates bringing together different stakeholders (i.e., community residents, community leaders, emergency management personnel, government officials) to determine what are the needs of the community and how best those needs can be met (Federal Emergency Management Agency, 2014) in a disaster event. This perspective can be integrated with the above mentioned perspectives to produce a multi-stage, all-encompassing method of addressing disaster preparedness and management.

DEVELOPING A PROPOSED DISASTER PREPAREDNESS PLAN FOR DISABLED POPULATIONS

Developing any disaster preparedness plan is a complex undertaking (National Highway Administration, 2013), regardless of what population or location it is designed to protect and support. There are multiple actors and constituencies involved, with differing perspectives, concerns, and resources that they can mobilize in times of disaster. It is also a multi-tiered affair, involving the interaction and coordination of efforts by individuals and families, and organizations and institutions at the local, state, and national levels (Centers for Disease Control, 2012). Disaster preparedness is a dynamic process that requires forethought and anticipation, testing, evaluation, and revision even before a disaster event strikes, as well as evaluation and revision during (as unexpected contingencies can emerge) and after a disaster (Kramer & Bahme, 1992). Moreover, there are factors that impede the successful implementation of even the best prepared plans (Thevenaz and Resodihardjo, 2010). With natural disasters like hurricanes, despite technological advances in detection and prediction of weather elements, there is still some degree of unpredictability of such events.

When developing disaster preparedness plans for the disabled, there are additional complications to the process. There are multiple types and combinations of disabilities; some are physical limitations while others involve cognitive and emotional issues. The extent of impairment also varies widely, from taking medications to dependence on technology to perform vital functions (American Red Cross, retrieved 2014). Disability sometimes co-exists with other limitations such as poverty, racism, limited educational attainment, access to timely information, accessible housing, and limited political influence (Atkins & Guisti, 2004). Technologies and other infrastructure that the disabled rely upon may not be readily and widely available (Feeney, 2012). Along with these limitations, the disabled often encounter a general lack of awareness of their concerns (Westcott, 2012b).

However, it is imperative that society recognizes this population and takes steps to prepare and protect them from disasters. Evidence from previous disasters (i.e., Hurricane Katrina and Indian Ocean Tsunami) suggests that the disabled are disproportionately harmed by disasters (Bethel et al., 2011; Hans, retrieved 2014). Moreover, as the population ages, a larger proportion of society will become disabled in some way later in life. Advancements in medicine and technology have made it possible for the severely disabled to survive beyond birth deformities, disease, and/or accidents (Iezzoni, 2014). It will also cost less in the long run to protect the disabled than to respond to their disaster-induced illnesses, injuries, and losses post-disaster (National Council On Disability, 2009). Finally, we have a moral obligation to care for others, especially those who face challenges in caring for themselves (Zack, 2012; Hans, retrieved 2014).

Based upon disaster preparedness information available, we propose a disaster preparedness and management plan for disabled populations. This plan examines disaster preparedness and management in terms of the four stages of disaster: Pre-Disaster, Disaster Imminent, During Disaster, and Post-Disaster. It also examines disaster preparedness at the different levels in society: Household, Community, and Societal. Many disaster preparedness plans tend to focus on what individuals should do, pre-disaster, to get themselves and their families ready for a disaster. With this plan, we are integrating these recommendations with research findings about what people experience during and after a disaster. We are also introducing into this plan what community organizations and societal institutions (i.e., governments and higher education) can do to assist individuals in planning for and surviving a disaster. While the proposed plan is detailed, we do not argue that it is fully comprehensive and exhaustive in nature; but rather, we believe the items mentioned in these plans illustrate some of the issues that need to be considered. The plan is presented in Tables 3.1 through 3.4.

Stage 1: Pre-Disaster Stage

The Pre-Disaster Stage is defined as the period of time prior to any disaster event, before any indications of a disaster are apparent. The Pre-Disaster Stage tackles issues dealing with disaster mitigation. The mitigation phase includes activities that

Table 3.1. Disaster Preparedness Plan, Pre-Disaster Stage[1]

Household Tier	Community Tier	Societal Tier
Do a personal assessment of one's needs. Create disaster kit. Check kit periodically throughout year and replace dated items. Create list of important contact numbers. Identify potential evacuation sites. Identify means of evacuation. If evacuating by personal vehicle, have gas and other vehicular supplies. Identify evacuation routes. Identify what needs to be done to secure residence. Identify where to relocate any pets. If one has service animals, create kit of supplies for them. If one has children, assist them in preparations. Have multiple means to be notified of impending disaster and to receive regular updates. Provide members of personal social support network a copy of one's Preparedness Plan. Create a set of instructions if they are needed for others to assist in the evacuation. Make safety improvements on residence. Sign-up for Special Needs Registry if one exists. Practice disaster plan. Join on-line planning community.	Know what hazards and risks exist in area. Create registry of disabled population. Know the types and extent of disability represented in the population. Train emergency response personnel how to interact with and serve disabled. Equip evacuation shelters to meet needs of disabled. Have back-up devices available for power, water, etc. Have evacuation transportation that are disability friendly and can be called quickly into service.. Have multiple notification systems that can be activated to reach disabled of all types. Clearly convey, via PSAs, the potential hazards and their risks for the area. Understand how culture may affect perception of risk. Recognize impacts of disability may be compounded by other issues such as poverty. Have disabled involved in developing community preparedness plans. Make information about disaster preparedness for households and community readily available. Create relationships between organizations and agencies. Create an on-line prescription storage program. Practice disaster plan at regular intervals.	Increase number of emergency management degree programs at higher education institutions. Dedicate research efforts to understanding disaster issues for the disabled. Have qualified professionals staff FEMA and other agencies. Have regular training exercises for disaster response personnel. Create channels of communication and resource distribution between community organizations and state/federal level agencies. Have national Public Service Announcements (PSAs) regarding disaster and disability to increase public awareness. Produce public policies that reduce the vulnerability of the disabled to disasters.

[1]See notes at end of chapter for references.

prevent the occurrence of a disaster, diminish the odds of a disaster, or reduce the damages likely to result from a catastrophic event that are implemented before the onset of any disaster in order to ensure societal welfare (Mileti, 1999). In reducing its impact, long-term actions and preventive measures are taken to combat human loss and environmental damage. In the case of hurricanes, this could be the months outside of the hurricane season (December through May) or before any tropical activity that could potentially impact a community is forecasted during the hurricane season period. One of the first things that a household should do as part of its disaster preparedness is have all members meet together and discuss each member's potential needs in a disaster situation and how those needs might be achieved. The household can also put together a disaster kit of basic supplies to be used in time of disaster.

Likewise, the local community should have a meeting of its members to discuss what hazards and risks exist, what segments of the community are vulnerable, and to develop Public Service Announcements to inform the community how they can prepare for disaster. In these meetings, the disabled and other important community stakeholders should be involved in developing disaster plans. The community can also begin creating and updating a registry of disabled persons and their specific needs in times of disaster.

At the same time, the society can develop educational programs to train personnel for managing disaster situations and develop public policies that reduce the vulnerabilities of the disabled. These policies should create workplace and other economic opportunities, as well as measures that politically empower the disabled. At this phase, governmental agencies play an instrumental role because they institute and enforce rules that ensure public safety in the event of a disaster. See Table 3.1.

Stage 2: Disaster Imminent Stage

The Disaster Imminent Stage is defined as the period of time prior to the disaster event, starting when the first signs of a potential disaster are present until the actual disaster event occurs. In the case of a hurricane, it can be considered the time when the first storm track projections showing possible impact are issued until the storm's major wind/rain/wave effects strike a location. One of the first things that a household should do in this time period is to stay aware of the latest disaster developments, such as changing storm direction and strengthening. The household should also contact those in the personal network about the household members' changing physical location.

Likewise, the community should keep the public informed of the disaster's status through multiple communication medium, to make sure everyone is aware of the dangerous situation. This includes contacting the disabled directly in the community to see if they need any assistance in preparing for the disaster strike. A component that is related to this stage is the preparedness phase. The preparedness phase encompasses activities that prepare the entire community on how to respond to a hazard that is expected to occur. During this phase, resources needed to get people ready to safely react to a disaster are available before the event occurs so as to improve people's chances of survival (Mileti, 1999). Examples of preparedness activities include developing, pretesting, and executing emergency preparedness plans before a disaster strikes; training emergency responders and volunteers on how to respond in times of danger; utilizing media outlets to communicate with the public about the onset of a disaster; providing them with safety tips; advising them on evacuation notices; evacuation routes and so forth. At the societal level, communications between local, state, and national agencies and organizations should commence, with the state and national organizations monitoring the situation to see what assistance they can provide to communities. See Table 3.2.

Table 3.2. Disaster Preparedness, Disaster Imminent Stage[2]

Household Tier	Community Tier	Societal Tier
Load disaster kit and other supplies into evacuation vehicle. Assist any children, disabled family members, or other dependents with evacuation. Secure residence. Evacuate, following directions and routes recommended by law enforcement and other emergency personnel. Be aware of latest disaster developments. Contact those in one's personal support network about one's changing location. Stay calm, level-headed. Stay connected on social media and media outlets.	Activate notification systems. Contact disabled directly. Activate evacuation shelters. Activate emergency personnel to assist with evacuations. Activate evacuation transportation. Keep public informed of the disaster's status through multiple communication mediums and channels.	Mobilize communication between community and state/national agencies and organizations. State and national agencies and organizations monitor the emerging situation. State and national agencies and organizations distribute resources to communities as needed for the evacuations and emergency shelters.

[2]See notes at end of chapter for references.

Stage 3: During Disaster Stage

The During Disaster Stage is defined as the time period when the disaster event's effects are strongly felt by the community. This stage is closely related to Mileti's (1999) response phase of the emergency preparedness phase. The response phase involves the deployment of resources and emergency measures to cope with an ongoing disaster. The primary purpose of response actions is to ensure the preservation of human/animal life, personal possession, the environment, and the society at large. At this phase, emergency responders must assess the disaster situation and constantly communicate their assessment with the public. In the case of a hurricane, it can be considered the time when strong winds, waves, and flooding rains occur. It is also the time when the potential loss of life and property is highest. While the household is waiting the disaster out, it should try to maintain as normal of a routine as possible. This includes regular bed and meal times and other daily activities.

Table 3.3. Disaster Preparedness, During Disaster Stage[3]

Household Tier	Community Tier	Societal Tier
Try to maintain as normal of a routine as possible Seek professional help if trauma and other symptoms emerge. Mentally and emotionally prepare for the unexpected Anticipate post-disaster environment. Be aware of latest disaster developments. Monitor use of supplies.	Make sure the needs of those in emergency shelters are being met. Encourage those residing in emergency shelters to stay in place. Keep notifying the public about the latest development of the disaster. Allow disabled's special assistants (service animals and personnel) to reside in emergency shelters.	Continue to monitor the disaster situation. Maintain continuous communications with local officials about unfolding events and emerging needs.

[3]See notes at end of chapter for references.

The community should encourage those residing in emergency shelters to stay in place, until the disaster has passed. The community should also communicate with shelter residents, to make sure their needs are being met. Communication of the latest disaster event developments should also be made. At the societal level, continuous communication between local, state, and national agencies and organizations about the latest disaster developments and needs should occur.

Stage 4: Post-Disaster Stage

The Post-Disaster Stage is defined as the period of time, beginning immediately after a disaster event and lasting until household and community recovery have occurred. The post-disaster phase corresponds to Mileti's (1999) recovery phase. During the recovery phase, measures are taken over an extended period of time to restore the community back to its original state or a better state before the disaster occurred. In doing this, reconstruction of physical surroundings such as rebuilding damaged roads and bridges, cleaning up disaster debris will have to be embarked upon to show citizens that recovery activities are taking place. Within this stage, processes are implemented to rehabilitate people suffering from physiological, psychological, emotional, and financial losses such as financial assistance programs, therapeutic treatment, etc. Depending upon the extent of damage, this period can last a few months to a decade or more (Kates, Colten, Laska, & Leatherman, 2006). For households, individuals should return back to their residences only after it has been declared safe to do so by authorized personnel (law enforcement and other emergency personnel). Community members should prepare themselves mentally for what they will see as they return home, and seek professional assistance with any on-going trauma and depression. They should also be prepared for delays in the return of transportation, electrical, water and other services. Community assistance organizations should contact community members to see the needs that people have and how they might assist them.

Table 3.4. Disaster Preparedness Plan, Post-Disaster Stage[4]

Household Tier	Community Tier	Societal Tier
Return home only after it is declared safe to do so by authorities. Identify means to return home. Identify means to travel around area. Restock necessities before extra supplies depleted. Realize delays and interruptions in services are likely. Assess damage to property. Contact insurance company about insured properties. Recognize threats posed by wild animals displaced during disaster. Begin repair process. Acquire alternative housing, if needed. Seek professional help if experiencing trauma and stress. Be wary of con artists. Return to school and/or work when possible.	Assess locations and extent of damage. Assess the risks associated with damage. Determine if locations are safe for people to return, especially those with disabilities. If safe, assist disabled in returning home. Provide follow-up to determine if disabled need any medical or counseling services. Determine if electrical, phone and other essential services are and continue to be operational. Make alternative housing available. Make sure FEMA and insurance people have been in contact with disabled or vice-versa. Analyze what processes went well and what areas need improvement. Make any needed modifications to disaster plans and their execution prior to the next disaster. Get businesses operating as soon as possible.	Send state and national resources to assist with recovery and reconstruction. Have disability rights advocates monitor the recovery process. Have an on-going conversation about what worked and what didn't work so improvements can be made before the next disaster. Involve the disabled in this conversation. Share knowledge gained from disaster experience with other communities and nations.

[4]See notes at end of chapter for references.

At the societal level, state and national agencies and organizations should send resources where they are most needed to assist with recovery. They should also begin recording information about what processes went well before, during, and after the disaster and what processes need to be improved upon. All stakeholders and constituent groups affected by the disaster should be involved in this information collection and sharing process. Moreover, "Lessons Learned" from the disaster should be shared with other communities in an effort to improve societal-wide disaster resilience. See Table 3.4.

POLICY RECOMMENDATIONS

At the core of a preparedness plan for disabled individuals is the desire to change participants' attitudes and behavioral disposition towards how preparedness information is provided to this group. Therefore, we outline a preparation scheme for emergency management participants that consist of: pre-disaster planning, pre-disaster evacuation planning and aftermath preparation that cater purely to disabled people.

Pre-Disaster Planning

Issues related to the accurate assessment of risk in the mitigation and preparedness phase are critical tasks governmental institutions, volunteers, community members, private organizations, schools, and NGOs have to review before the onset of a disaster. Based on our reconstructed disaster plan, we posit a four step process appropriate in assessing risk for the disabled population. These are identifying (1) possible hazards, (2) degree of danger posed, (3) level of vulnerability, and (4) extent of impact. A hazard is a situation that can potentially harm populations and their environments (Weinstein & Pillai, 2001). When identifying hazards in an area, emergency management teams must consider all the potential trigger events for different types of disasters. This means examining the type and frequency of different climatological and geological events (such as tornadoes, earthquakes, and so forth), as well as different types of manufacturing and warehousing facilities (such as combustibility of chemicals) and political relations within and across nations.

Second, emergency management teams must consider the degree of danger posed to the disabled community. If an oil spill occurs, how toxic is it to persons with disabilities? Third, one must examine how many disabled people would be affected if the hazardous event strikes, as well as if they will be likely to suffer the largest consequences. This would mean factoring in those directly impacted and those indirectly impacted (i.e., unemployed because tourism industry declined in an area).

Fourth, the extent of impact must be considered. This entails not only estimating the numbers of individuals impacted directly and indirectly, but also the different types of impacts sustained. Hurricane Sandy impacted hundreds of thousands of people living in the mid-Atlantic region in terms of lost lives, injuries, damaged/destroyed housing and places of business, and interruptions in education and health care delivery.

Pre-Disaster Evacuation Planning

Pre-disaster evacuation plans refer to the systematic process used in preparing and ensuring that processes are in place to address the safe movement of lives during periods of heightened alert and eminent danger.

While almost every metropolitan city has currently managed to draft a general emergency preparedness plan for its citizens, embarking on a successful evacuation plan focused on ensuring the well-being and safety of the disabled population must require the beforehand collaborative effort of several institutions, governing bodies, responders, private organizations, local municipalities and disabled people themselves. Also, city officials must be mindful of devising evacuation plans that recognize the challenges and needs the disabled community face during such precarious situations.

In order to draft an evacuation process best suitable for the disabled population, we recommend a six stage preparatory initiative in anticipation for a safe and quick evacuation: (1) Determining the number of disabled individuals in the population, (2) Pre-notification of disaster, (3) Immediate response, (4) Provision of basic amenities, (5) Provision of medical care, psychological and spiritual services, and (6) Provision of updated information.

Determining Number of Disabled Population by Disability Type

It is impossible to carry out a safe and successful evacuation without knowing how many people need to be evacuated. There should be no surprises or guesses when planning for an evacuation, especially when dealing with highly vulnerable people. Ignoring the actual human count of disabled people in an area and the type of disabilities they suffer from jeopardizes not only their safety, but the well-being of responders who risk their lives to ensure full evacuation in times of disasters. The first step in preparing for an evacuation for people with disabilities before a disaster hits involves pre-determining the number of disabled people needing evacuation by district. Acquiring this information can be made easy if facilitated from the state level at several points of contact. One point of contact may involve requiring people with disabilities to pre-identify their disabilities when obtaining a state authorized license. Having such information at the local and state level will give relief agencies, responders, and local officials a means of communicating directly to disabled people and/or caregivers before the onset of a disaster using direct communication. It will also ensure that when evacuation pre-trainings are being held, those who need the information have access to it.

Pre-Notification of Disaster

The beforehand notification process signals the presence of danger and the immediate necessity to evacuate. No one can be ready for an evacuation if they are unaware of the atmospheric conditions that pose eminent hazards to their lives. Yet when it comes to evacuation notifications, systems currently in place by the government, non-governmental agencies, mass media, and businesses to communicate messages to the public are typically geared towards able bodied individuals (Romo-Murphy, James, & Adams, 2011). Take for example, the weather alert sirens, the National Weather Service Announcements, or public service media alert notifications (television and radio). These three mediums have often been labeled the fastest means of contacting the general public before a disaster hits. However, the problem with all three notification systems is their failure to take into consideration the needs of the hearing and neurological impaired. Hearing impaired individuals cannot hear sirens. Individuals who are sight impaired cannot see flashing lights. Even online websites that are established to provide homeland emergency assistance to the public often lack the web assistive technologies and usability programs that cater to the needs of the disabled, especially the visually impaired. The intent of evacuation warnings is to alert the general public of a pending disaster and to ensure appropriate preparation. However, if disabled people lack equal access to such information ahead of time simply due to inaccessible web designs and online barriers, then the presence of such information is a complete waste.

We emphasize the need for adequate communication strategies. The utilization of communication outlets is inevitable in the preparedness phase because it gives people access to information about the disaster and its magnitude. The promotional aspects of getting the right message out will require the use of mass and specialized media, paid and unpaid sources to ensure the highest impact factor of reaching the disabled members of society and preparing them for the worst (Kotler & Zaltman, 1971). Media outlets can also be used to educate people on what they need to do to reduce human and property damages. Increasing the number of positive media images of disable people (e.g., Marlee Matlin; David Paterson) speaking about preparedness plans through public service announcement will expose and help disabled people relate to the message more due to the source.

Since types of disability vary across individuals, multiple approaches of notification should be used. To ensure accessibility, the information must be available from different sources (such as social media, websites, television broadcasts, radio, telephones, word-of-mouth, mobile aps, etc.) and be in formats that the disabled can receive (audio format for visually disabled; visual format for hearing disabled, and so forth). We found that there needs to be an integration of information provided across impacted areas. Promotion of the availability of this service for the disabled must be positioned in a fashion that can be seen/heard/read, and generally understood. This suggestion corresponds with Mileti and O'Brien's (1992) process of warning that follows a subsequent progression from *hear—confirm—understand—believe—personalization.* In addition, the cost for obtaining this information needs to be minimized as well—using existing technologies that most disabled people would already have in place to transmit the information.

Since the general public regardless of human impairment heavily depends on marketing communication from the government to inform them about potential disaster, it may be time that law makers consider mandating policies that facilitate equal access, particularly web access for all. Slight changes on existing disaster preparedness websites such as text magnification for people with poor vision, audio transmission for the blind, audio captioning and sign-language interpreters for the deaf, and adaptive keyboard tools for the physically impaired may help the disabled access evacuation notices faster. In addition, special provisions geared directly towards the disabled community in times of disasters may help improve access to notification warnings. For example, creating a central website and hotline purely dedicated to the disabled community may help improve evacuation response rate. These resources should contain clear and timely messages via multiple formats accessible to the disabled regarding what to do and how to respond to different disasters based on disability type.

Immediate Response

Immediate response addresses the way out of danger for disabled people. At this stage, disabled people should consider how they should evacuate, what evacuation routes to use, and what resources are needed to evacuate safely. Answers to these questions must be provided ahead of time on the websites of emergency response organizations. In addition to the above questions, disabled people should predetermine if they can evacuate on their own or if help is needed. Furthermore, they should specify the type of assistance needed beforehand in order to ensure that plans are in place to safely maneuver social and environmental barriers. Preexisting plans that ensure the safe removal of disabled children from schools, disabled patients from hospitals, and disabled employees from offices have to be pre-established to guarantee their safety. To further facilitate this process, pre-evacuation training showing emergency evacuation videos and actual practice drills that address different disability types will enhance disabled peoples knowledge of building escape paths (National Fire Protection Association, 2007).

Currently, a major problem city officials often deal with in times of disasters is getting disabled individuals engaged and responsible for their own personal wellbeing. Having a local or state evacuation order does not imply that all disabled persons will comply with such mandates (Guion, Scammon, & Borders, 2007). Much of the lack of personal engagement from the disabled community can be blamed on their sometimes heavy dependence on caregivers and family members for assistance during catastrophic events. The need for assistance underscores the frustration many disabled people feel, but also stresses the importance of emergency assistance programs. Pre-registering for emergency assistance with local emergency management officials will aid in identifying those that need help and what assistance they will need during a disaster evacuation (Rooney & White, 2007). While many communities do not provide such programs, those that do offer these programs still lack the appropriate messaging channels needed to relay the information to its intended target market. Another important activity in this stage is the pre-identification and proper training of disaster relief personnel and volunteers who can help disabled people respond to a disaster.

Provision of Basic Amenities

An additional element that has to be taken into consideration if the disabled are to be safe after an evacuation relates to the provision for basic human amenities. The timeline for such provisions, short or long, will depend closely on the aftermath of the disaster and extent of the disaster damages. Certainly the scope and size of the damages will ultimately dictate how long before disabled people can return to their homes. Conventionally, people are often advised to stock up their pantries, fill up their car tanks, charge cell phones and keep extra supplies around the home in the event of a disaster. But when it comes to evacuations, the basic amenities needed for the disabled may extend beyond transportation, shelter and food.

In considering potential sheltering areas, emergency management personnel need to determine if structural barriers (such as steps, limited parking space, narrow toilet stalls without bars) exist for the disabled. Moreover, shelter personnel should be evaluated to see if they have the necessary skills/expertise to serve the various disabled groups. If not, additional training should be provided in advance of potential disasters. These shelter areas should also be supplied with refrigerators, generators, and a variety of communication devices/methods. Refrigeration of extra medication, walkers for the blind, batteries for electric wheelchairs users, respirators, and supplies for service animals constitute some of the basic needs the disabled may require to survive in an evacuation. Blind individuals may need someone to read printed notices to them. Under the Americans with Disability Act of 1990, shelters are required to provide assistance to disabled individuals. This assistance may be in the form of locating the restroom or food line. Considerations need to be made when disabled individuals return home. If a hurricane destroyed a wheel chair ramp, it will need to be replaced before mobility impaired person returns home. For deaf individuals, TTY devices will need to be supplied with new phones.

Provision of Medical Care, Psychological and Spiritual Services

Studies have found that individuals often experience short or long term psychological trauma before, during, and after a disaster (Galea, Nandi, & Vlahov, 2005; Norris, et al., 2002). But for some disabled people, especially the cognitively impaired and children who lack support from adults and family members, the psychological impact of a disaster may led to additional attitudinal and behavioral consequences such as post traumatic stress, somatic complaints, sleep interruptions, and worsening clinical conditions (Norris, Friedman, Watson, Bryne, Diaz, & Kaniasty, 2002; Peek & Stough, 2010). Due to the potential long term effects of psychological trauma and its associated outcomes, emergency evacuation plans must incorporate provisions for immediate therapeutic interventions, peer counseling, medical care, spiritual support, and motivational guidance. In the face of a potential pandemic, health officials must provide updates of information to the media, encourage mass distribution of vaccines, and encourage those most susceptible to contracting illnesses to take extra sanitary precautions. Those who become ill must be removed from the disabled population and treated.

Provision of Updated Information

Public policy officials must advocate for the utilization of communication sources to provide disabled people with accurate and current information concerning the disaster. Provision of this sort of information will guide people's behavior in both the short and long run.

Aftermath Preparation

Preparing to accommodate disabled persons after a disaster requires an assessment of the extent, nature, and location of damages in order to determine repair/construction/cleanup costs. Acquiring a clear understanding of the aftermath of a disaster involves classifying the scale of its impact (Harper, 2004). Scale can be discussed in terms of the degree of damage (none, light, moderate, severe) and scope of impact (localized versus widespread). A tornado may totally demolish anything in its path (severe damage), but its path may be only a few hundred feet wide (localized damage). On the other hand, a hurricane may damage some (but not all) structures over several states. Understanding the population affected, particularly the number of disabled people impacted during a disaster is important because it allows the government to determine recovery time. The length of the impact in terms of time to full recovery/reconstruction may increase the economic burden many disabled individuals currently experience.

Additionally, policymakers have a role to ensure that zoning regulations are updated to encourage disabled families to build in less damage- prone areas or to take construction measures that will make their residences more storm resilient. Educational mandates about including preparedness plans in school curriculum can help disabled children better respond to a looming disaster. Educational institutions should be encouraged to develop courses and degree programs that train individuals to prepare and respond to disasters. These programs should include elements that address the needs of the disabled. Continued and updated training of preparedness participants such as responders, school officials, volunteers, etc will facilitate future disaster preparedness when the disabled is concerned. The use of public service announcements urging the disabled to be prepared and ready to handle a disaster will raise beforehand awareness and alter behavioral dispositions towards such a social issue.

CONCLUSION

In closing, we introduce a disaster preparedness model based upon the disabled's experiences after Hurricane Sandy. We show that a comprehensive qualitative plan must synchronize a Pre-Disaster, Disaster Imminent, During Disaster and Post-

Disaster Stage across multiple tiers including household, community and society. We also emphasize the need for these three tiers to share information concerning practical measures and policies that can aid in the successful preparedness and management efforts in the event of a disaster. In addition, we highlight avenues that policymakers can take to address proper preparedness plans for disabled individuals.

Notes

1. References for Table 3.1 are American Red Cross (n.d.) for items 1A, 2A, 4A, 5A, 6A, 7A, 9A, 10A, 11A, 13A, 14A, 15A, 16A, 17A, and 18A; Centers for Disease Control (2012) for items 3A, 1B, 8B, 10B, 14B, 15B, and 5C; Chatham Emergency Management Agency (2014) for item 8A; Disasters R Us (n.d.) for items 5A, 13A3, 16A, 19A, 4B, 12B, and 1C; Dyson (2006) for item 3C; Federal Emergency Management Agency (2014) for items 1A, 4A, 6A, 10A, 11A, 13A, 14A, 15A, 16A, 4B, 7B, 11B, 12B, 13B, 16B, 4C, 5C, and 7C; Hans (n.d.) for item 2C; National Fire Protection Association (2007) for items 6A, 10A, 11A, 13A, 14A, 18A, 3B and 12B; National Organization On Disability (2009) for items 6A, 14A, 17A, 18A, 19A, 5B, and 12B; St. Louis County MO Office of Emergency Management (2010) for 6B; and. U.S. Department of Justice (n.d.) for items 6A, 10A, 11A, 13A, 14A, 17A, 18A, 5B,9B, and 12B. For the items listed above, the item's number and letter indicates its location in the table. The letter indicates which column the items appears (e.g., column C is the third column from the left). The number of the item indicates its position from the top of the list (i.e., 3 indicates the third item from the top).
2. References: American Red Cross (n.d.) for items 1A, 2A, 3A, 6A, and 7A; Centers for Disease Control (2012) for items 1B, 2B, and 6B; Federal Emergency Management (2014) for items 4A, 5A, 4B, 5B, 1C, 2C, and 3C.
3. References: American Red Cross website (n.d.) for items 1A, 2A, and 4A; Disasters R Us (n.d.) for item 6A; General Dynamics (2013) for item 2C; Mersheeva and Friedrich (2013) for are household is waiting the disaster out, it should try to maintain as normal of a routine as possible. This includes regular bed and meal times and other daily activities. item 1C; National Fire Protection Association (2007) for item 3A; National Organization On Disability (2009) for items 4A, 5A, and 4B; U.S. Department of Justice (n.d.) for items 4A and 5A.
4. References: Becker (2009) for items 11B and 5C; Federal Emergency Management (2011) for items 1B, 4B, 5B, 6B, 8B,1C, 2C, 3C, and 5C; Frailing and Harper (2012) for item 12A; Hans for item 4C; McMillan (1998) for items 1A, 6A, 7A, 8A, 2B, 3B and 4B; National Organization On Disability (2009) for items 4A and 9A; U.S. Department of Justice (n.d.) for items 4B and 7B.

The authors would like to thank Dr. Jessica M. Doucet for her comments on a previous draft of this chapter.

REFERENCES

American Red Cross. (n.d.). Disaster preparedness for people with disabilities. Retrieved from http://www.hhs.gov/od/documents/disabilityAmericanRed Cross.pdf

AmeriCares. (2013). Unmet needs remain for Sandy survivors with disabilities. Retrieved from AmeriCares website: http://www.americares.org/who-we-are/newsroom/news/hurricane-sandy-survivor-disabilities-unmet-needs-remain

Associated Press. (2012). Hundreds of elderly and disabled New Yorkers evacuated during Hurricane Sandy are still homeless. Retrieved from the *New York Daily News* website: http://www.nydailynews.com/new-york/elderly-disabled-sandy-victims-homeless-article-1.1227517#ixzz2rLnGTUZi

Atkins, D., & Guisti, C. (2004). The confluence of poverty and disability. Retrieved from http://www.housingforall.org/rop0304%20poverty%20and%20 disability.pdf

Becker, C. (2009). Disaster recovery: A local government responsibility. *ICMA Publications, 91*(2). Retrieved from the ICMA website: http://webapps.icma.org/ pm/9102/public/cover.cfm?author=christine%20becker&title=disaster%20recovery%3A%20%20a%local%20government%20responsibility

Beekman, D. (2013). NYC discriminated against people with disabilities during Sandy, judge rules. Retrieved from the *New York Daily News* website: http://www. nydailynews.com/new-york/nyc-discriminated-disabled-sandy-judge-article-1.1510316

Bethel, J. W., Foreman, A. N., & Burke, S. C. (2011). Disaster preparedness among medi cally vulnerable populations. *American Journal of Preventative Medicine, 40*(2), 139–143.

Braddock, D., Rizzolo M.C., Thompson, M., & Bell, R. (2004). Emerging technologies and cognitive disability. *Journal of Special Education Technology, 19*(4), 49–56.

Brault. M.W. (2012). Americans with disabilities: 2010 household economic studies. Retrieved from http://www.census.gov/prod/2012pubs/p70-131.pdf

Burchardt, T. (2005). The education and employment of disabled young People. Retrieved from http://www.jrf.org.uk/sites/files/jrf/1861348363.pdf

Centers for Disease Control. (2012). Crisis emergency risk communication manual, 2012 edition. Retrieved from http://emergency.cdc.gov/cerc/pdf/CERC_ 2012edition.pdf

Chatham Emergency Management Agency. (2014). Find your evacuation route. Retrieved from Chatham Emergency Management Agency website: http://www.chat hamemergency.org/evacuation-information/find-your-evacuation-zone.php

Cutter, S. L., Barnes, L., Berry, M., Burton, C., Evans, E., Tate, E., & Webb, J. (2008). A place-based model for understanding community resilience to natural disasters. *Global Environmental Change, 18*, 598–606.

Davis, K. (1990). A social barriers model of disability: Theory into practice: The emergence of the "seven needs." Retrieved from http://www.leeds.ac.uk/disability-studies/archiveuk/DavisK/davis-social%20barriers.pdf

Department for International Development. (2011). Defining disaster resilience: ADFID approach paper. Retrieved from https://www.gov.uk/government/uploads/ system/uploads/attachment_data/file/186874/defining-disaster-resilience-approach-paper.pdf

Disasters R Us. (n.d.). Get a plan. Retrieved from the Disasters R Us website: http://www. disastersrus.org/MyDisasters/disability/disability_preparedness.htm

Disabled World. (2014a). Definition of disabilities. Retrieved from the Disabled World website http://www.disabled-world.com/disability/types/

Disabled World. (2014b). Physical and mobility impairments facts news and information. Retrieved from the Disabled World website http://www.disabled-world.com/disability/types/mobility/

Dyson, M. E. (2006). *Come hell or high water: Hurricane Katrina and the color of disaster.* New York, NY: Basic Books.

Federal Emergency Management Agency. (2014). Individuals with disabilities or access & functional needs. Retrieved from the Ready.gov website: http://www.fema.gov/plan/prepare/specialplans.shtm

Federal Emergency Management Agency. (2011). *A whole community approach to emergency management: Principles, themes, and pathways for action.* Washington, DC: FEMA. Retrieved from http://www.emd.wa.gov/about/documents/FEMA_Whole_Community.pdf

Feeney, S. A. (2012). Disabled people especially vulnerable in calamities such as Sandy. Retrieved from the AM New York website: http://www.amny.com/urbanite-1.812039/disabled-people-especially-vulnerable-in-calamities-such-as-Sandy

Filmer, D. (2008). Disability, poverty, and schooling in developing countries: Results from 14 household surveys. *World Bank Economic Review, 22*(1), 141–163.

Fox, M. H., White, G. W., Rooney, C., & Rowland, J. L. (2007). Disaster preparedness and response for persons with mobility impairments, *Journal of Disability Policy Studies, 17*(4), 196–205.

Frailing, K., & Harper, D. W. (2012). Disaster phases, structural vulnerability and crime. In L. A. Eargle & A. Esmail (Eds.), *Black beaches and bayous: The BP deepwater horizon oil spill disaster* (pp. 231–247). Lanham, MD: University Press of America.

Fujiura G.T., Yamaki, K., & Czechowicz, S. (1998). Disability among ethnic and racial minorities in the United States: a summary of economic status and family structure. *Journal of Disability Policy Studies, 9*(2), 111–130.

Galea, S., Nandi, A., & Vlahov, D. (2005). The epidemiology of post-traumatic stress disorder after disasters. *Epidemiologic Reviews, 27*(1), 78–91.

General Dynamics. (2013). Maintaining public safety communications in disaster situations: Key requirements for uninterrupted, interoperable communications. White paper. Retrieved from http://www.gdc4s.com/Documents/NotInNavDocs/GD_Disaster_Response_Communications_White_Paper_FINAL_26-8-13.pdf

Griffith, C., Jeffers, C., & Gardner, P. (2012). Creating and strengthening community-based disaster coalitions. Retrieved from the Centers for Disease Control website: http://blogs.cdc.gov/publichealthmatters/2012/04/creating-and-strengthening-community-based-disaster-coalitions

Guion, D. T., Scammon, D. L., & Borders, A. L. (2007). Weathering the storm: a social marketing perspective on disaster preparedness and response with lessons from Hurricane Katrina. *Journal of Public Policy and Marketing, 26*(1), 20–32.

Hans, A. (n.d.). Disaster management and disability: Promoting a research agenda. Retrieved from http://www.preventionweb.net/files/9706_DisasterManagement.pdf

Harper, C. L. (2004). *Environment and society: Human perspectives on environmental issues* (fifth edition). Upper Saddle River: Pearson/Prentice Hall.

Hoag, C. (2011). Disaster plan for people with disabilities needed for Los Angeles. *Huffington Los Angeles*, Retrieved from Huff Post website http://www.huffingtonpost.com/2011/02/11/los-angeles-disaster-plan-for-people-with-disabilities_n_822265.html

Hoffman, S. (2009). Preparing for disaster: protecting the most vulnerable in emergencies. *UC-Davis Law Review, 42*(5), 1491–1547.

Iezzoni, L. I. (2014). Policy concerns raised by growing US population aging with disability. *Disability and Health Journal, 7*(1), S64-S68.

Jenkins, S. P., & Rigg, J. A. (2003). Disability and disadvantage: Selection, onset, and duration effects, Retrieved from http://eprints.lse.ac.uk/6323/1/Disability_and_ Disadvantage_Selection,_onset_and_duration_effects.pdf

Kates, R. W., Colten, C. E., Laska, S., & Leatherman, S. P. (2006). Reconstruction of New Orleans after Hurricane Katrina: A research perspective. Retrieved from http://belfercenter.hks.harvard.edu/files/xstandard/kates_pnas_katrina_2006.pdf

Kotler, P., & Zaltman, G. (1971). Social marketing: An approach to planned social change. *Journal of Marketing, 35*, 3–12.

Kramer, W. M., & Bahme, C. W. (1992). *Fire officer's guide to disaster Control* (second edition). Saddle Brook, NJ: PennWell Books.

Livio, S. K. (2014). Group a 'light' for disabled people still reeling from Hurricane Sandy. *The Star Ledger.* Retrieved from http://www.nj.com/politics/index.ssf/2014/01/group-a-beacon-for-disabled-people-stillstranded-by-hurricane-sandy.htm

Mays, J. (2012). For disabled New Yorkers, effects from Hurricane Sandy to linger for months. *DNA Info New York.* Retrieved from http://www.dnainfo.com/new-york/20121113/kensington/for-disabled-new-yorkers-effects-from-hurricane-sandy-linger

McClure, L.A., Boninger, M. L., Oyster, M.L., Roach, M.J., Nagy, J., & Nemunaitis, G. (2011). Emergency evacuation readiness of full-time wheelchair users with spinal cord injury. *Archives of Physical Medicine and Rehabilitation, 92*(3), 491–498.

McMillan, C. R. (1998). Natural disasters: prepare, mitigate, manage. Retrieved from http://www.csa.com/discoveryguide/archives/ndht.php

Mersheeva, V., & Friedrich, G. (2013). Continuous monitoring problem for disaster management. Retrieved from http://uav.lakeside-labs.com/fileadmin/user-upload/papers/CMP_VeRoLog2013.pdf

Mileti, D. S. (1999). *Disasters by design: A reassessment of natural hazards in the United States.* Washington, DC: Joseph Henry Press.

———, & O'Brien, P. W. (1992). Warnings during disaster: Normalizing communicated risk. *Social Problems, 39*(1), 40–57.

Morgan, M. G., Fischhoff, B., Bostrom, A., & Atman, C. J. (2002). *Risk communication: A mental models approach.* Cambridge, UK: Cambridge University Press.

National Council On Disability. (2009). *Effective emergency management: Making improvements for communities and people with disabilities.* Retrieved from http://www.ncd.gov/publications/2009/Aug122009#ch14

National Fire Protection Association. (2007). Emergency evacuation planning guide for people with disabilities. Retrieved from http://www.nfpa.org/assets/files/pdf/forms/evacuationguide.pdf

National Geographic News. (2005). The deadliest tsunami in history. Retrieved from http://news.nationalgeographic.com/news/2004/12/1227_041226_tsunami.html

National Highway Administration. (2013). Using highways during evacuation operations for events with advance notice. Retrieved from http://www.ops.fhwa.dot.gov/ publications/evac_primer/19_components.htm

National Organization On Disability. (2004). 2004 NOD annual report.Retrieved from http://nod.org/about_us/our_history/annual_reports/2004_annual_report/#

———. (2009). *Functional needs of people with disabilities: A guide for emergency managers, planners and responders.* Washington: National Organization On Disability. Retrieved from http://www.nod.org/assets/downloads/Guide-Emergency-Planners.pdf

National Research Council (1989). Improving risk communication. Washington, DC: The National Academies Press

Norris, F. H., Friedman, M. J., Watson, P. J., Bryne, C. M., Diaz, E. & Kaniasty, K. (2002). 60,000 disaster victims speak: Part 1. An empirical review of the empirical literature, 1981–2001. *Psychiatry, 65*(3), 207–239.

Patrick, S. M. (2012). Man-made cities and natural disasters: The growing threat. Retrieved from the Council on Foreign Relations website: http://blogs.cfr.org/patrick/2012/08/14/man-made-cities-and-natural-disasters-the-growing-threat/

Peek, L., & Stough, L.M. (2010). Children with disabilities in the context of disaster: A social vulnerability perspective, *Child Development, 81* (4), 1260–1270.

Phillips, B. D., & Morrow, B. H. (2007). Social science research needs: Focus on vulnerable populations, forecasting, and warnings, *Natural Hazards Review, 8*(3), 61–68.

Randall, J. L. (2013). State bills would establish post-Hurricane Sandy confidential registry to aid stranded disabled. *Staten Island Live.* Retrieved from http://www.silive.com/news/index.ssf/2013/11/state_bills_would_establish_po.html

Reedy, J. (1993). *Marketing to consumers with disabilities.* Chicago, IL: Probus Publishing Company.

Richardson, C. (2012). Hurricane Sandy floodwaters destroyed a disabled New York City lawyer's vital transportation, but he soldiers on. *NY Daily News.* Retrieved from http://www.nydailynews.com/new-york/brooklyn/disabled-nyc-attorney-battles-back-hurricane-sandy-losses-article-1.1210386

Romo-Murphy, E., James, R., & Adams, M. (2011). Facilitating disaster preparedness through local radio broadcasting. *Disasters, 35*(4), 801–815.

Rooney, C., & White, G. W. (2007). Narrative analysis of a disaster preparedness and emergency response survey from persons with mobility impairments. *Journal of Disability Policy Studies, 17*(4), 206–215.

Santora, M., & Weiser, B. (2013). Court says New York neglected disabled in emergencies. *The New York Times.* Retrieved from http://www.nytimes.com/2013/11/08/ nyregion/new-yorks-emergency-plans-violate-disabilities-act-judge-says.html?pagewanted=1

Social Security Administration. (2013). Social security basic facts. Retrieved from http://www.ssa.gov/pressoffice/basicfact.htm

St. Louis County MO Office of Emergency Management. (2010). The five phases of emergency management." Retrieved from http://www.stlouisco.com/LawandPublicSafety/EmergencyManagement/TheFivePhasesofEmergencyManagement

Thevenaz, C., & Resodihardjo, S. L. (2010). All the best laid plans . . . conditions impeding proper emergency response. *International Journal of Production Economics, 126*(1), 7–21.

Troy, D., Carson, A., Vanderbeek, J., & Hutton, A. (2008). Enhancing community-based disaster preparedness with information technology: community disaster information system. *Disasters, 32*(1), 149–165.

United Nations. (2006). Convention on the rights of persons with disabilities. Retrieved from United Nations website. http://www.un.org/disabilities/convention/conventionfull.shtml

U.S. Census Bureau. (2013). Workers with a disability less likely to be employed, more likely to hold jobs with lower earnings, Census Bureau Reports. Retrieved from the U.S. Census Bureau website: http://www.census.gov/newsroom/releases/archives/american_community_survey_acs/cb13-47.html

————. (2010). Facts for features: 20th anniversary of American with Disabilities Act: July 26. Retrieved from the U.S. Census Bureau website: http://www.census.gov/newsroom/releases/archives/facts_for_features_special_editions/cb10-ff13.html

U.S. Department of Justice. (2009). A guide to disability rights laws. Retrieved from http://www.ada.gov/cguide.pdf

————. (n.d.). An ADA guide for local governments: Making community emergency preparedness and response programs accessible to people with disabilities. Retrieved from http://www.ada.gov/emerprepguideprt.pdf

Van Willigen, M., Edwards, T., Edwards, B., & Hessee S. (2002). Riding out the storm: Experiences of the physically disabled during hurricanes Bonnie, Dennis, and Floyd. *Natural Hazards Review, 3*(3), 98–106.

Weinstein, J., & Pillai, V. K. (2001). *Demography: The science of population.* Boston: Allyn and Bacon.

Wiener, J. M., & Tilly, J. (2002). Population ageing in the United States of America: implications for public programmes. *International Journal of Epidemiology, 31*(4), 776–781.

Westcott, L. (2013a). When disaster and disability converge. *Inter Press Service.* Retrieved from http://www.ipsnews.net/2013/08/when-disaster-and-disability-converge

————. (2013b). Poor and disabled when disaster strikes. *Inter Press Service.* Retrieved from http://www.ipsnews.net/2013/08/poor-and-disabled-when-disaster-strikes

Wisner, B., Blakie, P., Cannon, T., & Davis, I. (2004). *At risk: Natural hazards, people's vulnerability, and disasters* (second edition). New York, NY: Routledge.

World Health Organization. (2011). World report on disability. Retrieved from http://whqlibdoc.who.int/publications/2011/9789240685215_eng.pdf

Yeo, R., & Moore, K. (2003). Including disabled people in poverty reduction work: nothing about us, without us. *World Development, 31*(3), 571–590.

Yeo, R. (2005). Disability, Poverty and the New Development Agenda. Retrieved from http://r4d.dfid.gov.uk/PDF/Outputs/Disability/RedPov_agenda.pdf

Zack, N. (2012). Disaster relief. In D. Callahan, P. Singer, & R. Chadwick (Eds.), *Encyclopedia of applied ethics* (pp. 817–825). London: Academic Press

CHAPTER FOUR
HUGS, HANDS, AND HOPE DURING HURRICANE SANDY: THE PERSPECTIVE OF A NATIONAL RELIEF VOLUNTEER

Tanya M. Gulliver-Garcia

> The word "disaster" literally means the loss of a star, or the loss of your guiding light. Whether the disaster is large or small, intimate or collective, you don't see it coming. It is, by definition, a shock, a surprise. The disaster knocks you off your axis, jolts you out of your normal orbit (Clark, 2005, p. 384).

During a disaster community organizations are always one of the first to respond. During Superstorm Sandy, this was no different; in fact, many organizations had active disaster relief operations for several months after in the states of New Jersey and New York. As a volunteer with a large, national relief organization I was able to spend 130 days in New Jersey in direct disaster response and recovery. I spent my first two weeks managing three large evacuation shelters. The next four weeks I worked building community partnerships and connecting networks of support to provide goods and services for those affected. For the final 13 weeks I worked to help provide financial assistance for individuals and families recovering from damage to their homes.

As a PhD student at York University, in Toronto, Canada, working on themes related to disaster and urban sociology—particularly environmental justice, social vulnerability and community resiliency—Superstorm Sandy was an opportunity for praxis. During my two disaster deployments to New Jersey, I was able to take the theoretical and academic knowledge I'd gained from my studies and see it play out in front of me throughout my time in the state. As a student of disasters, this work provided me with an experience that most in academia are unable to access.

This chapter frames my experiences as a volunteer with a national, relief organization during Superstorm Sandy within the context of disaster vulnerability, resiliency and catastrophe. I argue that the impact on vulnerable populations clearly situates Superstorm Sandy as a catastrophe, not a normal disaster, within the disaster paradigm. This difference has clear implications for responders, as well as residents and communities, impacted by a disaster.

VULNERABILITY

Tierney (2006) says that vulnerability science sees disasters as a being influenced by a combination of three factors:

- Disaster agent—the hurricane, earthquake, technological event etc.;
- Physical setting—built environment and environmental factors—that can improve or worsen the impact of a disaster and;
- Population vulnerability (which many call social vulnerability).

One broad definition of vulnerability according to the United Nations International Strategy on Disaster Reduction is "[t]he conditions determined by physical, social, economic and environmental factors or processes, which increase the susceptibility of a community to the impact of hazards" (Phillips et. al., 2009, p. 35).

This is expanded upon by the most common working definition created by Blaikie et. al. (1994, in Oliver-Smith, 2006), "By vulnerability we mean the characteristics of a person or group in terms of their capacity to anticipate, cope with, resist, and recover from the impact of a natural hazard" (n.p.). To their use of the term 'natural hazard' could certainly be added acts of terrorism and environmental or technological events as well. There is a clear linkage to be made with the use of 'anticipate, cope with, resist and recover from' and the emergency management paradigm of preparedness, mitigation, response and recovery which will be explored later.

In both normal disasters and catastrophes, the impact of the disaster is felt the most at the individual/family level. Disasters tend to affect people differentially based on their circumstances prior to a disaster, and those that are most socially or physical vulnerable suffer the most harm. "The concept of vulnerability links the relationship that people have with their environment to social forces and institutions and cultural values that sustain or contest them," (Oliver-Smith, 2006, n.p.). There are two major forms of vulnerability before, during, and after a disaster: physical and social. Of the two, physical vulnerability is perhaps the easiest to solve—or at least create solutions for—whereas social vulnerability requires addressing a whole host of systemic issues that are usually bigger than the individual disaster.

As a sociologist my interest is in the area of social vulnerabilities. However, there is a link between physical and social vulnerability that cannot be ignored which has strong ties to issues of environmental justice and environmental racism. Oliver-Smith (2006) noted that "social systems generate the conditions that place different kinds of people, often differentiated along axes of class, race, ethnicity, gender, or age, at different levels of risk from the same hazard and suffering from the same event (n.p.)." Those that are most at-risk during a disaster due to their social vulnerability and lack of supports, tend to also be the same group that are most physically at-risk. They live in dangerous areas: in low-lying areas near flood plains. They live in sub-standard housing: trailers or structurally unsound buildings that face risks from wind and rain.

This can be seen though the example of real estate in a coastal area; either in a country like Sri Lanka affected by the Asian Ocean Tsunami or in the Gulf Coast states of the United States which are frequently impacted by hurricanes. A wealthy individual who maintains a fishing "cottage" on the Gulf or owns beachfront property in Sri Lanka, will be impacted by a natural disaster but the overall affect will be less than someone who has a subsistence existence.

The wealthy homeowner is more likely to have insurance for their home, resources to rebuild and as it is a secondary home may primarily live in an area that was not impacted by the disaster. For those whose family has lived and fished in the area for decades and depends on the coast for survival, they have lost their source of income as well as their primary residence. They may not have been able to evacuate due to lack of resources, lack of warning, or the need to protect both home and fishing vessel. As those with a low income, they might not have been able to afford adequate insurance coverage and won't have additional funds for rebuilding. They must rebuild their home and yet must sustain their income during that period as well—even if their primary income source has been impacted. People in these scenarios were impacted by the disaster but the those that were at-risk before the disaster are even more marginalized now.

Risk increases when faced with a catastrophe instead of a normal disaster. Not only have the numbers of disasters increased in recent years, so has the impact of, and significance of, disasters. This is likely to continue as a result of technology, climate change and continuing environmental degradation. An increase in the number of "catastrophic disasters" has meant that vulnerability and resiliency will play a greater role in recovery and response.

CATASTROPHIC VERSUS NORMAL DISASTERS

Normal disasters can create intense problems for communities especially those with limited resources. Catastrophic disasters result in extensive challenges for people and governments that are often beyond their ability to cope. Quarantelli (2006) said that early disaster researchers in the 1950s addressed ways in which "disasters as social occasions differed from everyday emergencies" (n.p.). He said that they defined four major differences including the need for co-operation and partnerships with and amongst a large number of unfamiliar organizations, the need to adjust to a loss of autonomy and freedom in actions, application of different performance standards and private-public interface that operates at a much closer level than usual.

However, catastrophic disasters—or what Garrett et. al. (2007) call "mega-disasters"—operate on a very different scale, and ergo by necessity, so must response. The U.S. Department of Homeland Security created a definition of catastrophic incidents in its 2004 National Response Plan which stated:

> Catastrophic incidents [are] any natural or manmade incident, including terrorism, which results in extraordinary levels of mass casualties, damages, or disruptions severely affecting the population, infrastructure, environment, economy, and national morale and/or government functions. A catastrophic event could result in sustained national impacts over a prolonged period of time; almost immediately exceeds resources normally available to State, local, tribal, and private sector authorities; and significantly interrupts governmental operations and emergency services to such an extent that national security could be threatened. All catastrophic events are considered Incidents of National Significance (emphasis added) (in Sylves, 2006, pp. 27–28).

It is critical that emergency planners, government officials and groups like the Red Cross, Salvation Army, Southern Baptists and others consider how best to construct emergency plans that apply to routine emergencies, disasters and catastrophes while recognizing the differences inherent in each. In particular, catastrophes are so immense and the impact so significant that many typical ways of functioning in normal disasters no longer apply (see Table 4.1).

Table 4.1 Normal Disasters Versus Catastrophes

Impact	Normal Disasters	Catastrophes
Likelihood	Probabilistic chance of occurrence	Possibilistic chance of occurrence
Frequency	Often predictable in nature, if not scope. Hazards repeat themselves.	Rarity breeds unfamiliarity. Occurrence is infrequent, so preparation and planning focuses on normal disasters.
Duration	Limited duration of event and then opportunity for response and recovery.	Event may have extended duration. Response/recovery is extended and magnified.
Households Preparedness	People are aware of what to do but often, hazards are normalized so preparedness is weak in some cases.	So rare that preparedness is usually ignored. "It won't happen here!"
Physical Impact	Damage is localized with pockets of extreme damage and areas of little to no damage.	Heavy impact to much or all of the built community structure.
Local Officials	Local officials are able to respond with limited (if any) limitations.	Local officials are unable to undertake their usual work role, and this often extends into the recovery period

Table 4.1 (Continued) Normal Disasters Versus Catastrophes

Impact	Normal Disasters	Catastrophes
First Responders	Victims of the disaster, or residents in the area of the disaster.	Victims of the catastrophe, or residents in the area of the disaster.
Timeliness of Emergency Response	Response is very quick.	Extensive delays in understanding scope of catastrophe and providing sufficient emergency response.
Isolation	Assistance is provided from internal resources and those of nearby communities.	Help from nearby communities cannot be provided because of an inability to access large areas affected by the disaster. Help will come from distant communities and take longer.
Migration	Is temporary, if it occurs at all. Permanent displacement most likely to be voluntary.	Is significant—affecting large numbers of people for a long duration. In many cases displacement (and sometimes migration) is forced.
Everyday Functioning	Disruption of social functions occurs but is not widespread or extensive.	Most, if not all, of the everyday community functions are sharply and concurrently interrupted
Media	Media is primarily local with brief reporting by cable and network media.	Media socially constructs the situation—especially nonlocal mass media i.e cable TV. Limited opportunity for analysis.
Politics	Politics plays a role but is primarily at the local level.	The political arena becomes even more important and involves higher ranking national politicians and bureaucrats.
Response Solutions	Response by local and neighboring NGOs and emergency responders.	Militarization/privatization of response by federal government.

Based on Clarke (2005), Garrett et. al (2007), Oliver-Smith (2006), Quarantelli (2006), Rodriguez & Dynes (2006), Rodriguez et. al (2006), Scanlon (2001), Sylves (2006), and Waugh (2006).

MY SANDY DEPLOYMENT

I lost the fall. And the winter. And all the holidays—Labor Day, my birthday, Halloween, Thanksgiving, Christmas, New Year's Day, Martin Luther King Day, Valentine's Day and St. Patrick's Day—in those seasons. Between Hurricane Isaac and Superstorm Sandy I spent over 155 days doing disaster response as volunteer between August 27th and March 17th.

As a Canadian temporarily based in Louisiana, my work with Hurricane Isaac was what I had expected when I first signed up and became involved with this national disaster organization. With a disaster in my own state, and having been given a leadership role in "Community Partnerships," I knew that I'd be there through most of the event. I helped out the first full day of the DR (Disaster Response) and I helped close one of the local offices down a month later.

Sandy was Different

Thursday, October 25th 2012

My role as a volunteer responder for this national relief organization to the Hurricane/Superstorm Sandy disaster started the way it often does. The email pinged at 8:40am with a message from my local chapter's manager in charge of deployment. "Hurricane Sandy is coming to the East Coast . . . We're not sure where or when Sandy will make landfall, but we know there will be communities who need our help. If you're able to deploy sometime in the next week for a period of 14 days or longer, please email me at [email redacted] with your name and availability. I will ensure your record is properly coded to "match up" with any recruitment opportunities based on your qualifications and interests."
I reply an hour later, "I'm free to go."
Over the next 30 minutes we exchange several emails to decide what activities I should consider deploying in. My region believes in cross-training its volunteers so I was qualified in client casework, community partnerships and sheltering. Pre-landfall the biggest need is always for sheltering; it's important that people are kept safe during a storm. But it's time to wait to see what the system pops up.

Friday, October 26th 2012

During Hurricane Isaac I had served as the lead for the Southeast Louisiana for this same national relief organization working in the Community Partnerships area. My colleague N.H. and I had shared the work of leading the local teams in Southern Louisiana; he focused on the Baton Rouge area and I focused on New Orleans. He was staff, I was a volunteer. We worked under a staff reserve leader who is on-call to the organization at least six months out of the year in order to ensure that critical and skilled leadership is in place. Our team had been strong and productive. The three of us had worked on Hurricane Isaac for over a month between late August and late September and were joined for short periods by more than a dozen volunteers specialized in partnering from across the country and Canada.
Friday afternoon the staff lead emails N.H. and I. "Want to come and play hurricane again? New Jersey, let me know. Trying to put a team together before they close airports. . ."
Over that afternoon I coordinate with the staff lead and the chapter's volunteer manager. N.H. needs to stay and work in Louisiana; he can't be released from work

for another disaster so soon. I confirm that I am absolutely available to go. While I want to go out and "play hurricane" with the staff lead in Jersey, I will be sent wherever the need is greatest. There is no guarantee that it will be New Jersey or what my role will be.

I start packing my bags. Digging up cold weather clothes while in Louisiana requires some work. I can't remember the last time I was out of shorts and sandals. I visit a local dollar store to buy snacks. Disasters often mean long days without a chance to grab regular meals so I buy some protein bars, granola bars and quick sugar treats.

Saturday, October 27th 2012

At 10 a.m. another email arrives confirming my deployment. By mid-afternoon I'm on a plane to Philadelphia where I grab a car and drive up to central Jersey. I've been sent as a supervisor in the sheltering program. The organization uses a series of abbreviated letters to assign your focus area, type of job and level of responsibility or position. These letters are one of many acronyms that the relief organization loves to use—along with its many sayings and slogans—but learning them is important. You use it, and your volunteer number, on almost every piece of paperwork you sign and it helps create a chain of command in an operation.

This national relief organization creates standardized national training packages. It doesn't matter where you live, you'll receive the same training and information. While local chapters might create adjustments in their own responses —one chapter puts coffee makers in their shelter start-up kits, another chapter doesn't—this standardization means you can fly a dozen volunteers in from across the country and almost instantly create a functional team.

This is critically important. The majority of people who respond to disasters with this organization are volunteers. They give up their vacation time, take time off work, leave their families behind and travel to a disaster affected area. Most deployments are two weeks; some people are able to stay for three. With a long disaster response this can mean a constantly changing group of volunteers; knowing their roles and functions from the get-go is necessary. During the pre-landfall stage particularly, there aren't always enough volunteers to go around. There definitely isn't time for lengthy training.

This was abundantly clear during Hurricane Isaac. The storm was predicted to hit Florida before it suddenly shifted west. The majority of volunteers and supplies had been sent to Florida to be ready for immediate response during and just after landfall. They ended up having to chase the storm westward which meant local volunteers and those who did get deployed later in the cycle had to short-handedly provide response. Members of a local Rotary club that I had trained on Thursday, August 23rd were in place as shelter volunteers at a Washington Parish shelter at 6 a.m. Tuesday, August 28th.

Sunday, October 28th 2012

After a couple hours of sleep I head to the Princeton NJ chapter where people from several different areas, mostly reserve and paid staff filling the highest level positions, were operationalizing the planning that had taken place in the community and the state. Local chapter staff and volunteers work year-round with local officials to ensure that emergency plans and responses are developed and coordinated, well in advance of a disaster. New Jersey was "lucky" in that it had been able to start rolling-out its plans during Hurricane Irene in the fall of 2012, but suffered only minimal impact during that storm. It was a good test run to see what worked and what needed improvement. The disaster management cycle—preparedness, mitigation, response and recovery—is very critical to the operations of this relief organization.

Preparedness

In each local chapter volunteer and community preparedness is an ongoing endeavor. Preparedness in the emergency management context is generally considered to be a focus on being ready to respond if, or when, an emergency or disaster occurs. It is generally localized, of a specific duration and crisis-situation specific (Lakoff, 2006). Preparedness at an emergency response or community level tends to have more of a structural focus rather than a population-specific focus. Community organizations help fill that gap by also focusing on the individual.

Preparedness, according to Yarnal (2007) "involves taking measures in advance of a local hazard to ensure effective response to it is impacts. It includes issuing timely and effective early warnings and temporarily evacuating people and possessions from threatened areas" (p. 252). Evacuation is a challenge; Garrett et. al. (2007) report that 92 percent of Americans are hampered from immediate evacuation—even if ordered to do so—because of the need to "ensure the safety of dependent family members—children (48 percent), elderly (47 percent), disabled (45 percent), and pets (34 percent), (p. 193).

Lakoff (2006) stated that currently preparedness focuses on the logistical issues i.e., ". . . hospital surge capacity, the coherence of evacuation plans . . ." (n.p.) but that doing that in isolation from the broader issues of vulnerability and security amongst the population creates challenges.

To a certain degree this is where this national relief organization steps up. They understand the needs of the local community and addresses issues that affect vulnerable populations. Potential shelter spaces are examined for safety requirements including size, access to bathrooms and cooking facilities, composition of the building (i.e., stability of the structure including the roof, ability to shelter during hurricane or tornado landfall in an area without glass) and geographical location (i.e., access, elevation, situation in relation to a flood plain, history of past flooding events).

The organizations knows that many of the people who use its shelters will be the most vulnerable populations so provisions are made to create a shelter with diverse staffing. A shelter team is often composed of shelter management, dorm supervisors, disaster health and/or mental health staff and a local police official for security. Partnerships with groups like Save the Children provide support for kids in the shelters, while some shelters are open to hosting animals, often through cooperative partnerships with local animal welfare organizations. Shelter posters are widely available in both English and Spanish but materials are accessible in many other languages depending upon a community's need. The organizations ensures that food is available; usually heater meals or cold snacks during a landfall event, but quickly afterwards partners with Southern Baptist Relief, Salvation Arm or another aid group to get feeding programs up and running. Each kitchen or trailer can put out hundreds, if not thousands, of meals a day.

Many researchers feel that households that are the most vulnerable are not prepared for disasters. The 2007 US Preparedness report from Redlener et. al. (2007) found that while nearly 47 percent of people surveyed believe that within the next five years they "will personally experience a major disaster such as a terror attack or a catastrophic weather emergency" (p. 3) only one-third are actually prepared for it. 43 percent actually have no intention of making any preparations.

Education is a critical component to effective preparedness as is evidenced by Cuba's work in reducing the number of deaths and injuries. Their system includes education in elementary school which "allows children to understand the basic concept of risk from hurricanes at an early age, and use this as a foundation for learning such skills as first aid and storm preparedness" (Garrett et. al., 2007, p. 194). Additionally, hurricane drills occur annually helping both the community and the household prepare for a disaster.

The organization does this work very effectively in many communities through participations in community fairs and events, media, training and publications. In the South Louisiana area one of the initiatives is aimed at helping kids prepare for an evacuation by decorating a pillowcase with items they might need including items not usually found on an evacuation list including photos of their friends, books, school work, toys and stuffed animals. Students were given pillowcases on which they could color items needed during a disaster evacuation. Giving them an easy way to collect their belongings before evacuating to a shelter helps them feel in control and helps their stay at the shelter be a little more comfortable and secure.

Another program is focused on helping businesses, community groups, faith-based organizations and services prepare to step-up in a disaster. People are trained ahead of time to staff the various organizational functions and corporate and community response plans are developed. When disaster strikes local volunteers are ready to go until other national volunteers can get to the scene.

Mitigation

According to Etkin and Stefanovic (2005) mitigation is "sustained actions to reduce or eliminate the long-term impacts and risks associated with natural and human-induced disasters" (p. 468). They stated that mitigation is a process to either reduce or transfer/share risk including "a blend of policies, educational programs, structures (such as dams), design of resistant or resilient systems, retrofitting (such as reinforcing buildings to ground shaking) or land use planning (such as restricting development within flood plains)" (Etkin & Stefanovic, 2005, p. 468). These risk reduction techniques primarily focus on physical vulnerability rather than social, however there is certainly a link. People who are most marginalized often tend to be living in poorer housing and in more vulnerable areas.

Mitigation to social vulnerability is critical. Quarantelli (2003) noted that disaster mitigation should be considered "as much of a priority in planning and application as emergency preparedness, response and recovery" (p. 6). That addresses both physical and social vulnerability, but he added that "there is a need to more closely integrate disaster planning to the developmental planning or social change processes of the social system involved" (p.7).

For most chapters of the organization mitigation is a lower priority than the other categories but they are still involved through education and community partnerships. This is particularly visible in the educational and social media tools it uses.

Response

Yarnal (2006) stated that response is "the emergency assistance that takes place during or immediately after a disaster. Its purpose is to save lives and meet the most fundamental needs—water, food, and shelter—of the people affected by the event" (p. 252). In catastrophes—and in many cases normal disasters—the first responders are other victims of the event. The extent of a catastrophe is so large that outside help and professional help isn't always available.

The ability for people to evacuate is dependent on many factors including finances, access to a vehicle, security concerns, etc. Sometimes, the problem in evacuation/sheltering stems from the government. In the Dominican Republic during Hurricane Georges fear of 'professional victims' caused the government to keep the locations of shelters secret until the last minute. However, "in order to not give away the location of the shelters until it was absolutely necessary, the shelters were also not stocked adequately with food, water and medical supplies," (Olson et. al., 2001, p. 21). Since the most vulnerable people are the ones most likely to seek shelter, this precautionary approach resulted in great hardship for many.

For this organization, response is perhaps the area where they are best known. They are able to step in when invited by a local, state or federal government to ensure that people are fed and shelter, to help determine the level and impact of the disaster, to coordinate and build partnerships with local government and NGOs or volunteers, to play a role in local government emergency operations centers and to share information with the public about the disaster. These functions are critical in order to operate an effective and efficient disaster response that addresses the immediate and emergency needs of a community.

I began my Sandy experience that Sunday working in the office to help determine the demographic composition of each New Jersey county. This information–part of building future partnerships—is useful for response planning. It helps identify which communities have the most vulnerable populations and therefore, who may need the most help post-landfall.

But I had deployed in as a shelter supervisor, so soon enough I was sent to Rutgers University in Piscataway as a shelter manager (not enough managers had made it to the state yet). NJ operates a variety of shelter types during a disaster. Some are managed by community organizations or volunteer relief organizations like mine, while others are state-run. My shelter was one of the latter. Named SISI shelters—State Supported Shelter Initiative—my intended role as a partner organization was to manage registration and help keep order in the dormitory.

When we arrived evacuation buses from Atlantic City were already there. I met with a representative from FEMA who told me he thought this was a turn-key operation. He was expecting me to arrive with a team of a couple dozen people (I brought one other fairly new volunteer) and food and that the organization would completely take over the shelter operation. We both made contact with our superiors: known as "running it up the chain." A decision was made to bring in a National Guard troop to provide additional support but that I would take the lead of the overall shelter.

The dormitories of our shelter are four side-by-side basketball courts in the recreation center's gym. Cots are lined up with just a few inches around them and there is no other place to eat. In Louisiana we aim to have enough cots for 10 percent of the population pre-landfall. They are reserved for the disabled, elderly and pregnant. The goal is to give people a safe place to ride out a storm. Post-landfall, there will be enough cots for everyone. However, in New Jersey, everyone gets a cot. The lights at the emergency setting are still as bright as daylight. For safety reasons we can only reduce them to 75 percent so people get used to living in 24-hour brightness.

We have access to the bathrooms, hallways and a small lounge. While there is power people are able to watch the storm come in on the television. I'm not sure that it's helpful but the news is mostly showing New York City so no one is getting too anxious.

With our odd hours, staff need a separate area to sleep so we take over the hallways of a racquetball court area. Over the next few days all the courts are put to full use. We host a Disaster Medical Assistance Team (DMAT) that deployed from Tennessee. They set-up a full-fledged, 24-hour medical clinic, including nurses, doctors, pharmacists and mental health professionals.

By midnight, we have over 300 people staying in the shelter. About 75 are children; another 75 are frail elderly. There are people on oxygen, folks in wheelchairs and seniors who are bed bound. One woman is blind, three people need regular dialysis, several people are Hispanic and speak no English, two women are between eight and nine months pregnant and several people are on methadone and need treatment. There are a lot of people with mental health issues. Many residents of an assisted living facility were evacuated without their support workers. We have a cross-dressing Atlantic City boardwalk performer who causes concern amongst the parents because he loves hanging out with the kids. I address issues of communal living, diversity and respect over and over.

The vulnerability of shelter residents wasn't a surprise to me; as a disaster sociologist focusing on vulnerabilities I understand all too well that shelters are a last resort and are primarily for those without networks and social capital. But seeing it up close and personal was a reminder that theory is one thing, experience is another.

Monday, October 29th 2012

We are a fine-oiled machine now. We are extremely short-staffed but you wouldn't know it. My team is functioning on very little sleep; I track mine—I get 17 hours over the first seven days of the storm. But students from Rutgers University are starting to come in by the handful.

I organize a bunch of the kids into a "Food Patrol." They help distribute food and clean-up the plates from the elderly and disabled clients. It's hard for them to get in and out of their cots and we have no dining area; everyone eats in their bed. Bed-wetting amongst the elderly is a serious issue too. The National Guard is changing out up to 25 cots a night. We can't get out to purchase any supplies until the storm blows through though.

The kids need something to do and I need help. They give orientation tours to the new volunteers and staff, run errands and help out where needed. I create a list of duties and rules and tack it to the wall. The kids sign it and one calls it their "terms and conditions." In Fight Club style, the first rule is "Rule #1 is Food Patrol always WALKS!!" I also have a rule about being in your cot early at night which is greatly appreciated by the state police and National Guard supervising the dorms.

I hear two elderly clients talking. "Don't worry," says the one. "If you don't understand something, just ask one of those kids with the name tags. They know everything." After a day or two of the kids helping out, more and more of the adults start taking on additional responsibilities as well. Creating a sense of belonging and ownership within a shelter by giving people something to do is one of the tenets of the organization's training.

The Salvation Army sets up a kitchen and makes coffee. My organization sends in catered breakfast and Salvation Army provides hot dogs and hamburgers for lunch and spaghetti for dinner. Everyone is excited to have real food instead of heater-meals—the kind you shake to warm them up. They are only a few hundred calories and aren't providing enough sustenance, especially for the many diabetics we have.

The storm hits. We lose power but the back-up generators kick in. We are very lucky; many facilities don't have generators and during landfall coping with hundreds of people in the dark can be a challenge. But we discover that back-up power doesn't make all of the outlets in the gym work. We are down to a handful of power sources and we have people on 24-hour oxygen. We prioritize the outlets: full-time oxygen and oxygen treatments have ultimate priority. After a few break-downs of wheelchairs and scooters, we give them secondary priority. Charging any devices such as cell phones, gaming machines and radios is last. Someone finds a power bar which makes everyone much happier.

I'm doing lots of media, mostly for outlets back in Toronto. I do a number of calls to radio and television. Listening later I'm surprised how calm I sound and how much of a southern accent I seemed to have developed from my time in Louisiana.

The Globe and Mail puts out an article late Monday night entitled "York graduate student runs shelter with mix of competence, empathy." They seem to have really captured the mood at the shelter.

It says, "But for all the time taken up by these logistical tasks, Ms. Gulliver spoke most often of the more human side of her job Monday: helping those who need a hand getting around the shelter, for instance, or comforting those people worried about the condition of the homes they left behind in the path of the storm. On Sunday night, Ms. Gulliver said she got just 90 minutes of sleep, but you wouldn't know it from talking to her. Upbeat and articulate, she said first-hand experience dealing with storms has informed her research. "I've taken courses in disaster response, but you can't really visualize it until it rolls out—what roles people fill, how they work together," she said (Morrow, 2012)."

Tuesday, October 30th 2012

The mood darkens in the shelter. People are getting texts telling them that their home is flooded or destroyed. When the power finally goes back on the TV returns. Jersey is now being shown in the news: Hoboken has people being evacuated by helicopter, the boardwalk in Atlantic City has been damaged, the ferris wheel in Seaside Heights is toppled over in the water.

One woman runs up to me crying. "T, they just showed my house on TV. It's under water." We sit and chat for a while. Once she is calmer, I ask if she wants to talk to the mental health professionals on the DMAT team. They help her explore her options.

There had been an expectation in the shelter pre-landfall, that a return home would happen Monday night or Tuesday morning once the storm had passed. As the reality hits, people realize that they aren't going to be going home immediately; the roads aren't passable and many have nowhere to go. Halloween is tomorrow and the kids are frantic; luckily the governor postpones Halloween and we are given a large donation of candy and decorations from the Walgreens pharmacy chain. We make plans with the Rutgers students to help us out the next day.

When the relocation to Atlantic City finally occurs a few days later, over half of the residents merely move from one shelter to another. But being relocated to a shelter closer to their home and their social support networks is helpful, especially for those who are the most vulnerable. They need access to their friends, family and community supports in order to think about regaining and restarting their lives.

Weeks later, I'm in Atlantic City and see a shelter resident I called Mr. T crossing the street. I call out to him and he comes running across. "Miss T, it's so great to see you. I've found a new place, I'm doing great!" He gives me a long hug. I'm excited to see that he is rebuilding his life.

VULNERABILITY WITHIN PREPAREDNESS, MITIGATION, RESPONSE, RECOVERY

Whether a rich or poor nation, those that are poorest and most marginalized are also the ones most vulnerable to disasters, and the ones that are least able to react to the disaster despite their own awareness of risk. This speaks to a clear link between social vulnerability, disaster risk and concepts of social—and environmental—justice (Phillips et. al, 2009, p. 36). It is possible to predict who will be most at risk and therefore to create preparedness, mitigation, response and recovery plans with those that have the highest vulnerability in mind. Unfortunately, this does not always—or even often—happen.

Aldrich (2012) feels that "social resources, at least as much as material ones, prove to be the foundation for resilience and recovery" (page viii). Those that were in our shelters were generally people without other options and resources. Many of them had been evacuated from assisted living facilities or single-room occupancy hotels.

The Role of Social Networks and Social Capital

Community resiliency—and to an extent individual resiliency—is achieved largely in part though social networks and social capital. People who have the least often depend on institutions to provide support for normal functioning and this is amplified in times of crisis. This broad framework of institutions including "shops, schools, the police, medical, transportation, communication and banking systems" (Lukes, 2006, n.p.) are important to all of us but especially to those who lack the means to evacuate or cope on their own during a disaster. However, the complete breakdown of these systems of support has an unequal impact and "a divide appears between those who have access to means of escapes and survival and those who, until help arrives, have not" (Lukes, 2006, n.p.). The ability of an individual to connect to resources is an indicator of the extent of their social networks and their own personal, social capital.

In a normal disaster a network of stronger ties/dense sectors—i.e., those networks in which most people know each other, are similar, have kinship connections—aids greatly in recovery. However, in a catastrophe there is so much more need for support—schools, jobs, housing etc.—that a broader network in which the connections/ties may be weaker but provide access to a wider-range of sectors is more useful. Therefore, in catastrophes in particular, the existence of an "optimal network" structure—a combination of "stronger ties/dense sectors with weaker ties/wider-ranging sectors"—(Hurlbert et al., 2006, n.p.) before the event or the ability to create one post-catastrophe will greatly aid in recovery.

Hurlbert et. al. (2006) stated that "the structure of an individual's social networks prior to [Hurricane Andrew] affected the degree to which they activated network ties for help in the preparation and recovery phases" (n.p.). In the recovery phase, social support networks also led to better physical and emotional health. The researchers defined the most successful networks as those that were higher-density, had more gender diversity, and had "higher proportions of men, kin and younger individuals" (Hurlbert et. al. 2006, n.p.). It is generally easier for someone who is more affluent to maintain this kind of network—"residents of poor urban areas participated in smaller networks of restricted range (less access to weak ties, lower diversity)" (Hurlbert et. al. 2006, n.p.) and therefore are less likely to be able to retain their network following a catastrophe as well.

Social Vulnerability

Social vulnerability provides greater insight into the manner in which the decisions we make as a society influence our differential experience of hazard events. Social vulnerability stems from limited access to resources and political power, social capital, beliefs and customs, physical limitations of the population, and characteristics of the built environment such as building stock and age, and the type and density of infrastructure and lifelines (Schmidtlein et.al., 2008, p. 1100).

In contrast to physical vulnerability, social vulnerability affects people at a very individual level in terms of their family and household. Individual factors can make them more or less vulnerable during a disaster. However, many of these factors are systemic in nature so there is a community component that needs to be addressed to reduce social vulnerability, not just to disasters but to life circumstances.

According to Tierney (2006) population vulnerability can be seen as:

a complex construct that includes such factors as: proximity to physical disaster impacts; material resources (e.g., income and wealth), race, ethnicity, gender, age; knowledge concerning recommended safety measures; and factors associated with social and cultural capital, such as routine involvements in social networks that can serve as conduits for information and mutual aid, as well as knowledge that enables community residents to interact successfully with mainstream societal institutions (p. 208).

In his book *Heat Wave*, Klinenberg showed how the disaster in Chicago was socially constructed, and ignored by many because those who were killed among the groups often ignored and isolated: the frail, the elderly, people living in poverty, people of color etc. In fact, he said that increased vulnerability amongst Americans who are poor and old can be traced to four trends:

1. a demographic shift—the increasing number of people living alone, and, in particular, of seniors who are aging alone, often with disabilities and barriers to mobility and sociability;
2. a cultural condition—related to crime, the coupling of a 'culture of fear' stemming from the violence and perceived violence of everyday life with longstanding American valuation of privacy, individualism, and self-sufficiency, particularly among the elderly and men;
3. a spatial transformation—the degradation, fortification, or elimination of public spaces and supported housing arrangements such as public housing clusters or SRO dwellings, especially in areas with concentrated poverty, violence, and illness;
4. a gendered condition—the tendency for older men, particularly single men without children, and men with substance abuse problems to lose parts of their social networks and valuable sources of social support as they age. (Klinenberg, 2002, p. 48)

These factors were all evident in New Jersey, at this first shelter and the next two I served in. They remained evident throughout the length of my deployment. The supports needed by each person and family were different. But those who had the least before the storm remained those who had the least after the storm.

Thursday, November 8th 2012

My two weeks are over and I'm wrapping up work at my third shelter. I can outprocess and fly back to New Orleans tomorrow. I'm trying to decide if I will go home or stay deployed. This last run, though short, was a nightmare situation in many ways. The county or the state—it was never clear—made the decision to relocate people from several shelters to one that was located in a large tented compound. This wasn't a decision made by the organization I'm volunteering with, nor were they originally there to provide support. When my second shelter closed we were in fact originally told to stay there to conduct tear-down. But then I was sent, by myself, to this new tent shelter. When I arrived, a nor'easter was just starting to blow in, a woman went into labor on the bus and chaos reigned.

The shelter, named "Camp Freedom", was designed for electrical and outdoor workers to give them a place to crash for a few hours. The for-profit management company had believed that they would be providing spaces for homeless (prior to Sandy) people who didn't have a place to ride out the storm. Instead, they were sent busloads of Sandy evacuation shelter residents, many of whom like those at my second shelter) had been told they were going to a much better facility. My second shelter had been in a hockey arena attached to a school and had been without power (except for emergency back-up) for longer than a week. I didn't think there was much that could be worse. I was wrong.

The tent—think big, white wedding tent—was cold. The heaters weren't pumping out enough heat to keep pace with the storm. Snow was piling up on the roof; at one point I was worried that it was going to collapse. In the panic of near hysteria I started laughing, thinking at least I'd get a good video for "America's Funniest Home Videos."

Solnit (2009) says, "Disasters provide an extraordinary window into social desire and possibility, and what manifests there matters elsewhere, in ordinary times and in other extraordinary times" (p. 6). Never was this more true for me than at Camp Freedom.

As I pulled into the facility I met two of the organization's senior disaster staff. For the next couple hours, we were the only supports from the organization on the ground with a couple hundred clients. But, over the next couple of days the true heart of the organization became evident. AmeriCorps—a voluntary program for young adults—participants showed up bringing their youth and enthusiasm. Senior management, local volunteers and deployed staff from the organization's Southern NJ disaster center worked all night to bring in supplies: blankets, clothing, hygiene kits—anything they could find to make the residents' stay more comfortable. Many of them had already put in a full day's work on their normal disaster duties but heeded the "all hands on deck" call.

Residents of the shelter, who already had shown that they could look out for each other, began to do so in big and small ways. Every cot not in use was relocated to the edges of the shelter where the tent flaps met pavement to create a barrier against the snow and wind. The food tent was a couple hundred yards away; a challenge in a blizzard for those with low mobility so clients took turns fetching food and beverages for higher needs clients. There was anger that they had been put in such a situation but there was also an understanding that we all needed to pull together to get through the night and the next few days.

Eventually, the organization was able to negotiate with local officials to get the shelter moved to the inside of the racetrack we were stationed at. I was gone by then but heard stories of how much better it was compared to the tents.

Saturday, November 10th 2012

I've considered my options and decided to stay. But I get out of shelters. That last shelter did me in, so I switch over to the building partnerships program, finally catching up to my staff lead from Hurricane Isaac. I spent the next two days on the road covering most of the eastern coast of New Jersey. I hit Atlantic City and Cape May in the south, and up to several little towns in the north. The organization is distributing supplies: coats, shovels, rakes, bleach, gloves and other essential clean-up items. We check on the delivery sites and check in with locals to find out what the needs are.

Then I get sick. Really, really sick. I guess spending a night wet in a freezing tent will do that to you. The on-site nurse suggests that I consider going home. But my staff lead wants me to say so he sends me to Atlantic City for a couple days of bed-based research on my laptop. There is a lot of information still needed and as a graduate student, and someone with experience in building community partnerships, I know what to look for and how to find it.

For the next three and a half weeks I work with several teams in the partnerships area. We cover hundreds of miles, network with dozens of people and work to ensure that vulnerable communities are being well-served in the disaster. I get to see the extent of the damage in the various communities. There aren't words for how bad it is in some places. Living in New Orleans, and having just gone through Hurricane Isaac, I'm used to it in one way. At the same time, a sadness settles on my heart when I see the extent of the damage. I know what it will be like to try to rebuild and recover.

Thursday, November 22nd 2012

Thanksgiving comes. We work all day and then have a "family" dinner in the evening. Buddy "the Cake Boss" Valastro sends in a cake. It's plain white—we use tinsel to decorate it—but it's oh-so-delicious. I ask my roommate to make sure I don't fall into a diabetic coma in the middle of the night. Maybe I shouldn't have had a corner piece!

This is a critical time. We need to ensure that everyone's emergency needs have been met and that communities have the supports that they need in place to start providing their own responses. Economically, it's better for the local community if the meals come from restaurants so we close up our kitchens and our meal delivery programs. I eat at one restaurant where the owner says "It's nice to serve people from your organization instead of being given meals by them."

We work hard to identify special needs communities within the state: those living in poverty, undocumented residents and people of color or from other marginalized communities. We build partnerships with the local chapters helping to give them tools and strength to continue the response after we leave. We connect to faith-based communities and non-profits, some that have sprung up overnight, to make sure the community capacity will exist after we leave. Long-term recovery committees—supported by United Way and FEMA—are springing up and we share resources and information.

By early December, things are winding down on the operation. Most people are leaving and heading home for the holidays. My final day will be December 7th and I'll home on the 8th, 6 weeks after deploying for what I thought would be 14 days. The response period is finally over and it's time for a move to recovery operations which my organization is rarely involved in.

RECOVERY

Vulnerability continues to play a role in the recovery stage as well. Aldrich (2012) says " . . . social engines and connections form the core engine of recovery after even the most devastating of events" (page viii).

Recovery is the processes—short and long term—of repairing what was damaged. Yarnal (2007) said,

> In the short run, this phase of emergency management means restoring important infrastructure and services, like sewage, electricity, transportation and communications. In the long-run, it means rehabilitating and rebuilding physical structures. Ideally, recovery should not only restore pre-disaster living conditions by rebuilding the physical setting, but also should better those conditions by improving the social setting. It should provide opportunities to make physical and social changes that reduce the risk of, and vulnerabilities to, future disasters (p. 252).

Redlener (2008) stated that recovery is often somewhat of an afterthought and that "recovery inadequacies are far more grave than the failures of the initial response" (p. 791). Investment in communities is critical and he said that "investing in community support systems, income stability and access to appropriate services should be part of effective and comprehensive disaster planning" (Redlener, 2008, p. 792).

One continuing theme throughout disaster readings is the need to build resiliency into recovery planning, and to look at how to recover before the catastrophe even happens. In other words, recovery planning should be pro-active, rather than simply reactive.

In terms of social vulnerability, any recovery work needs to take into account the special needs of marginalized populations. In talking about Katrina, Waugh (2006) says we need to look at how to fix "the flaws in the nation's support networks for the poor, elderly, and disabled—that were revealed by the disasters. How can we deal with the racism that contributed to the slow response to devastated African American communities?" (p. 11). Marginalized populations are at-risk in most disasters—before, during and after. Like Katrina, the same was true for Superstorm Sandy.

Tuesday, December 12th 2012

I've been home for only four days—one of which I spend managing a local shelter after a tornado went through—when I get a call from my chapter. "Your name came up in the system as a potential caseworker. Do you want to go back out again?" I agree that I will go back but I need a few days at least. My luggage got lost in Atlanta on the trip home and still hasn't arrived.

Saturday, December 20th, 2012

I head back out; Baton Rouge to Atlanta to Philly to New Jersey. The operation which had all but shut down when I left a week and a half ago is ramping back up.

The organization has moved into the recovery phase. While this organization is occasionally involved in recovery during large disasters that usually occurs as part of the long-term recovery process of rebuilding that begins months later. This time, we are focused on those people who are still in hotels and motels paid for by FEMA because of the extensive damage to their homes. It's been 2 months; families need to get back to a normal—or at least a "new normal"—way of life, and that can't happen when they are living out of a hotel room.

The Only Constant is Change

Over the next few days, everything changes on an almost hourly basis. It's a philosophy of the organization to be flexible and responsive to change. We are constantly revamping our forms and processes to try to figure out how best to do the immense amount of work before us. I'm technically a supervisor in casework assistance but I'm almost immediately thrown into a role as an Assistant Manager due to the workload and the lack of staff. It's a couple days before Christmas; I'm not surprised we are short on staff.

Monday, December 24th 2012

For Christmas, I have G.B., a fellow volunteer, come over from the New York City disaster response. We worked together in the shelter at Rutgers University for a few days. He went home after a couple of weeks but is back again as well. He's a professional Santa Claus so on Christmas Eve he dresses up and goes door-to-door in the hotel, giving my staff chocolates and candy canes. It's a small bright spot for those who are hundreds of miles away from their families at the holidays.

Daily, more people begin arriving at the headquarters. Most are coming in for the client assistance program, but there is also a roll out of support functions: staffing, health and mental health services, transportation, logistics and disaster services technology. As the leadership changes—both at the operational level and of the client assistance area—the process and direction changes again.

January 2nd 2013

In early January, we're told that a funding formula and plan has been created. We now have the ability to provide financial support for families still living in the hotels. Our goal is to help them establish themselves in housing and provide some of the basic necessities—what they need versus what they want—to rebuild their lives. This is what has been needed for many of the people still in hotels. They had the desire to move but not the resources.

Smith, (2006) said that, "In every phase and aspect of a disaster—causes, vulnerability, preparedness, results and response, and reconstruction—the contours of disaster and the difference between who lives and who dies is to a greater or lesser extent a social calculus" (n.p.). This is true not just for life and death but for who recovers quickly and who is stuck in a fairly awful situation for a lengthy time.

Evidence of vulnerability is front and center for the next couple months even when the physical impact of the storm is out of sight. We drive from the hotel to the headquarters and back, often in the dark. One time, I get off work a bit early and think I have gotten lost as I don't recognize anything on the side of the road. I realize it's the first time I've done the drive in daylight. Outreach teams are still seeing the damage though.

I'm sent south for a day to interview a client who has been referred from a local politician's office. Her case requires kid gloves because it includes a tale of sexual assault in her recovery phase. I drive around the neighborhood by her home; it's an area I had visited frequently throughout November. It's quiet. While there isn't as much debris piled by the side of the road anymore, where once the remains of houses stood, now there is cleared land. It's deserted.

But in the stories we hear—the team I'm supervising has over 150 clients —vulnerability is ever present. We bring a mental health worker onto our team for a few days; she helps both the clients and the volunteers. It's hard hearing these stories over and over.

- "I lost everything."
- "My son committed suicide after the hurricane came through."
- "My wife and I have separated because of the storm."
- "My kids are having nightmares."
- "We all huddle under the covers when it rains because we're afraid."

We also start to wonder about fraudulent cases. All of a sudden we're getting continual calls from the same town, one that experienced isolated flooding but not to the extent that would justify the cases we're receiving. They all have a similar tone. "I moved everything in my house into the basement before the storm arrived. Everything is gone." A local community recovery center has posted a flyer with full details of the assistance program we are providing. People are asking us for assistance using the weird wording found in a couple of our guidelines. "I'd like 'small appliances (including a microwave)'." Our price list says that but it's not how someone would normally ask for support.

I send caseworkers out to visit a few of these homes. They state they have no heat, while the caseworkers feel warm air blowing and everyone is in short-sleeves. They state they have no beds or furniture, but everyone has a place to sit and beds are visible through open doorways. As a charity, the organization is very careful with the donor dollar. While the response from the world has been phenomenal in terms of donations received, due diligence is still required. We need to spend money carefully. We check with FEMA; these families didn't file for assistance or we discover that FEMA has investigated to find no damage at all.

But more often, we are successfully helping people to get out of the hotels and into their old, or new, homes. When checks start arriving we let caseworkers deliver them to the clients. The reward of seeing a client smile, of seeing the realization dawn on their face that they are going to get to start a new life, makes the two or three weeks of being away from their own families well worth it.

My co-worker S.T. and I deliver a check—or as I liked to write in my case notes to the chagrin of my American colleagues a "cheque"—to one family, still living in a hotel room in February. We leave after profuse thank-yous but through the closed door we hear "Thank you Jesus. Thank you Lord. We are getting a home now. We are getting out of this hotel." Another woman collapses in my arms when she sees the amount of her assistance. It is bare bones, covering only the essentials, but she says "I've always wanted to buy one of those "bed-in-a-bag" sets from Walmart. Now I'm going to be able to get new furniture for the first time in my life. I'm going to have sheets that match. I can replace what I lost." She tells us that she, her daughter and grandchild will be forever grateful to the organization and will pray for us daily. S.T. and I are fighting back our own tears, but this is why we do this work.

More and more, the caseworkers who are coming back are those who have been deployed already in one function or another. People are extending their deployments as well. While normally the 14 or 21 day deployment is typical for all but the local paid staff or reserve volunteers, there are several of us who hit the 100 day mark. The mental health team continually reminds us to take care of ourselves. Disaster stress can impact workers as well as clients. We need to be in top form in order to hear these stories and do this work. While the hours are better than during the immediate aftermath of the disaster—12-16 hours days have decreased to 10 hour work days—some of us are taking work home. Most of us are taking mental stress home nightly.

We start having Saturday night parties at the hotel to relieve some of the stress. A client shows up in the middle of one to find me. He was staying in the same hotel and had some questions about his case. I begin to think about the concept of "resiliency" a key area for my PhD dissertation. While I had always framed this in terms of community resiliency, I realize that personal and individual resiliency is just as important. So is my own resiliency and that of my volunteer colleagues.

Resiliency

According to Gaillard (2007) the United Nations International Strategy for Disaster Reduction defines resilience as: "[. . .] the capacity of a system, community or society to resist or change in order that it may obtain an acceptable level of functioning and structure" (p. 523). Most resiliency literature looks at community or systems resilience rather than exploring individual or family resilience. In the case of vulnerable populations this is very important because individual resiliency is extremely challenging for an individual to achieve without the government or society providing adequate social supports. In part, this is because an individual's social capital—particularly someone who is highly vulnerable—is low and their ability to self-mobilize support is hampered.

Etkin & Stefanovic (2005) say that vulnerability reduction is achieved by either "increasing resistance (by changing design criteria to protect against more extreme events) or by increasing resiliency (by creating the capacity to 'bounce back' more quickly and easily after a damaging event occurs" (p. 470). Increasing resistance most often looks at physical vulnerability whereas increasing resiliency is more often a combination of physical and social vulnerability. For many who are socially vulnerable, resiliency during and after disasters is impossible to achieve on their own. They do not have economic assets or social networks sufficient to sustain themselves.

Resilience and vulnerability are interrelated. Resilience addresses capability and coping mechanisms, whereas vulnerability explores the risk and extent to which people may suffer harm. However, "both concepts may rely on the same factors (demographic, social, cultural, economic, political, etc.) which may however vary on different scales" (Gaillard, 2007, p. 523).

At the same time and contrary to many media-perpetrated disaster myths, disasters can bring out the best in people. Solnit (2009) says, "When all the ordinary divides and patterns are shattered, people step up—not all, but the great preponderance—to become their brothers keepers. And that purposefulness and connectedness bring joy even amid death, chaos, fear, and loss . . . Horrible in itself, disaster is sometimes a door back into paradise, the paradise at least in which we are who we hope to be, do the work we desire, and are each our sister's and brother's keeper" (p. 3).

While the various levels of government certainly have a role to play "community-based risk reduction" is also critical. The input of local residents—and the buy-in for the plan that can accompany it—is important for success (Ilan, 2008). "Community-based risk reduction is needed because it is the most effective approach for tackling disasters, even when the government is competent, not only for saving lives and money, but also for enhancing sense of community with further sustainability benefits" (Ilan, 2008, p. 2).

One challenge to risk mitigation is what Kunreuther (2006) called the 'natural disaster syndrome' which refers to the fact that many individuals and businesses don't take pro-active, risk reduction methods and are therefore unprepared when a disaster strikes. At the same time they do access relief payments afterwards. One of the reasons for this syndrome Kunreuther said is that because catastrophes are low-probability high-consequence events people feel that they are not at risk. "As a result, they do not feel the need to invest voluntarily in protect measures, such as strengthening their house or buying insurance. It is only after the disaster occurs that these same individuals claim they would like to have undertaken protective measures" (2008, p. 209). After all, as Etkin & Stefanovic (2005) said that "risk is increased when people or communities act as if safety has been assured, when in fact it has not" (p. 471).

Sunday, March 17th 2013

I fly back to Louisiana today. The disaster recovery phase has one more week left to it and then it will migrate to long-term recovery with paid caseworkers. I apply for and am offered a job with the long-term recovery team. In the end, although it was offered, I turn it down to concentrate on my studies. I wanted to see out that last week but my passport is about to expire and I need to get back to Canada before it does.

I will miss everyone I have been working with, but it is time to leave. I can feel myself facing total exhaustion. It's been 13 weeks this run. I've been on hand for 19 out of just under 21 weeks since I first came out or 130 days of the 142 days the disaster operation had been in place. Sandy hit 140 days ago.

We have given out significant amounts of money but have barely made a dent in the need. This process will continue for many years to come. I say a prayer that the new hurricane season, just a few months away, will pass New Jersey by this year and give it a chance to recover, rebuild and grow more resilient.

REFERENCES

Aldrich, D.P. (2012). Building resilience: Social capital in post-disaster recovery. Chicago, IL: University of Chicago Press.

Bankoff, G. (2006). The tale of the three pigs: Taking another look at vulnerability in the light of the Indian Ocean Tsunami and Hurricane Katrina. Retrieved from http://understandingkatrina.ssrc.org/bankoff.

Blaikie, P., T. Cannon, I. Davis and B. Wisner. (1994). At Risk: Natural Hazards, People's Vulnerability, and Disasters. London and New York: Routledge.

Clark, N. (2005). Disaster and generosity. The Geographical Journal, 171(4): 384–386.

Clarke, L. (2005). Worst Cases: Terror and Catastrophe in the Popular Imagination. Chicago, IL: University of Chicago Press.

Etkin, D. and Stefanovic, I. L. (2005). Mitigating natural disasters: The role of eco-ethics. Mitigation and Adaptation Strategies for Global Change, 10:467–490.

Gaillard, J.C. (2007). Resilience of traditional societies in facing natural hazards. Disaster Prevention and Management, 16(4): 522–544.

Garrett, A.L., Grant, R., Madrid, P., Brito, A., Abramson, D. & Redlener, I. (2007). Children and megadisasters: Lessons learned in the new millennium. *Advances in Pediatrics* 54, 189–214.

Hurlbert, J.S., Beggs, J.J. and Haines, V.A. (2006). Bridges over troubled waters: What are the optimal networks for Katrina's victims. Retrieved from http://understandingkatrina.ssrc.org/Hurlbert_Beggs_Haines/

Ilan, K. (2008). Myths of Hurricane Katrina. *Disaster Advances*, 1(1): 1–7.

Klinenberg, E. (2002). Heat Wave: A Social Autopsy of Disaster in Chicago. Chicago: University of Chicago Press.

Kunreuther, H. (2006). Disaster mitigation and insurance: Learning from Katrina. *ANNALS of the American Academy of Political and Social Sciences*, 604: 208–227.

Lakoff, A. (2006). From disaster to catastrophe: The limits of preparedness. Retrieved from http://understandingkatrina.ssrc.org/Lakoff/.

Lukes, S. (2006). Questions about power: Lessons from the Louisiana hurricane. Retrieved from http://understandingkatrina.ssrc.org/Lukes/

Morrow, A. (2012). "York graduate student runs shelter with mix of competence, empathy." *The Globe and Mail*, Monday, October 29th 2012. Retrieved from http://www.theglobeandmail.com/news/national/york-graduate-student-runs-shelter-with-mix-of-competence-empathy/article4752020/

Quarantelli, E.L. (2003). Programs and policies that ought to be implemented for coping with future disasters. Preliminary Paper #332. University of Delaware Disaster Research Center.

———. (2006). Catastrophes are different from disasters: Some implications for crisis planning and managing drawn from Katrina. Retrieved from http://understanding katrina.ssrc.org/Quarantelli.

Redlener, I., Abramson, D., Stehling-Aziza, T., Grant, R., and Johnson. D. (2007). The American preparedness project: Where the US public stands in 2007 on terrorism, security and disaster preparedness. Retrieved from http://hdl.handle.net/10022/AC:P:8848

———. (2008). Population vulnerabilities, preconditions, and the consequences of disaster. *Social Research*, 75(3), 785–792.

Rodriguez, H., and Dynes, R. (2006). Finding and framing Katrina: The social construction of disaster. Retrieved from http://understandingkatrina. ssrc.org/Dynes_Rodriguez

———, Trainor, J. & Quarantelli, E.L. (2006) Rising to the challenges of a catastrophe: the emergent and prosocial behavior following Hurricane Katrina. *ANNALS of the American Academy of Political and Social Sciences*, 604: 82–100.

Scanlon, J. (2001). Lessons learned or lessons forgotten: The Canadian disaster experience. Institute for Catastrophic Loss Reduction: Paper #1. Retrieved from http://www.iclr.org/images/The_Canadian_disaster_experience.pdf

Schmidtlein. M.C., Deutsch, R.C., Piegorsch, W.W. and Cutter, S.L. (2008). A sensitivity analysis of the social vulnerability index. *Risk Analysis*, 28(4): 1099–1114.

Smith, N. (2006) There's no such thing as a natural disaster. http://understanding katrina.ssrc.org/Smith

Solnit, R. (2009). A paradise built in hell: The extraordinary communities that arise in disaster. New York, NY: Penguin Group.

Sylves, R.T. (2006). President Bush and Hurricane Katrina: A presidential leadership study. *ANNALS of the American Academy of Political and Social Sciences*, 604: 26–56.

Tierney, K. (2006). Foreshadowing Katrina: Recent sociological contributions to vulnerability science. Contemporary Sociology, 35(3), 207–212.

Waugh, W. L. (2006) The political costs of failure in the Katrina and Rita disasters. *ANNALS of the American Academy of Political and Social Science*, 604, 10–25.

Yarnal, B. (2007). Vulnerability and all that jazz: Addressing vulnerability in New Orleans after Hurricane Katrina. *Technology in Society*, 29, 249–255.

CHAPTER FIVE
MITIGATION FOR UNIVERSITY HEALTH SYSTEMS AND TRANSFER TRAUMA: HURRICANE SANDY AS CASE STUDY

Dana M. Greene

ABSTRACT

In the aftermaths of Hurricanes Katrina, Rita, Irene, and Sandy, as well as other natural and technological disasters (wildfires, tornadoes, tsunamis, earthquakes, and terrorist attacks), University health systems have led the way in both continuing to care for inpatients, as well as working to triage those affected by both forecasted and "surprise" events. As a result, medical manpower is stretched thin, and healthcare professionals working predominately in research units within University health systems experience a shift in responsibilities away from credential specific (simply MD or RN) to being "jacks of all trades," and taking on responsibilities of orderlies, lab techs, emergency technicians, life-flight paramedics, and ICU doctors and nurses. In such a scenario, the most critical patients in ICU are those who require the most supervision, and who often fall prey to the greatest consequences when University health systems (e.g., New York University Health System, Tulane University Hospital, and Louisiana State University Health System) lose power and must move patients to other facilities that can take over responsibilities for providing critical care. This paper draws upon data collected from Hurricane Sandy and her impact on New York University's Health System (which lost power during the storm), and examines the impact of the transfer trauma experienced by patients that had to be moved away from a top research hospital to a secondary facility. Given that the greatest ramification of transfer trauma is mortality, I will discuss this risk with regard to the Changes in Health, End-Stage Disease and Symptoms and Signs (CHESS) measures. Further, I will provide recommendations for greater disaster preparedness, coordination and mitigation for University Health Systems, so that critical care patients will experience better health outcomes by being able to remain at these hospitals without compromised care.

INTRODUCTION

The United States is no stranger to catastrophic natural disasters; as past history with storms like Hurricanes Andrew, Katrina, and Rita have provided the government, aid organizations, and citizens with strategies for coping with the most dangerous of events. While many thought that the United States had learned valuable lessons from all that went wrong during Hurricane Katrina, Superstorm Sandy provided additional challenges to aid infrastructures, disaster preparedness plans, and placed significant stressors on hospitals charged with caring for the most critically ill patients. This paper focuses on the issues faced by University Hospitals (typically the institutions that are charged with caring for the most critically ill patients) in New York City during the Superstorm, and on the impact of transfer trauma (the impact of moving critically ill patients when the primary treating hospital cannot continue to treat patients because of being rendered incapacitated by the brunt of the storm) on patients in those hospitals. To this end, specific emphasis will be placed on the primary ramifications of transfer trauma on patients (mortality) by recommending better greater disaster preparedness, coordination and mitigation for University Health Systems, so that critical care patients will experience better health outcomes by being able to remain at these hospitals without compromised care.

Superstorm Sandy was the eighteenth named storm during the 2012 hurricane season, and proved to be the deadliest and most-destructive storm to hit the United States (second to Hurricane Katrina).[1] Sandy was an extremely unique storm in many ways. Beginning initially as a hurricane, Sandy presented significant risks to Cuba and the Caribbean before embarking on an unprecedented track that took the tropical cyclone up and into New Jersey and New York, while also merging with an intense low-pressure weather system that caused the storm to increase dramatically in size and magnitude as it hit landfall. This unique intersection of significant weather patterns all converging at once created a storm of unprecedented danger —both in terms of the increased size of the storm as well as its impact when Sandy made landfall. Indeed, this unique merged significant weather patterns and created a storm that was far more dangerous to an area that does not normally deal with these kinds of weather events, as the storm combined hurricane and post-tropical cyclone.

Superstorm Sandy made landfall along the southern New Jersey shore on October 29, 2012, causing historic devastation and substantial loss of life. The National Hurricane Center (NHC) Tropical Cyclone Report estimated the death count from Sandy at 147 direct deaths. In the United States, the storm was associated with 72 direct deaths in eight states: 48 in New York, 12 in New Jersey, five (5) in Connecticut, two (2) each in Virginia and Pennsylvania, and one (1) each in New Hampshire, West Virginia, and Maryland. The storm also resulted in at least 75 indirect deaths (i.e., related to unsafe or unhealthy conditions that existed during the evacuation phase, occurrence of the hurricane, or during the post-hurricane/ clean-up phase).[2] As a result of such catastrophic damages, Sandy became the deadliest hurricane to hit the U.S. mainland since Hurricane Katrina in 2005. Further, the National Weather Service (NWS) and the National Oceanic and Atmospheric Administration (NOAA) classified Hurricane Sandy as "the deadliest hurricane/post-tropical cyclone to hit the U.S. East Coast since Hurricane Agnes in 1972."[3]

Given the storm's largesse, NOAA classified damage estimates from Hurricane Sandy to be in excess of $50 billion, having impacted 24 states. The NWS noted that the tropical damage estimates from Sandy exceed $50 billion, with 24 states impacted by the storm. Storm force winds extended over an area about 1,000 miles in diameter,[4] while also "water levels to rise along the entire East Coast of the United States from Florida northward to Maine."[5] Most significantly, however, was the storm surge that was generated. The storm surge hit record levels in New Jersey, New York and Connecticut, but hit the New York City metropolitan area the hardest, causing flooding greater than eight feet of water in New York City. This flooding knocked out power and rendered roads impassable. As a result, university hospitals located in the flood zone experienced significant problems including power outages and damages to emergency generators that were located in the basements of these hospitals (and were thus rendered unusable by the flood waters), thereby increasing the threat for hospitalized critically ill patients in the New York University Hospital. Without power to operate generators for those patients requiring advanced life support and other medical technologies, hospitalized patients were inadvertently placed in significant jeopardy and required considerable attention and individualized care in order to survive.

THE IMPACT OF SUPERSTORM SANDY ON NEW YORK UNIVERSITY LANGONE AND TISCH HOSPITALS

Within hours of the storm making landfall in New York City, problems with power outages and flooded basements (where emergency generators were located) became an unanticipated emergency for which there was not an alternative emergency plan. As a result, critically ill patients' lives (ranging from patients in the neonatal intensive care units to those in the adult intensive care units) were threatened by the interruption in critical care that was regularly delivered via machines that run on electric power. As such, while Superstorm Sandy hit metropolitan New York in the early afternoon on October 29, 2012, decisions to transfer critically ill patients to other hospitals that still had both power and the capacity to care for the sickest patients were made by 7:45 PM on that very same day. While NYU did not expect heavy flooding in Sandy's wake, and thus elected not to evacuate all of its patients prior to the storm (as they did with Hurricane Irene one year earlier), it became readily apparent that evacuation of the most critically ill patients was indicated when the hospital's basement, lower floors and elevator shafts filled with 10 to 12 feet of water, and the Hospital lost all of its power (and generators). While emergency generators did kick in initially, no sooner than two (2) hours later, approximately 90 percent of the power went out, and the hospital(s) decided to evacuate. The flooding that NYU's hospitals experienced was unprecedented, and thus there weren't any disaster plans in place to address possible evacuation of patients in the event of a hurricane or other such natural disaster.

Evacuations from affected hospitals began with the youngest and most ill first, as electricity failed and the battery life for respirators and other critical life preserving equipment was limited to only several hours. As a result, oxygen tanks and hospital personnel were stationed at each ventilator patient's bedside, as a precaution, and "any IV drip that could be converted to subcutaneous injection was changed."[6] (Ofri 2012: 2265) Further, given the lack of electricity, critically ill patients who were being treated for serious illnesses had to be carried down staircases, with nurses serving as human shields against the wind to protect not only the patients, but also the IVs and other important equipment. Adding insult to injury was another emergent problem: the hospital water supply runs on electricity, and uses gravity to provide water to various hospital units. The flooding incapacitated the pumps that provide water throughout the hospital. Without water, even those patients who were not considered critical faced potential worsening of their conditions. As a result, mass evacuation of patients from New York University Hospitals to other hospitals that were not affected by Superstorm Sandy was indicated medically, even though concerns were voiced over the impact of transfer trauma on patients being moved. Transfer trauma is the involuntary relocation of patients for medical reasons. Often, the transfer is not only unwanted, but it also causes increased stress on the patient, which often leads to higher rates of morbidity and mortality (the topic of transfer trauma will be discussed in greater detail later in this paper). In the case of Superstorm Sandy, the risks associated with transferring patients to other hospitals for continued treatment far outweighed the realities that, if left in a hospital that was crippled by the storm, the mortality rates from the storm would certainly be higher than were recorded. Because of the need to move patients as expeditiously and safely as possible, EMS services were coordinated with New York City Police and Fire Departments to have ambulances lined up to take patients to other hospitals in the area. As such, critically ill patients were evacuated via these ambulances and mobile intensive care units to other area hospitals.[7]

Over 200 critically ill patients from New York University's Langone's Medical Center were evacuated on October 29, 2012 to nearby hospitals. Among these patients were twenty (20) infants in the neonatal intensive care unit. Four (4) of the infants had breathing tubes, and were thus carried down more than seven (7) flights of stairs with their intravenous (IV) lines, oxygen, and monitoring devices still attached to them.[8] Significantly, one 29 week-old infant was carried gingerly by a nurse who held an oxygen mask to his face, and was manually inflating it to keep the child alive.[9] Coordinated evacuation efforts by doctors, nurses, interns, assistants, orderlies, pharmacy personnel, police, fire, National Guard, and volunteers seamlessly evacuated patients to waiting ambulances.

THE EVACUATION PROCESS

The process of evacuating New York University Hospitals was nothing like the evacuation of the Superdome in New Orleans following Hurricane Katrina. Instead of haphazardly sending patients to this or that hospital, patients were inventoried, classified according to the type of condition for which they were being treated, and clinical records were sent together with the patient to waiting ambulances. Due to flooding in the elevator shafts and the lack of electricity, patients had to be evacuated from wards on higher floors of each hospital building via stairwells. For those patients who were immobile or were too weak or unable to walk, the National Guard set up sleds. Medical personnel accompanied patients who were evacuated on sleds.[10] Once patients were loaded into ambulances, EMTs and paramedics were responsible for presenting patients' full medical histories and treatment plans to the receiving hospital and staff. Evacuated patients were taken to other area New York City hospitals including Mount Sinai Hospital, the Memorial Sloan-Kettering Cancer Center, St. Luke's Hospital, New York Presbyterian/Weill Cornell Medical Center and Long Island Jewish Hospital.[11]

In sum, 215 patients were evacuated from New York University Hospitals. These patients suffered from various conditions including needing oxygen, nebulizer, dialysis, and ventilator treatments, without which they could not live. Other patients were being treated for "shortness of breath, carbon monoxide poisoning, heart attacks, and other emergent disorders."[12] This was an emergency of unprecedented proportions.

While New York University Hospital facilities were designed to withstand floods, Superstorm Sandy left seven (7) hospital buildings flooded with between seven (7) and ten (10) feet of water. This calls into question the level of preparedness that emergency facilities such as hospitals maintain and why such flooding took place at a level-one trauma units. Typically, mitigation for disaster medicine includes planning, surveillance, and response. Certainly, for most hospitals, "emergency preparedness" means being ready to treat a surge of patients from an earthquake or terror attack—disasters outside their walls. Even the Federal program that coordinates hospitals' preparedness at the Department of Health and Human Services has this mindset: it focuses on planning for mass fatalities and quickly reporting their number of available beds, not having redundant electrical systems."[13] Unfortunately, while hospitals may draw up emergency plans and institute mandatory training drills for greater preparedness in the event of a natural or technological disaster, Superstorm Sandy made one thing abundantly clear: virtually no emergency drills simulate a disaster inside a hospital.

DISASTER MEDICINE

Herchiser & Quarantelli (1976) and Pine (1974) conducted several studies about hospitals and the delivery of emergency medical services to disaster victims, but little has been done since the mid-1970s to focus on disaster preparedness for hospitals who might either have inpatients who may need to be transferred to other facilities in the event of the incapacitation of a treating hospital's infrastructure. Significantly, therefore, research on this type of phenomenon has focused on either treating the injured and dead (as victims of disaster) or on inpatients in nursing homes and long-term care facilities. The research, however, has not focused on inpatients in level-one trauma centers or those who are hospitalized and in need of continuous medical monitoring and care. These patients may have suffered injuries, have different chronic illnesses needing special monitoring, have cancer, heart, or other serious ailments needing continuous medication, be in psychiatric wards, neonatal intensive care units, or be in isolation as a result of such procedures as bone marrow transplants (in which patients must be kept in a "clean and sterile" environment without which death could be imminent). As such, Superstorm Sandy made it exceptionally clear that a focus must be placed on how to better prepare primary and secondary medical facilities, so that patients can continue uninterrupted treatment for their conditions and not have their bodies and treatment plans disrupted by transferring patients to other (unknown) facilities for the continuation of their treatment. The impact of transfer trauma on patients leads to higher rates of morbidity and mortality, and thus must be mitigated in such a way as to limit the necessity to transfer patients from a familiar facility with recognizable caregivers to new locations that are less familiar with the intricacies of a patients' care plan.

While disasters generally follow a cycle that consists of prodrome, impact, rescue, recovery, and quiescent, this cycle does not include mitigation for patient care and the impact of transfer trauma when hospitals fall victim to disasters, themselves. Prodrome consists of initial awareness of the disaster threat and preparation for a response with activation of a variety of internal and external resources. Impact involves the actual disaster event and damage as well as mitigation activity as the event unfolds. Rescue involves deployment of resources to aid victims of the disaster. Recovery includes rebuilding and application of additional resources to infrastructure needs. The quiescent stage is the period after the recovery when preparedness for future disasters occurs. It is here that hospital administrators need to focus on the potential for transfer trauma to be a serious problem for inpatients, in the event that hospitals become incapacitated by disaster. To this end, the World Health Organization (WHO) has urged increasing focus on disaster risk reduction, especially where it involves the loss of health care in disasters.[14] Further, while the literature indicates that "hospital evacuations occur globally; however, there is a paucity of published data on policy,[15] and policies are often developed after the event."[16] Certainly, hospitals with a regular risk of "predicted" disasters prepare differently than hospitals facing "unpredicted" disasters. Further, with respect to "predicted" disasters, plans should address not just staff coverage, but also coverage for patients who can or can't be evacuated easily. If Superstorm Sandy drove any message home, it is that the impact of transfer trauma on patients must not only be considered, but also included in institutional disaster plans. This is not an optional issue; rather it is a life-saving imperative.

Transfer Trauma

While the majority of research on transfer trauma has been conducted on nursing homes and long-term care facilities, and focuses on the impact of moving patients from one facility to another without consent or appropriate care plans in place. While transferring patients away from New York University Hospitals became an imperative during Sandy, the movement of patients created stress on those who were moved to other facilities. It is this stress and any resulting damage (change in treatment plans, loss of nebulizer or ventilator treatments, resultant injury, etc.) that causes leads to increased patient morbidity and mortality and is known, in disaster circles, as transfer trauma. Studies on the physical and psychological effects of transfer on older adults have indicated increased mortality rates, "increased dissatisfaction levels, together with significant declines in physical and mental health."[17] This increased stress is also compounded by lack of patient control over their surroundings and care, thereby decreasing the likelihood that patient care will be continuous and uninterrupted, and increasing the likelihood that the stress of movement from one medical facility to another will both inhibit recovery from illness and increase stress that could lead to both secondary infection and increased morbidity and/ or mortality.

Yet, what occurred during Superstorm Sandy was nothing short of miraculous. Even without practiced disaster mitigation plans, when the storm hit and caused catastrophic losses in electricity and functionality for the hospital, the staff, understanding their diminished capacity to treat patients under such conditions, effectively triaged and evacuated the sickest patients first (accompanied by medical personnel from New York University Hospitals so that continuity of care would not be an issue for critically ill patients). As a result of the superior actions on the part of medical and hospital staff, zero (0) patients died as a result of being transferred to area hospitals: a feat that has never been accomplished in any other disaster during which hospitals have become encumbered and incapacitated by situations beyond their control. The NYU team realized that keeping patients in a risky situation (no electricity or water) was more dangerous and costly (in terms of human life) than the cost of transporting patients out of the risk zone. As such, the right decision was made to privilege human life above finances as the breaches to the hospital's structural integrity were such that simply trying to treat patients "as they were," would undoubtedly lead to catastrophic loss of life for the most ill, and increased morbidity for those who were receiving treatment in the hospital that could not be given at home. Certainly, important lessons were learned from watching what occurred with Charity Hospital, long-term care facilities (and other health care institutions) during Hurricane Katrina (where there was significant loss of life as a result of the failure to evacuate in advance of the storm), and hospital staff made certain that similar errors in judgment and patient treatment were not made during Superstorm Sandy. While news broadcasters always like to point out the "heroes" during major disasters, in the case of Superstorm Sandy, it was the medical and administrative staff at New York University Hospitals who worked together seamlessly to ensure that there wasn't any loss of life, even though patients were transferred to other medical facilities to continue their treatment. This situation, coupled with pairing patients with members of treatment staff to travel with the patient, cut down on the stress that could have exacerbated a patient's underlying condition and open them up to greater stress-related illness and injury.[18]

CONCLUSION

Superstorm Sandy presented a wide range of challenges for the New York University Hospitals' staff when the Hospitals lost power and water. It was at this time that the most vulnerable population to disaster (the patients) had to be evaluated and evacuated in a timely, efficient, and manageable manner. Medical personnel and hospital workers drew used the Changes in Health, End-Stage Disease, Signs, and Symptoms Scale (CHESS) to triage patients. This scale evaluates patients on the basis of Activities for Daily Living (ADLs) in concert with symptoms and need for advanced medical care (included machinated care) to determine who was most ill and thus who needed to be evacuated first.[19] What occurred in terms of medical decision making was right on target, but the lack of a coherent and codified plan for patient evacuation remains problematic. Clearly, hospital inpatients are extremely vulnerable populations when disasters strike, as all control is stripped from them, and they are at the mercy of their treatment staff for everything: medication, treatment, tests, food, etc. As a result, this population must continue to be studied, and disaster mitigations plans put in place to accommodate the specialized needs of hospitalized patients.

Scholars in disaster studies often provide a list of recommendations for how to improve disaster response and preparedness, and I am certainly no different. After studying what occurred at the New York University Hospitals, it is clear that several strategies should be built into hazard mitigation plans (for both natural and technological [man-made] disasters). As such, emergency preparedness planning for disaster preparedness for hospitalized populations should:

1. Use community capacity-building strategies as an approach to, and foundation for, emergency preparedness with vulnerable populations;
2. Involve a diverse representation of stakeholders: those who work with or are vulnerable populations in emergency preparedness planning;
3. Address different levels of preparedness, including community-level preparedness and individual-level preparedness; and,
4. Focus on structural, logistical, and systems level issues.

While this analysis has focused solely on Superstorm Sandy as a case study for evaluating transfer trauma, the findings discussed herein are different than those for nursing homes, long-term care facilities, and other hospitals that could be affected by disasters in the future. Certainly, the personnel at New York University Hospitals were aware of the risks and benefits associated with transfer trauma, and it was their efforts that saved the 300 patients who were safely and effectively evacuated from danger and into a safer treatment environment. What remains to be seen, however, is how New York University Hospitals will integrate mitigating transfer trauma into their hazard and evacuation plans. They have shown that effective and safe transfer of patients can be done when under the gun, but how administrators effectively codify, train, practice, and implement such procedures after the fact, largely remains to be seen.

NOTES/REFERENCES

1. Hurricane/Post-Tropical Cyclone Sandy, October 22–29, 2012 (Service Assessment). United States National Oceanic and Atmospheric Administration's National Weather Service. May 2013. p. 10. Archived from the original on June 2, 2013. Retrieved June 2, 2013.
2. Ibid., pp. 1–2.
3. Ibid.
4. Ibid.
5. Ibid.
6. Ofri, Danielle. 2012. "The Storm and the Aftermath" in *The New England Journal of Medicine* 367; 24, 2265.
7. http://www.cbsnews.com/8301-201_162-57542295/evacuations-after-major-nyc-hospital-loses-backup-power/
8. http://www.cbsnews.com/8301-505263_162-57542362/inside-nyc-hospitals-near-disaster-during-sandy/
9. Ibid.
10. Ofri, Danielle. 2012. "The Storm and the Aftermath" in *The New England Journal of Medicine* 367; 24. 2266.
11. http://www.huffingtonpost.com/2012/10/30/nyu-hospital-evacuation-hurricane-sandy_n_2044026.html
12. Ibid.
13. http://www.insurancejournal.com/news/national/2012/11/06/269512.htm
14. World Health Organization. Hospitals Safe From Disasters: Reduce Risk, Protect Health Facilities, and Save Lives. Available at http://www.safehospitals.info.php?option=com_frontpage&itemid=103. Accessed June 30, 2012.
15. Bagaria J, Heggie C. Abrahams J. et al. Evacuation and sheltering of hospitals in emergencies. A review of international experience. *Prehosp Disaster Med.* 2009; 461–467.
16. Little M., Stone T, Stone R, Burns J et al. The evacuation of Cairns Hospitals due to severe tropical cyclone Yasi. *Academic Emergency Medicine.* 2012; 1088–1098.
17. Robert, Janet M. Involuntary Relocation of Nursing Home Residents and Transfer Trauma. 24 St. Louis U. L.J. 758. 2012; 1979–1981.
18. http://www.foxnews.com/opinion/2012/10/31/superstorm-sandy-and-hospital-heroics/
19. Hirdes JP, Frijters D, Teare G. 2003.The MDS CHESS Scale: A New Measure to Predict Mortality in the Institutionalized Elderly. Journal of the American Geriatrics Society 51(1): 96–100.

CHAPTER SIX
FAST AND SLOW CAPITALISM
AFTER HURRICANE SANDY

Stan C. Weeber

ABSTRACT

Fast capitalism is Ben Agger's term to describe an Internet-based capitalism in which buying, selling, and advertising occur 24 hours per day, seven days per week without relief. Fast capitalism took a hit on the East Coast after Hurricane Sandy when cell phone towers were inoperable and other critical infrastructure was completely destroyed. Eventually fast capitalism returned as infrastructure reconstruction projects were funded and repair work began at a frantic pace. However, for average citizens—small business owners and middle and lower class homeowners—the pace of recovery was much slower. Slow capitalism is my term to describe the sluggish pace of recovery at the micro or family level as experienced after a natural disaster such as Hurricane Sandy. Recovery is a slow, problem filled process where access to goods, services and privileges needed to rebuild are contingent upon stiff bureaucratic qualifications and coordination of effort among several stakeholders. The fast/slow capitalism dichotomy was not unique to Hurricane Sandy as stories from Hurricanes Katrina, Rita, Ike and Tropical Storm Irene demonstrate.

INTRODUCTION

Fast capitalism denotes an Internet-based capitalism in which buying, selling, and advertising occur 24 hours per day, seven days per week on an accelerated basis (Agger, 1989, 2004; Kenway and Langmead, 1998; Holmes, 2000). For the young especially, fast capitalism is a preferred method of commerce as it accommodates

103

rapidly changing styles and consumption patterns. Internet stores are open every day, all day. Social media provides a smooth unobstructed channel for capitalism to move quickly as buyers and sellers have instant access the commodities of choice. The discussions related to such commodities or commodified images— distributed freely on variegated social media—are so frequent as to be associated with a dysfunctional tendency to overshare information on social media (Agger, 2012). A related but clearly different dysfunction is the way in which personal boundaries clearly established in socially structured physical space may be obliterated in cyberspace. In particular, the usually well defined institutional spaces called "work" and "family" are wiped away by the closeness we can attain to both spheres through technology. Similarly, the boundaries that we may say we attain between a so called "steady state" of our lives and a condition of life called "disaster" also become intertwined in nuanced ways. In this chapter, I explore a complex understanding of fast capitalism as it pertains to the recovery and reconstruction processes after the disaster of Hurricane Sandy. At face value, fast capitalism after a disaster such as Sandy would be perceived as a good thing; rapid buying of products assists all stakeholders in the regional economy in recovering from the storm's effects. However, we will see that post-disaster capitalism is faster for some than for others. Further, fast capitalism has both negative and positive impacts on people, families, and businesses recovering from the disaster.

THEORETICAL FRAMEWORK

Fast capitalism is a sociohistorically distinct stage of capitalism in which the heretofore distinct social institutions such as work and family, education and entertainment have blurred to the point of near extinction in an accelerated, post Fordist stage of capitalism (Agger, 2004). The implication of this stage of history is that it is difficult for people to shield themselves from subordination and surveillance by political or corporate forces trying to mold human behavior. Every keystroke can be traced; one's online footprint can be packaged and sold, sometimes without our knowledge. The working day has expanded; time for relaxation has shrunk because work is always a phone call away. People can office anywhere, using laptops and cellular phones to stay in touch. Our privacy may be reduced by friends who "text" us, expecting an immediate response (Agger, 2012). Cramped as our lives appear to have become by these invasive technologies, the same level of technology can be used as a weapon to fight back again those who might seek to control us (Weeber, 2011, 2012). Beyond this, the Internet can be used to encourage an enlightened public sphere in which people express themselves and organize others (Parham, 2003; Van Laer and Van Aelst, 2010; Lerner, 2010; Carty, 2009; Brooks-Klinger, 2007; Della Porta and Mosca, 2005; and Capling and Nossel, 2001). Information technologies additionally afford unparalleled connection and mitigate isolation. Positive as these developments may be, what happens when fast capitalism (or fast technology) is suddenly not so fast due to a natural disaster? Who benefits and who suffers? Some proponents argue that a "slower" capitalism such as average citizens experience after a hurricane's destruction should be pushed as a viable alternative to fast capitalism (Honore, 2004).

Neo-liberal policy has provided a secure platform from which fast capitalism can take root in an accelerated media culture. Neo-liberalism can be traced to Adam Smith and David Ricardo who wrote important books on economic theory in the late eighteenth and early nineteenth century. Smith (1776) opposed "mercantilism," a strategy based upon state control and promotion of economic activity. He wanted to abolish state intervention in economic matters, asserting that markets regulate themselves and the natural balancing forces of the marketplace tend toward an equilibrium in which resources are used efficiently. David Ricardo (1817) added the idea that unrestricted trade between countries would be beneficial. When a nation trades for products and can obtain them at lower cost from another country, that nation is better off than if it produced the products at home (Hytrek and Zentgraf, 2008). Together, these two ideas formed the theoretical basis of "laissez-faire capitalism," an economic system in which the state does not impose restrictions on ownership, production, or trade (Friedman and Friedman, 1980).

In the United States, neo-liberalism began around 1980 with the election of Ronald Reagan. Though Reagan was not immediately identified as neo-liberal by the public or even by academics, Americans became familiar with such expressions as "Reagonomics" and "trickle down economics," ideas that were derived from the philosophies of Smith and Ricardo, and which we now know and recognize as neo-liberalism (Hytrek and Zentgraf, 2008).

Business friendly neo-liberal policies on disaster stress reconstruction over recovery. Although the two terms are often viewed as synonyms, even in the disaster literature (e.g., Kurth and Burkel, 2006), it is also recognized that at a higher level of complexity the terms can have nuanced meanings. A lucid discussion of these terms is provided by Edwards (2012; see also Mileti, Drabek and Haas, 1975). First, before either recovery or reconstruction can begin, there is an emergency or rescue phase where the primary tasks are saving lives, protecting property and providing for basic human needs such as food and shelter. This is the period immediately following a disaster in which there is often an outpouring of support in various forms and an influx of temporary help and helpers. Second, there is the recovery phase. This can last up to a year or more, in which there is a focus on helping victims resume normal, basic life activities. The third phase is reconstruction which lasts for years, during which organizations and communities may be reshaped and strengthened.

What happens under neo-liberal policy is that the reconstruction phase, on an accelerated basis, occurs before the recovery process begins and may run parallel to it for a period of time. Disasters are good for business in that contracts can be quickly signed for cleanup of debris and for construction of much needed infrastructure. After all, this infrastructure is necessary before displaced residents can return and businesses can get up to speed once again (APA, 2005). The buying of replacement goods to cover losses helps drive economic growth. Rebuilding sparks investment, construction and employment. Insurance payments and emergency benefits, in theory at least, should improve household budgets (Clancy, 2012). However, this also provides an opportunity to push an agenda to socially reorganize the depleted region on business friendly terms, and to restructure it in such a way that large companies can profit from similar disasters in the future. Disasters in general are viewed as opportune moments to change the public sphere and to promote exciting market opportunities (Gunewardena and Schuller, 2008; Saltman, 2007). Klein (2005, 2007) asserts that the purpose of reconstruction is to transform everything. She called this "disaster capitalism," a predatory form of capitalism that uses the desperation and fear created by the catastrophe to radically reinvent social and economic institutions. The reconstruction industry works with efficiency and dispatch so that privatizations and new land contracts get locked in before locals become aware of the consequences. All manner of disasters are fair game for such radical reconstruction, including tornadoes, floods, tsunamis, earthquakes, oil spills, and others (Klein, 2007; Weeber, 2011, 2012). In the meantime, families are left to fend for themselves based upon the fundamental concept of individual responsibility that is a hallmark of neo-liberalism (Hytrek and Zentgraf, 2008), that is, the individual family has the responsibility to be prepared for disasters; if not prepared, then your family must bear the circumstances.

As a neo-liberal economist Milton Friedman found disasters to be fertile grounds for social reorganization. Though viewing the displacement of New Orleans school children in areas across the America after Katrina as unfortunate and tragic, he also felt that the hurricane was a blessing in disguise because it opened the door for the radical reconstruction of the New Orleans schools by converting them into for-profit charter schools. This was just the beginning of the social transformations that neo-liberals had in mind for the city. Thirteen days after Katrina's landfall, the Heritage Foundation proposed thirty-two free market solutions for New Orleans, several of which were subsequently implemented by the Bush Administration (Klein, 2007).

Post disaster construction plans for New Orleans emphasized maximizing profits, the centerpiece of which were no-bid contracts to Halliburton, Fluor, Shaw, and CH2M Hill totaling $3.4 billion to provide mobile home to evacuees (Klein, 2007). Additionally, there was a lowering of the minimum wage; cheap labor was brought in by trucks from the outside; and there were plans to completely redesign the city. Some residents had legitimate concerns that these plans would destroy valuable aspects of New Orleans culture and bring about gentrification, making it impossible for them to return (Delgado, 2010).

A template for action by the reconstruction industry was constructed following Hurricane Mitch's landfall in Honduras in 1998. Two months after Mitch, with the country still reeling from the devastation, the Honduran congress initiated "speed sell offs" which allowed the privatization of airports, seaports, and highways. Additionally, there were fast tracked plans to privatize the state telephone company, the national electric company and part of the water sector. As a condition for the release of about $47 million in annual aid over three years and 4.4 billion in debt relief, the World Bank and the IMF demanded that the telecom company be privatized (Klein, 2005; Stonich, 2008).

With emphasis on reconstruction, recovery becomes a sorely neglected agenda, a public relations ploy to give off the impression that families are being helped when the grim reality is that many are falling through the cracks of the large, heavily bureaucratized operation. While FEMA issues reports that boast of activities accomplished and dollars spent, the harsh fact is that a substantial number of families end up getting little or no help at all (e.g., FEMA, 2006; Sullivan, 2005). Local, state or federal government reports fail to note these embarrassing statistics, and from a pro-business stance, too much help to families detracts from capital accumulation and profit. What's more, neo-liberals openly suggest that each family should be left to fend for itself, citing the idea of "individual responsibility" for each family to prepare for disaster. What evidence now exists to document the unwritten policy that the least help is the best help? Library shelves around the world are now full of volumes or documents that verify the lack of governmental response after Hurricanes Katrina, Gustav, Ike, and Tropical Storms Irene and Issac (Harriford and Thompson, 2008; Bullard and Wright, 2009; Brinkley, 2006; Horne, 2006; Dyson, 2006, 2007; Cooper and Block, 2006; Troutt, 2006; Hartman and Squires, 2006; Montana-Leblanc, 2008; Marable and Clark, 2008; Potter, 2007; Hidalgo and Barber, 2007; Saltman, 2007; Vollen and Ying, 2008; Brandon, Garman and Ryan, 2012; Russell, 2013; Standridge, 2010, Mayeaux, 2009; Weeber, 2008, 2009, 2011).

FAST CAPITALISM AFTER HURRICANE SANDY

The storm system that came to be known as Hurricane Sandy lasted for one week in late October, 2012 and proved to be the second costliest Atlantic hurricane on record (see NOAA, 2012). Appearing first as a tropical wave on October 22, the system to be named Sandy intensified to tropical storm strength on October 23 and drenched the coast of Jamaica the next day. After the system left Jamaica it rapidly intensified into a Category 3 hurricane with maximum sustained winds of 115 miles per hour. The storm would decrease in intensity to Category 2 just before beginning a western arc in the Atlantic that would lead to projections that the storm would hit the New Jersey shoreline. During this change in direction Sandy began its transition into an extra tropical cyclone, a process it completed before making landfall near Brigantine, New Jersey late on October 29. The extra tropical remnants weakened gradually overland, and the center of circulation was declared indistinguishable over western Pennsylvania two days later.

The storm surge produced by Hurricane Sandy pushed water to 13.88 feet in Battery Park, New York, setting a new all time high. Storm tide records were also broken in Sandy Hook, New Jersey and in Philadelphia, Pennsylvania. Sandy was the largest tropical cyclone in terms of gale diameter since records began in 1988.

Sandy was responsible for 72 direct deaths in the U.S., with storm surge being responsible for 41 of the 72 fatalities. Falling trees during the storm killed twenty people in the northeastern and mid-Atlantic states, even in locations experiencing winds of less than hurricane force. The storm and its remnants caused at least 87 indirect deaths; about 50 of these were the result of extended power outages during cold weather, which led to deaths from hypothermia, falls in the dark by senior citizens, or carbon monoxide poisoning from improperly placed generators or cooking devices.

An analysis of the wind field from Sandy showed that even at the time of landfall, some residual effects of the storm were being felt as far south as Florida and as far north as Nova Scotia. In Florida, there were reports of minor flooding and beach erosion while in Nova Scotia, 14,000 residents lost power (NOAA, 2012). Closer in, North Carolinians along the Atlantic shore lost 70 miles of protective dunes due to beach erosion and a key artery, Highway 12, was under water (Barnes, 2013). Businesses with multiple sites reported wide variations in the amount of damage along the coast (see Dow Jones News, 2012; Reuters, 2012). U.S. pipeline and storage company NuStar Energy reported no damage to its Virginia Beach, Virginia, facility, and it resumed operations soon after the storm passed. There was virtually no damage to its terminal at Dumfries, Virginia which came back online Thursday morning, November 1. Nustar's terminal in Andrews Air Force Base, Maryland, had no apparent damage. Closer to the center of the storm's circulation NuStar reported some flooding in the Piney Point, Maryland, terminal and some tank insulation damage but the facility did not lose power. High water, however, limited access to the pier.

Near the center of the storm along the New Jersey and New York coasts, capitalism traveled fast for some of the larger businesses because of the greater resources that could be mustered to get operations online or at least near capacity. Such businesses may suffer some direct losses in the hurricane zone for a time, but these losses can be offset by raising prices in other locations to cover the deficit. Personnel can be shifted and revenue streams continue, albeit at less than normal volume, despite the storm's impact. Information technologies can be relocated to another unit if needed to keep operations online. For some companies, the main computer operations are located at a site far from the disaster zone, thus avoiding catastrophic data losses.

The perceived importance of a business to the regional or national economy was a factor in getting certain firms back online quickly. The New York Stock Exchange was knocked out of service for only two days after Sandy, and major banks and financial services companies rushed to get back up to speed for the beginning of trading on Wednesday after the storm. Atlantic City casinos managed to get back online quickly, not wanting to suffer a large break in revenue streams. Socioeconomic status played a role in how quickly people got power restored; the Gold Coast area, an affluent part of New Jersey, had its power restored within 36 hours of Sandy's landfall (Grey, 2012).

Pipelines and refineries, deemed important because of their ability to deliver fuel, also recovered quickly (Dow Jones News, 2012). Colonial Pipeline Company's 825,000-barrel-a-day Line 3 pipe that carries gasoline and diesel from Greensboro, North Carolina, to Linden, New Jersey, resumed limited operations on November

2, four days after Hurricane Sandy. PBF Energy in Paulsboro, New Jersey was shut down briefly but ramped up operations on a reduced output basis by November 1. The same day, a facility owned by Philadelphia Energy Solutions and one owned by Delta Airlines facility in Trainer, Pennsylvania were already back producing at normal rates (Flynn, 2012). Such news provided a boost for the stock market which was shaken by the potential economic effects of the storm (Kim, 2012; Reuters, 2012).

Phillips 66 in Linden, New Jersey shut down its operation due to loss of power caused by flooding in low-lying areas of its refinery, but had plans to restore power in 24 to 48 hours of the storm's passing. New Jersey's primary electric company, Public Service Electric and Gas Company (PSEG) said on the Tuesday following that storm that it re-energized three of six flooded switchyards, including equipment that can deliver power to the Linden area and the Newark airport and the cities of Newark and Elizabeth, New Jersey. NuStar Energy said its Paulsboro, New Jersey, terminal suffered the most damage of all its facilities, but had hopes of being back in operation Tuesday evening, October 30. Magellan Midstream Partners completed preliminary assessment of its New Haven and Wilmington facilities in the hours after Sandy passed through and were in the process of implementing a reactivation plan. Truck loading operations were expected to resume late Tuesday, October 30. U.S. midstream company Buckeye Partners LP said many of its facilities in New York City, New Jersey and Connecticut were without power after the hurricane but would begin restoring power to several mid-point booster stations in Pennsylvania, and that several of those systems were scheduled to restart as early as Tuesday evening, 48 hours after Sandy passed through (Dow Jones News, 2012).

A variety of businesses not related to oil and gas also regained power quickly. Legrand, a maker of electrical equipment in Fairfield, New Jersey had power restored the day after the storm. Ace Hardware stores in New York City opened the same day as did Aetna Insurance in Hartford, Connecticut (Schwartz, 2012).

SLOW CAPITALISM AFTER HURRICANE SANDY

New Jersey Governor Chris Christie acknowledged that capitalism traveled faster for some than for others after Sandy demolished the Jersey Shore in October, 2012. At a ribbon cutting ceremony to celebrate the reopening of beaches and boardwalks in May, 2013, he said:

> (Recovery is) an eight in some places and a four in others (on a scale of ten) . . . Here on the boardwalk, people will see it as an eight out of ten when they start coming here in June, but for a lot of the homeowners of the state, it's going to take the better part of the next year to get them back. . . . This was the easiest one to get done first. The homeowner part is much more difficult because people have decisions they want to make about whether they want to rebuild, how they want to rebuild, and how much they want to elevate (Stump, 2013).

In the neighborhoods along the Jersey Shore where recovery was slower, the median household income is about $33,000 per year. A majority of the dwellings there are single family homes built before 1960 (U.S. Census, 2010). For the most part, these homes are owned by third, fourth, or fifth generation residents who chose to live there or to rent their homes out to tourists or to temporary workers in the tourism industry. Some of these homeowners also run "Mom and Pop" style small businesses catering to the tourist crowds that gather on the Jersey Shore each summer. Back in the 1940s and 1950s, these home owners and business owners were not required to buy flood insurance and failed to see the need for it as hurricanes and tropical storms were exceedingly rare events until recently. It is a great understatement to say that these small firms were not in the same competitive position as big box companies and other Fortune 500 corporations when it comes to recovery after a disaster such as Sandy. Among other advantages, the larger businesses are able to transfer their information technology hardware and software to a remote site far away, if necessary, from the storm. On the other hand these smaller businesses, if computerized at all, may have a local IT platform that does not have data backup capabilities, and if so, were in a position to lose all data due to flooding.

In spite of a mandatory evacuation order, many residents did not leave. Some were unable to leave due to physical restrictions. Others felt that they had no place to go, or that they did not understand the storm to be different from previous storms that hit the area. People who did not evacuate faced dire circumstances. Some had to be rescued by boat (Annese and D'Anna, 2012). We know from studying past disasters that "attachment to place" is a factor that plays a significant role in explaining why some do not evacuate from a storm. (Barber, Hidalgo, Haney, Weeber, Pardee and Day, 2007; Weeber, 2009; Wilkinson and Ross, 1970). In the South along the Gulf Coast attachment to place was hypothesized to be strong due to the tendency of extended families in the region to have long, proud traditions of living in a particular place for a long period of time up to several decades. This type of social dynamic appeared to play a role in the reluctance to evacuate ahead of Hurricane Sandy. Some third, fourth, or fifth generation residents of the Jersey Shore did not want to abandon the belongings that they had spent decades accumulating, fearing looters might try to break in and steal them—a legitimate fear.

The Waiting Game

For those residents fortunate enough to leave town in time before Sandy's impact, the first question on their mind is, "How is my house?" Getting information about the condition of one's dwelling from long distance is very difficult to obtain immediately after a storm passes. National and even regional news reports may not be reporting upon one's own town or specific area along the coastline. Or, some messages passed along via Internet, for example, to evacuee message boards, may be inaccurate (Weeber, 2008, 2009). If you evacuated four or more hours away from where the storm made landfall, local radio or TV stations may not be reporting on the storm at all, feeling it would not be a strong topic for locals in their broadcast area to know about. Trying to call people in the area near landfall is difficult due to the frequent failure of cell phone towers after a hurricane. Thus, it may be difficult or impossible to find out the condition of your dwelling without seeing it yourself.

This leads to a second question, "When will I be able to return to my town to survey the damage to my home?" This has been a source of great irritation at least since Hurricane Frances hit Florida in 2004, and local police began restricting access to locals until towns could be deemed secure and safe for people to return to their homes (Barton, 2004). The general belief among residents in such a situation is that the amount of time that public officials keep residents out is much too long. At a raucous, contentious meeting held at the Holiday Inn in Toms River on November 9, eleven days after Sandy, residents from Seaside Heights and Lavellete wanted to go home to collect personal belongings and salvage whatever they could before mold and mildew firmly took root. However, public officials claimed that the towns—especially the roads going in and out—must be secured and repaired and debris cleared before they can allow citizens back in even on a limited basis to make a preliminary assessment of the damage to their homes. Safety appeared to be the top priority (O'Neill, 2012). Based upon what we know of evacuee experiences after storms in the 2000s, citizens who return without receiving an "all clear" message from city officials risk not being protected by police, fire, or emergency services while they are inside the city limits (Weeber, 2009).

Once back in town on a temporary or permanent basis, the first task is to do a preliminary assessment of damages to your home. If there's not much damage and your home is obviously livable, then it is possible to remain there and repairs can begin immediately. If there are structural issues that compromise the safety of your home, city officials are responsible for determining if the residence should be condemned and torn down. This process can take months. In the meantime, temporary housing must be located for residents whose homes were heavily damaged and beyond repair (Weeber, 2009).

The next important question is, "when will power be restored?" Life is at a standstill until power is returned. On this measure of post-storm well-being, homeowners definitely did not fare as well as large businesses. Those households with generators or access to generators coped better, assuming that their dwellings were livable, because generators can provide electricity to at least a portion of the home, and can power TVs, refrigerators, air conditioning or heating units, and other creature comforts until such time as power is turned back on (Weeber, 2008, 2009).

The long wait for power did have some positive outcomes. Young people and their parents, usually relentlessly tethered to their electronic gadgets, actually spent some serious "face time" with each other. Impromptu family gatherings took place as extended family members, also without power, were invited in to share in the misery. Or, family members with power took in those that did not. In any event, family ties were strengthened to a degree by such interactions and neighbors no longer took each other for granted (Krayewski, 2013).

For some families, the wait for power can be measured in weeks. Needless to say, the long wait was a sore spot for some, but citizen anger at the utility companies did nothing to hurry up the speed of having electricity reconnected. The companies had priorities. Ralph LaRosa, President and Chief Operating Officer of PSEG told a New Jersey Senate Committee:

> We try our best. We start with the hospitals first—that was our primary concern. We also had additional issues during the storm that we hadn't seen before, so we had a big focus on getting the refineries back up and running—which is not normally in the process. And those types of requests come from the (State) OEM offices. So we have a set list that we've worked on, and it starts with the critical infrastructure the Department of Homeland Security has identified. And then we work our way down that list to where we actually listen to the county OEMs; and after the county OEMs, the municipal OEMs (State of New Jersey, 2012a: 24–25).

Another problem identified by returning residents was a lack of consistent information from the power companies about when power would come on. The news they received, if they got any at all, was incomplete or contradictory. Ralph LaRosa explained the problem:

> Everybody has different information among the (PSEG) hierarchy. . . . And it's more up to date depending upon where you are in that hierarchy. The more we have the information and technology for this (e.g., use of social media to provide close to real time updates) the better. None of the utilities want to provide bad information (State of New Jersey, 2012a: 36–37).

Insurance Problems

As part of the recovery process, residents must make initial calls to FEMA and to insurance companies, and must fill out the required paperwork. As some applications can be lengthy, public libraries became popular places for evacuees to hang out, fill out insurance forms and warm up, as the late season hurricane left many out in the cold (Bayliss, 2012). In some cases, FEMA came to the disaster zone and set up claims centers in certain towns, although some critics suggested the claims centers were too far away from senior citizens centers and provided assistance only in English (Strike Debt, 2012). This was a particular problem in ethnic neighborhoods where native languages were spoken and many could not read or speak English. Residents reported that they were generally satisfied with this interaction and that the FEMA employees were good people (State of New Jersey, 2012b). Then, these same residents received bureaucracy letters which rendered the whole episode (i.e., the application process) to be an exercise in futility because FEMA generally will not pay until insurance companies have paid. It appears to some that FEMA is structured in such a way that initial claims are always denied. FEMA officials claim that, after an initial denial, the customer must appeal to a higher level of FEMA, though this is rarely if ever communicated to customers in writing. At a meeting of the New Jersey Senate Budget and Appropriations Committee (State of New Jersey, 2012b: 15) Mayor Frank Nolan of Highlands remarked:

> (A)lmost everybody I know who I have talked to—they got a letter saying they're not getting any money, and that's determined, in my mind, as a denial. When you ask FEMA, they say it's not a denial; it means you have to go to the next level. But it doesn't say that in the letter. And, quite frankly, if you're spending 50 minutes on the phone doing that to get to know to go the next level—just tell me who to call in a letter and we'll take care of it.

For residents, interaction with FEMA representatives began to take on the social dynamic of interacting with an insurance company. (To a degree FEMA is an insurance company because they administer the National Flood Insurance Program). With insurance companies, the standard drill is for resident to sign a contract in which they believe that they will be covered for any expenses they incur after a disaster of Sandy's magnitude. It is reasonable to expect that a claim must be filed for any damages incur. Then, there was an expectation that a check would arrive, unless the loss is not covered or you do not have sufficient documentation to prove a loss, in which case the insurance company owes you nothing. Thousands of residents found that FEMA did not provide them with any actual assistance (except for immediate help in the days following the disaster) until they had been denied coverage by their insurance companies. And many found they were not really insured, had a lower level of insurance than was needed to rebuild and fully replace their losses, or that they were denied coverage because of obscure passages in their insurance coverage. Mayor Nolan testified before the Senate Committee:

> I've read about 20 letters here today. . . . The issue that's really confounded me the most is this issue of flood insurance. I have more people saying, "Well, we've loyally purchased flood insurance for the last 10, 20, 30 years," and then they do, during a crisis or a flood, and they find out the carrier saying, more times than not, 'Well, you're really not covered, or you have some other issue" (State of New Jersey, 2012b: 19).

New Jersey Senator Kevin O'Toole remarked, "So I will tell you, in my opinion, they're trying to hold on to the money as long as they can and then dispense it when they have to." (State of New Jersey, 2012b: 20).

One very obscure aspect of the insurance business left many residents stuck in the "wind versus water" controversy, where neither home owners insurance nor flood insurance would pay for damages to their dwelling. Hurricane Katrina brought this problem to the forefront of the public's attention like never before. Many of the lawsuits filed by policyholders who were denied coverage by their homeowners' insurers focused on whether property damage from Katrina was caused by wind or objects propelled by wind—both of which are covered under the standard property insurance policy—or by water or flood, which is excluded (Haney, 2007). Several families in New Jersey reported that they were caught in this dilemma. Susan and Ahmad Sharif, who lived and owned a home in Brick Township, had a standard homeowners' policy on their house, which Sandy pushed off its foundation. They didn't have separate flood insurance policy from the National Flood Insurance Program. But they say they were never informed that their homeowners' policy would not cover hurricane storm surge destruction, so they sued their insurance company, as did hundreds of their neighbors in similar circumstances (Cushman, 2013; Beeson, 2013).

Another insurance issue that emerged during the aftermath of Sandy was the "earth movement" controversy. When some residents returned from the hurricane, they found their floors were buckled and there was severe foundation damage. Insurance adjusters told the residents that the damage was preexisting or that flood insurance does not cover damage from soil shifting regardless of whether or not the soil shifting was caused by flood. As it turned out, this is a fairly standard, but obscure, provision of standard flood policies. There is an exclusion in flood insurance policies for a loss of property caused "directly by earth movement even if the earth movement is caused by flood," according to the standard policy. In plain English, this means that if water moves the soil and that movement of soil cracks a house's foundation, that damage is not covered by insurance. Because this policy was seen as unreasonable, intense anger was directed at FEMA. Michele Mittleman told a reporter (Pitzi, 2013):

> Losing the house was heartache, losing everything we owned was heartache, and now realizing the federal government is defrauding us and taking our money, after paying premiums for years, is the heartache here. Its been ten months of living in a one bedroom apartment, with my son sleeping in a closet, that's the heartache.

Mittleman's home was flooded so badly that it was condemned. She was greatly surprised when FEMA declined her claim on the basis of "earth movement." She thought this ruling was outrageous as flood waters had obviously led to the damages to her home. Michele took to Facebook to vent her anger:

> I was so outraged when I got this letter that I immediately got on Facebook. I have never been on Facebook before. My son is on Facebook all the time. But I got on there because in my gut I knew they were not singling my claim out (Pitzi, 2013).

Mittlemen went on to form a Facebook group called Sandy Victims Fighting FEMA, many of whom are still homeless or soon to be homeless as their temporary assistance runs out.

Robert Trautmann, a Red Bank attorney representing Sandy victims battling insurance companies, said he has reviewed about 30 to 40 earth movement cases. Trautman said that adjusters for insurance companies are following FEMA's directions on claims "to a fault," fearful of the repercussions if they get something wrong. Trautmann maintains that FEMA has told those adjusters that the agency will be looking to the adjusters to reimburse the federal government, not the homeowners, if a mistake is made. "They're really looking for any reason to deny in case FEMA comes back to them" (Jones, 2013).

Richard and Stephanie Diehl of Union Beach had their flood insurance claim for a cracked foundation denied because the adjustor said that their damage was preexisting, a charge that the couple vehemently denies. Though the Diehls did receive some insurance money to rebuild their home, it was not enough money to pay for the repairs to the foundation, a necessary step before repairs to the remainder of the home can begin. They received an $86,000 loan from the Small Business Administration, but felt that they did not have the means to pay the loan back. As a result, they are strongly considering walking away from their home on Eighth Street (Serrano, 2013).

It is difficult to determine how many victims fit the profile of the Diehl's. There are no hard numbers collected by government or private agencies. But many victims say the payments from insurance companies and state grants are woefully inadequate in providing enough money to help them move back into their homes. Keyport bankruptcy attorney Warren Brumel said that he sees a repeat of the Diehl's story every day. "It's very common . . . the combination of the FEMA benefits, and flood insurance and homeowners' insurance payments is just a fraction of the total cost of rebuilding the house. Clients are telling me, 'I have $80,000 in checks but it's going to cost $130,000 to rebuild.'" (Serrano, 2013). One resident with a story similar to the Diehls posted the following message to a Hurricane Sandy discussion board:

> Our house was destroyed and we received $67,000 from our initial flood insurance claim. The township sent us a letter stating the house was substantially damaged. We had the house taken down and the lot cleared. We have been saving up to cover the gap of about 50K to replace the house. And it's not with granite counter tops and tile floors. Now Wells Fargo wants the moratorium money, 22K, and wants us to pay the mortgage every month going forward (Serrano, 2013).

A few statistics could help to explain why this problem is now so widespread. About 100,000 homes needed to be elevated in New Jersey, according to the state Department of Environmental Protection. As of summer, 2013 only 7,500 home-owners received grants to lift their homes, which shows among other things the financial struggles within households to come up with the funds to rebuild in accordance with the new height regulations. Robert Trautmann said insurers working for the National Flood Insurance Program are paying 24 to 26 cents on the dollar of actual damage. For the 74,387 flood insurance claims made in New Jersey, the average payment with a closed claim was $52,617, according to the NFIP (Serrano, 2013).

Rebuilding

Even if residents were fortunate enough to avoid such devastating problems, rebuilding was clearly an exercise in patience as several complex obstacles needed to be cleared. Residents who wanted to rebuild soon discovered that there were multiple stakeholders in the recovery process, each with stiff bureaucratic requirements that had to be met, so that rebuilding was not so straightforward as choosing a contractor and then proceeding to rebuild. Homeowners must wait for new flood maps that are issued after each hurricane. These maps will show the specific requirements needed to rebuild, such as the required height at which buildings should be built so as to survive a similar storm of Sandy's magnitude. The wait for maps can last for months. The homeowner is responsible for complying with the new regulations. Then, city licenses are needed before building could proceed (Porpora, 2013). Trying to get all interested parties in line and ready to move forward led to delays, which in turn slowed the overall economic recovery that is fueled at least in part by the reconstruction process.

The costs involved in complying with the new federal construction guidelines —or face highly inflated flood insurance rates—led some to consider walking away from their properties just as the Diehls were considering rather than jumping through the hoops necessary to comply with the regulations. New federal flood maps revealed in June, 2013 added 68,000 structures in New York City and thousands more in New Jersey to flood zones. Affected homeowners are being forced to make drastic changes to their residences, such as elevating them on pilings, or incur punishing new insurance premiums that will take effect by mid-2015 (Leitsinger, 2013).

Making such emotional and painful decisions had the effect of delaying the rebuilding (or not rebuilding) process, and such delays for families meant delays in the overall fiscal recovery of New Jersey and New York. Even when construction was able to move forward, the process was delayed by state regulations. After Katrina, truckloads of immigrants were shipped in to work to accelerate recon-struction. After Sandy, the assistance of some workers brought in from out of state was rejected. Union workers did most of the cleanup, but at higher cost and in longer time frame than the contract labor would have provided the services (Tillison, 2013).

Homeowners with liens on their properties found that mortgage lenders tended to hold on to any disaster relief checks instead of forwarding them to customers, thus slowing down the rebuilding process. Instead of disbursing the insurance money as a lump sum, lenders were holding on to the money to disburse it as a series of construction loans, asking for contractor bills or verification of work actually completed before monies will be sent to the homeowner (Willis, 2013).

The delays in recovery translate to hard times for local businesses and lower revenues for state and local coffers. The tourism industry was a vivid example. With communities still recovering, tourism revenues were down by as much as 40 percent, according to Governor Christie who cited anecdotal evidence from business owners and residents in North Wildwood. A local businessman cited evidence that confirmed the Governor's statistics. Rentals are off by 30 percent to 40 percent, and home sales are down by an even wider margin. Beach tags—the daily or seasonal passes purchased for beach access—are another indicator of the tourism industry's health. Beaches in central and northern New Jersey—which bore more of Sandy's brunt than South Jersey shores – are seeing declines averaging 16 percent. Some beach communities are seeing a decrease of more than 80 percent in beach tag sales. (Hamilton, 2013).

Broader Indicators of Slow Capitalism

Individual stories of woe eventually accumulate into summary statistics that provide a broader indicator of how slow capitalism has been for individual families. One such indicator of comes from the fact that aid to cover what FEMA and private insurers would not cover arrived about nine months after the storm. The state of Connecticut learned in summer of 2013 that it will get nearly $72 million in federal grants to help pay for storm damages. The federal government has approved the funding to assist homeowners and business owners whose damages were not covered by insurance. This money was for average families and for municipalities: $30 million to help homeowners repair damage; $26 million to rehabilitate and rebuild low and moderate-income multifamily homes; $4 million to assist a wide range of businesses affected by the storm; $4 million to address infrastructure needs that post health and safety risks; and $2.2 million for public building repair (McNamara, 2013).

New construction statistics provided another indicator. In an update of July 3, 2013, new construction data shows the recovery process was well underway in many areas. The number of demolition permits in places like Toms River, spiked dramatically in March and April, a clear indication that even the hardest hit areas of the state were beginning the process of getting back on their feet. Where demolitions were able to take place earlier, such as Sayreville and Brick, the number of building permits being issued for new construction and alterations to homes was on the rise as families begin rebuilding follow the storm (Sandy Recovery Scorecard, 2013).

As late as September, 2013, some residents were still stranded away from their homes, living in hotels as part of FEMA's Transitional Sheltering Assistance program, which pays for hotels and rooms for Hurricane Sandy victims. After an extension requested by the State of New York such victims had until September 16 to vacate their transitional housing (Porpora, 2013).

FEMA's Slow Response

FEMA's response time to help victims was notoriously slow (see generally Strike Debt, 2012). It took FEMA days to show up in Staten Island after the storm, provoking an angry admonition from the borough president. When workers finally got there, they provided very little of the resources most needed to initiate a process that might eventually return the community to normal. Instead of using their enormous resources to provide hot meals, they provided only freeze-dried food and bottled water. Instead of going where the people needed help, they stationed themselves in schools and parking lots, expecting the elderly and infirmed to travel to them.

The majority of those impacted by the storm in Red Hook, Brooklyn were either small business owners or residents of single-family houses. Residents complained that FEMA was more focused on local businesses than on residents. Angel Ylufo, who lives in a high-rise project housing building on Dwight Street, expressed frustration with the state and allocation of recovery efforts in Red Hook: "I've got no power, no water and can smell sewage in my building and there is definitely more attention to the local businesses than for us in the projects. I'm all for local business, but what about the rest of us citizens who are living here?" (Strike Debt, 2012). However, local businesses were also dissatisfied. Many were still waiting to see if their loan applications will be approved or not, but did not see taking on additional debt as a solution for the disaster. Instead, many started "crowd-source" funding pages to raise money for repairs, stating that if the condition of reopening is debt, then they cannot afford to reopen.

Once the storm passed in Coney Island, Brooklyn, a major need was for the elderly, disabled and ill to be identified and provided with basic necessities. The consensus of an accumulation of local reports from the area was that no such direct effort by city, state or federal agencies or even the Red Cross was noted in the weeks immediately following the storm. Many residents spent weeks in dark, cold apartments without food, water and prescribed medical treatments. As with many low-income neighborhoods and areas where public housing is prevalent, much of the area has been underserved by supermarkets and drug stores. Many of the bodegas were flooded and looted in the wake of the storm, leaving residents without access to even a bare minimum of necessities like food, cleaning supplies, baby formula and diapers.

FEMA's presence finally began to be visible in the Coney Island community over a week after the storm hit, but even then their trailer was located in the historic far west end of Coney Island, far from the majority of NYCHA housing in which many elderly and disabled residents were trapped. Despite a significant population of Russian speakers, FEMA materials were not available in Russian.

The entirety of the Rockaways in Queens was hit hard, but certain sections were the focus of FEMA's resources. Observers claimed that FEMA's efforts were primarily in the higher-income area west of 116th Street, where repair to the beachfront had already begun. There was little to no activity to the east, where middle and lower income people of color live.

Overall, aid from fellow citizens proved better and more reliable than that from governments. According to several reports, mutual aid networks were on the scene days if not weeks in advance of federal, state and city run efforts, delivering needed care and support that in many cases official relief efforts have yet to step up and provide. In Staten Island, for example, Occupy Sandy Relief has created a central distribution hub at the Church of Margaret Mary at 1128 Olympia Blvd. This hub provided volunteers, hot meals, cleaning supplies, blankets, heaters and a variety of tools necessary for demolition work. It also acted as the central hub of the community and facilitated community meetings.

A long term implication of the FEMA assistance given (or not given) to residents was the widening gap between the well off and the poor in the Northeastern region affected by the storm. By only offering loans to already struggling homeowners, FEMA and the SBA shift the burden of disaster to individuals and send profit to the loan servicers who make $1 billion in profit annually off these loans. While the residential community was clearly in need of resources such as physical help with the massive job of cleanup and ongoing financial support to begin the process of recovery, they were only offered debt on top of that sustained by the storm. Moreover, only the better off qualified for the loans whereas the less resourced were left without any path to recovery.

KATRINA AND SANDY COMPARED

In United States hurricane history, Hurricane Katrina which struck New Orleans in 2005 is the high mark against which all other storms are compared. Katrina was the deadliest U.S. storm and also the costliest. As a meteorological event, it was a larger and fiercer storm, coming ashore as a Category 3 hurricane with winds of 125 miles per hour. Sandy, with as much devastation it caused, was not even a tropical storm when it made landfall. Consequently, the situation along the Jersey Shore and the Northeast could have been much worse if Sandy had been a storm of Katrina's magnitude. This gives planners cause for sober contemplation as the region prepares for the next hurricane to arrive.

After Katrina, the city of New Orleans fully embraced the neo-liberal policy of using the storm as a reason to generate profits and produce a social reorganization of the city, which was viewed as dysfunctional in the eyes of outsiders. As a Strike Debt (2012) report concluded:

The city's reconstruction was profitable to nearly all involved except for the actual disaster victims. The Department of Homeland Security, the umbrella organization that FEMA operated under, oversaw a free-for-all for large corporations like Halliburton and many others. Immediately following the storm The Shaw Group won several no-bid contracts totaling $600 million from FEMA, the Environmental Protection Agency, and the Army Corps of Engineers. Due to a series of subcontracts that outsourced the work being done, much less money than what corporations received went directly into reconstruction and local communities. Low-income residents were discouraged from returning to their neighborhoods—in part because they were often the last to get power, water and other services. Damaged schools were permanently closed, providing opportunities to replace them with privatized alternatives. Hospitals dedicated to the care of low-income patients were never reopened; instead, plans were made to replace them with higher-end, more profitable facilities (Strike Debt Report, 2012).

The report goes on to say that the social problems of New Orleans, especially the problems of the poorer neighborhoods, were washed away in the flood and wind damage from the hurricane as the storm essentially got rid of the affected population. As the communities of displaced individuals were selectively dismantled, there was less incentive for people to return.

After Sandy, the Jersey Shore and the state of New York did not embrace a capitalism that traveled quite as fast or as far as the fast capitalism in New Orleans after Katrina. Neo-liberal philosophers opined that several barriers to a quick fix to solve problems after Sandy in the Northeast would only slow the reconstruction and recovery process (Klein, 2012). Perhaps it did, but there was neither the large scale profit grab nor the social reorganization in the Northeast that existed in New Orleans after Katrina. It was, definitely, a slower capitalism.

Building back "faster and better" was a theme that was echoed after Sandy, but the emphasis of such rhetoric appeared to shift some since Katrina. Darren Walker, the incoming president of the Ford Foundation, said: "A successful response to Hurricane Sandy must build back better and stronger than ever before—reimagining not just our communities, but how those communities work for our families" (Housing and Urban Development, 2013). Note the new emphasis on the well being of families, something that was completely missing after Katrina.

Conclusion

Governor Christie saw from close range the slow, dysfunctional response of the federal government to the crisis of Hurricane Sandy. He expressed indignation when he learned that thousands of his constituents were not yet back into their homes. He blamed federal agencies for this predicament, saying that he was incredibly frustrated by the National Flood Insurance Program. He called the Small Business Administration "a disaster" worthy of intervention by the Federal Emergency Management Agency. When he learned of the devastating tornado in Moore, Oklahoma in the spring of 2013 and the dire need for help that those residents required, he said that those victims deserved swift and immediate help (Spoto, 2013; Dellisanti, 2013).

However, even if Governor Christie is elected President of the United States in 2016, he is unlikely to be able to reform the neo-liberal policies that led to the poor federal response after Sandy—a move that might free up resources so that more families can get help and get it sooner. Such neo-liberal policies are now so much a part of the institutional apparatus in the nation's capital that they are referred to as the Washington Consensus, favored by both political parties (Hytrek and Zentgraf, 2008).

The repercussions of the slow federal response to Sandy's destruction in the Northeast echo far beyond that region. The lack of concern for these citizens may come to be viewed as a betrayal of the public trust. A generalized belief may circulate that there is little real prospect of having a government which is fully committed to the well being of its citizens (Walzer, 2013). Cynicism and apathy, already at high levels, may begin to show in a decline of interest in voting and in other types of participation in civil society.

Sober, critical reflection upon the consequences of the storm might lead to the conclusion that the conditions that led to the disaster were decades in the making, and that it was in fact a "slow motion" catastrophe. Ultimately, the solutions to make the Northeast more resilient to hurricanes may take decades—also a decidedly slow process. A slower capitalism, with some deliberate planning to make the coastline more resilient, is something that could become a popular idea.

Having said that, the changes wrought by climate change are such that the region does not really have a great deal of time to be deliberative. With so-called hundred year storms becoming events that can occur every five years, it is very likely that the next big storm will arrive in the Northeast before the region is fully prepared to withstand it.

REFERENCES

Agger, Ben. 2012. *Oversharing: Presentations of Self in the Internet Age.* Oxford: Oxford University Press.
———. 2004. *Speeding Up Fast Capitalism.* Boulder: Paradigm Publishers.
———. 1989. *Fast Capitalism: A Critical Theory of Significance.* Urbana: University of Illinois Press.
Annese, John and Eddie D'Anna. 2012. "Staten Island's Coastal Communities in Chaos as Hurricane Sandy Flood Waters Rise." *Staten Island Advance,* October 29.
American Planning Association. 2005. PAS Report No. 483/484. Chicago: American Planning Association.
Barber, Kristen, Danielle Hidalgo, Time Haney, Stan Weeber, Jessica Pardee and Jennifer Day, 2007. "Narrating the Storm: Storytelling as a Methodological Approach to Understanding Hurricane Katrina." *Journal of Public Management and Social Policy* 13 (2): 99-120.
Barnes, Jay. 2013. *North Carolina's Hurricane History: Updated with a Decade of New Storms from Isabel to Sandy.* Chapel Hill: University of North Carolina Press.
Barton, Jill. 2004. "Floridians Begin Rebuilding Process After Hurricane." Associated Press, September 6.

Bayliss, Sarah. 2012. "Libraries Respond to Hurricane Sandy, Offering Refuge, WiFi and Services to Needy Communities." *School Library Journal*, November 1.

Beeson, Ed. 2013. "Hurricane Sandy to Spawn Storm of Lawsuits." NJ.com, January 20.

Brandon, Craig, Nicole Garman and Michael Ryan. 2012. Good Night Irene. Keene, N.H.: Surry Cottage Books.

Brinkley, Douglas. 2006. The Great Deluge: Hurricane Katrina, New Orleans and the Mississippi Gulf Coast. New York: Morrow.

Brooks-Klinger, Jeneve. 2007. "Anti-War Music Websites: Cultural Social Movement Activity in Cyberspace." Paper presented at the Annual Meeting of the American Sociological Association.

Bullard, Robert and Beverly Wright, 2009. Race, Place and Environmental Justice After Hurricane Katrina: Struggles to Reclaim, Rebuild and Revitalize New Orleans and the Gulf Coast. Boulder: Westview Press.

Capling, Ann and Kim Nossel. 2001. "Death of Distance or Tyranny of Distance? The Internet, Deterritorialization and the Anti-Globalization Movement in Australia." Pacific Review 14, 3: 443–465.

Carty, Victoria. 2009. "Bridging Contentious and Electoral Politics: MoveOn and the Digital Revolution." Paper presented at the Annual Meeting of the American Sociological Association.

Clancy, Gene. 2012. "Hurricane Sandy and Capitalism. Workers World, December 6.

Cooper, Christopher and Robert Block. 2006. Disaster: Hurricane Katrina and the Failure of Homeland Security. New York: Times Books.

Cushman, Ted. 2013. "Storm Warning: Here Come the Hurricane Sandy Lawsuits." *Coastal Contractor*, January.

Delgado, Sharon. 2010. "Responding to Hurricane Katrina." Earth Justice Ministries, June 5: 1.

Della Porta, Donattela and Lorenzo Mosca. 2005. "Global-Net for Global Movements? A Network of Networks for a Movement of Movements." *Journal of Public Policy* 25, 1 (May): 165–190.

Dellisanti. Angela. 2013. "Chris Christie in Oklahoma: Now Is 'Not A Time For Political Retribution.'" Huffington Post, May 22.

Dow Jones News, 2012. Online. Available: http://www.dowjones.com/ djnewswires.asp (retrieved September 1, 2013).

Dyson, Michael. 2007. Debating Race. New York: Basic Civitas Books.

———. 2006. Come Hell or High Water: Hurricane Katrina and the Color of Disaster. New York: Basic Civitas Books.

Edwards, Richard. 2012. "Editorial Note." Administration in Social Work 37, 1 (January-March): 1–2.

FEMA, 2006. "$4 Billion in the Hands of Disaster Victims." Federal Emergency Management Agency, January 4: 1.

Flynn, Phil. 2012. "Oil Balances Chinese PMI With East Coast Refinery Restarts." *FuturesMag*, November 1.

Friedman, Milton and Rose Friedman, 1980. Free to Choose: A Personal Statement. New York: Harcourt Brace Jovanovich.

Grey, Barry. 2012. "Hurricane Sandy and 'Free Enterprise.'" World Socialist Web Site, November 1.

Gunewardena, Nandini and Mark Schuller. 2008. Capitalizing on Catastrophe: Neoliberal Strategies in Disaster Reconstruction. Lanham, MD: Rowman and Littlefield.

Hamilton, Matt. 2013. "Christie Touts Post-Sandy Recovery, But Jersey Shore Tourism Drops." Los Angeles Times, August 31.

Haney, Tim. 2007. "Disaster and the Irrationality of 'Rational' Bureaucracy: Daily Life and the Continuing Struggles in the Aftermath of Hurricane Katrina." pp. 128–138 in D. Hidalgo and K. Barber (Eds.) Narrating the Storm: Sociological Stories of Hurricane Katrina. Newcastle, U.K.: Cambridge Scholars Press.

Harriford, Diane and Becky Thompson, 2008. "Say It Loud, I'm Black and Proud: Organizing Since Katrina." Fast Capitalism 4, 1.

Hartman, Chester and Gregory Squires. 2006. There is No Such Thing as Natural Disaster: Race, Class and Hurricane Katrina. New York: Routledge.

Hidalgo, Danielle and Kristen Barber (Eds.) Narrating the Storm: Sociological Stories of Hurricane Katrina. Newcastle: Cambridge Scholars Press.

Holmes, Douglas. 2000. Integral Europe: Fast-Capitalism, Multiculturalism, Neofascism. Princeton, N.J.: Princeton University Press.

Honore, Carl. 2004. In Praise of Slow. London: Orion Books.

Horne, Jed. 2006. Breach of Faith: Hurricane Katrina and the Near Death of a Great American City. New York: Random House.

Housing and Urban Development (U.S.). 2013. "Statement 081913." August 19.

Hytrek, Gary and Kristine Zentgraf, 2008. America Transformed: Globalization, Inequality and Power. New York: Oxford University.

Jones, Bart. 2013. "Flood Insurance Law Hurting Sandy Victims." Long Island Newsday, July 21.

Kenway, Jane and Diana Langmead. 1998. Fast Capitalism, Fast Feminism and Some Fast Food for Thought. Geelong, Victoria: Deakin Centre for Education and Change.

Kim, Susanna. 2012. "Stocks Rise as Markets Open After Hurricane Sandy." ABC News, October 31.

Klein, Naomi. 2012. "Hurricane Sandy: Beware of America's Disaster Capitalists." The Guardian, November 6.

———. 2007. The Shock Doctrine: The Rise of Disaster Capitalism. New York: Metropolitan Books.

———. 2005. "The Rise of Disaster Capitalism." The Nation, April 14: 1–3.

Kurth, Michael and Daryl Burkel. 2006. The Rita Report. Baton Rouge, LA: Louisiana Recovery Authority.

Leitsinger, Miranda. 2013. "$20,000 a Year for Flood Insurance? Sandy Survivors Face Tough Rebuilding Choices." NBC News, September 3.

Lerner, Melissa. 2010. "Connecting the Actual with the Virtual: The Internet and Social Movement Theory in the Muslim World—The Cases of Iran and Egypt." Journal of Muslim Majority Affairs 30, 4 (December): 555–574.

Marable, Manning and Kristen Clark. 2008. Seeking Higher Ground: the Hurricane Katrina Crisis, Race and Policy Reader. New York: Palgrave Macmillan.

McNamara, Eileen. 2013. "Hurricane Sandy Aid: $72 Million for Connecticut. North Haven Patch, August 4.

Mileti, D, T.E. Drabek and F.J. Haas. 1975. Human Systems in Extreme Environments. Monograph No. 021. Boulder CO: University of Colorado Institute of Behavioral Science.

Montana-Leblanc, Phyllis. 2008. Not Just the Levees Broke: My Story During and After Hurricane Katrina. New York: Atria Books.

NOAA, 2012. Online. Available: http://www.noaa.gov/

O'Neill, Erin. 2012. "Angered Residents of New Jersey's Barrier Islands Want to Know: When Can They Return?" The Star Ledger, November 6.

Parham, Angel. 2003. "The Haiti Forum and Transnational Solidarity: Opportunities and Limits of an Internet-Mediated Public Sphere." Paper presented at the Annual Meeting of the American Sociological Association.

Pitzi, Erica. 2013. "FEMA Denying Aid to Hundreds of Sandy Victims, Citing 'Earth Movement' As Reason." PIX 11, August 29.

Porpora. Tracey. 2013. "Hotel Housing Program for Hurricane Sandy Victims Extended Until September 16." Staten Island Advance, August 30.

Potter, Hillary. 2007. Racing the Storm: Racial Implications and Lessons Learned from Hurricane Katrina. Lanham, MD: Lexington Books.

Reuters, 2012. Online. Available: http://www.reuters.com/

Ricardo, David. 1817. On the Principles of Political Economy and Taxation. London: John Murray.

Russell, Jesse. 2013. Hurricane Gustav. Books on Demand, Ltd.

Saltman, Kenneth. 2007. Capitalizing on Disaster: Taking and Breaking Public Schools. Boulder: Paradigm Publishers.

Sandy Recovery Scorecard. 2013. "Update." NJ.com, July 3.

Schwartz, Nelson. 2012. "After Storm, Businesses Try to Keep Moving. New York Times, October 30.

Serrano, Ken. 2013. "Stay or Go? Union Beach Sandy Victims Face the Choice of Their Lives." Asbury Park Press, August 23.

Smith, Adam. [1776] 1970. The Wealth of Nations. Harmondsworth: Penguin Books.

Spoto, MaryAnn. 2013. "Christie Rips Small Business Administration and National Flood Insurance Program." NJ.com, August 28.

Standridge, Sarah. 2010. Hurricane Ike: The Life Stories of the Residents of the Bolivar Peninsula, Texas. Bloomington, IN: IUniverse.

State of New Jersey, 2012a. Committee Meeting of the Senate Budget and Appropriations Committee, Trenton, December 5.

———, 2012b. Committee Meeting of the Senate Budget and Appropriations Committee. Highlands, December 11.

Stonich, Susan. 2008. "International Tourism and Disaster Capitalism: The Case of Hurricane Mitch in Honduras." pp. 47–68 in N. Gunewardena and M. Schuller (Eds.), Capitalizing on Catastrophe: Neoliberal Strategies in Disaster Reconstruction. Lanham, MD: Rowman and Littlefield.

Strike Debt, 2012. Shouldering the Costs: Who Pays in the Aftermath of Hurricane Sandy? New York: Occupy Wall Street.

Stump, Scott. 2013. "Jersey Shore Reopens 7 Months After Sandy." NBC News, May 24.

Sullivan, Bob. "Contacting FEMA: Is Anyone There?" Red Tape Chronicles, November 1: 1.

Tillison, Tom. 2013. "Governor Christie's Political Dilemma: Should Unions Control Hurricane Sandy Money?" BizPacReview, January 20.

Troutt, David. 2006. After the Storm: Black Intellectuals Explore the Meaning of Hurricane Katrina. New York: New Press.

U.S. Census, 2010. Online: Available: http://www.census.gov/2010census/

Van Laer, Jeroen and Peter Van Aelst. 2010. "Internet and Social Movement Action Repertoires." Information, Communication and Society 13, 8, December: 1146–1171.

Vollen, Lola and Chris Ying. 2008. Voices from the Storm: The People of New Orleans on Hurricane Katrina and its Aftermath. San Francisco: McSweeney's Books.

Walzer, Michael. 2013. "The Last Page." Dissent, Winter: 112.

Weeber, Stan. 2012. "Resisting Corporatism: Citizens Fight Back Against the British Petroleum Oil Spill." pp. 263–280 in L. Eargle and A. Esmail (Eds.) Black Beaches and Bayous: The BP Deepwater Horizon Oil Spill. Lanham, MD: University Press of America.

———. 2011. "Leveraged Responses to Neo-Liberal Policies on Disaster Reconstruction: Observations from Haiti, the United States, and the Indian Ocean Region," *International Review of Modern Sociology* 37, 2, Autumn: 185–203.

———. 2009. Post-Rita Reflections: A Sociological Journey. Lanham, MD: Hamilton Books.

———. 2008. "A Weary Veteran Escaping the Storm Surge of 2008." *Orato*, October 20.

Wilkinson, Kenneth and Peggy Ross. 1970. Citizens' Responses to Warnings of Hurricane Camille. State College, MS: Social Science Research Center, Mississippi State University.

Willis, David. 2013. "Mortgage Servicers Tie Up Sandy Checks." Press on Your Side, January 20.

CHAPTER SEVEN
HURRICANE IMPACTS ON AND
ADAPTATIONS IN EDUCATION:
A COMPARISON OF THE KATRINA
AND SANDY DISASTERS

Lisa A. Eargle and Ashraf Esmail

When Hurricane Katrina hit in 2005, it became one of the most destructive disasters in US history. However, as Kai Erikson points out, it also has "the potential for being one the most instructive disasters" (Erikson, 2010, p. xviii), with lessons learned that could be used for future disasters that would occur (Erikson, 2010). One of those later disasters was Hurricane Sandy, which ravaged the mid-Atlantic coast in late 2012.

Like Katrina, Sandy had major impacts on communities, their social institutions, and residents. One of those institutions impacted was the education system, which includes primary and secondary schools, colleges and universities, other educational facilities such as hospitals and libraries, the faculty and staff who work within these organizations, and the students served by these organizations (Greubel, Ackerman and Winthrop, 2012). Often the schools are the central focus of communities and community life (Azad, 2014). Their ability to adapt effectively to the disaster is a key factor in communities' recovery (Greubel et. al, 2012).

This chapter examines the impacts that Hurricanes Katrina and Sandy had in their respective regions and how educational institutions adapted to those impacts. We make comparisons of those adaptations taken by educational institutions after Katrina and Sandy in order to see the similarities and differences of responses. Similar responses taken by educational institutions suggest not only the similarity of the disasters' impacts, but also points to the possibility of social learning, as part of the adaptation process, occurring between the two disasters. Different responses taken suggest not only potential differences in impacts, but also perhaps instances where knowledge learned from Katrina was not carried over to or used during and post Sandy.

However, before delving into the discussion of impacts on and adaptations by educational institutions, we briefly discuss the disaster process and where adaptation and social learning fit into that process. We also examine how social learning occurs and what factors contribute to social learning. Moreover, we relate how these factors are important in addressing disasters.

THEORETICAL BACKGROUND

The Disaster Process

One important theoretical model elaborating the disaster process is the Disaster Resilience of Place (DROP) model, developed by Cutter and associates (2008). This model argues that community resilience is determined by a series of features present in the community, which unfold over time to create, respond, recover, and mitigate disaster in the community. These features include precursor characteristics of the community, the presence of one or more hazards, the ability of the community to handle the hazards, impact of the hazards/disaster, adaptive capabilities of the community, degree of disaster recovery, and preparation and mitigation efforts towards future disasters (Cutter et. al, 2008).

While this model was developed to address community resilience, one could argue that these same ideas can also be applied to educational organizations and institutions within a community as well. When a disaster strikes a community, it also affects the functioning of local organizations and institutions in that community in various ways. This includes primary, secondary and higher education institutions in a disaster area. Moreover, like communities, local educational institutions themselves have precursor conditions that can impede or contribute to disaster and have different adaptive capabilities to deal with a disaster when it occurs. Part of these adaptive capabilities is engaging in social learning. Not only is social learning an important adaptive strategy for schools and institutions of higher education to recover from a disaster, it also provides a road map to prepare and mitigate future disasters (Greuber et. al, 2012).

Social Learning

Social learning refers to people adopting new attitudes and actions by observing what other people do and imitating what they observed the other people doing (Bandura, 1971). This concept has been expanded upon to include multiple means by which people learn and make decisions about behavioral options. One method of learning is through trial and error, having experiences first hand, where people learn which situational approaches work best. A second method of learning is through direct observation of how others address a situation. A third method involves copying another's actions and seeing the results of those actions. A fourth method is listening to others' encouragement to engage in a particular action. A fifth method of learning is receiving instruction from another person about a situation's characteristics and actions to take. Lastly, people can learn from watching others' emotional responses in a situation.

There is disagreement among scholars about which method is the most optimal for learning to occur, with some advocating trial and error as the most effective approach, while others propagate that trial and error is not the most feasible approach in all situations (Campbell, 1963). In the place of trial and error, some advocate simulation experiences as a method of learning, in the absence of or in preparation for, some real-life event in the future (that has not happened yet) where effective response is required. This is essentially the type of learning that takes place in fire or tornado drills, or homeland security or emergency management exercises. Still others have advocated for the use of computer-simulated exercises for learning, in addition to (blended-instruction) or in place of traditional in-the-field role play exercises (where for example, fire fighters have a building set on fire and then act to "rescue" supposed victims and extinguish the fire). Computer simulated exercises reduce risk of injury to participants, compared to traditional exercises, and allow for a greater number of practice sessions to be experienced by participants. Also, computer simulated exercises have been advocated on the basis of allowing multiple participants to engage in collaborative efforts and to measure and record participant performance (O'Reilly and Bradenburg, 2006).

Conditions that Promote Social Learning

One condition that promotes social learning is the presence of self-efficacy. Self-efficacy refers to one's belief that they can manage their own behaviors and handle whatever events that occur in their lives. Those individuals with a high degree of self-efficacy are better able to cope in stressful situations (like a disaster) and "adopt strategies and courses of action designed to change hazardous environments into more benign ones" (p. 1132). Individuals can be reactive, adapting to events after the fact, or act as proactive agents of change, where they seek to transform their environment prior to any potentially damaging situation emerging (Benight and Bandura, 2004).

Another important condition that promotes social learning is the presence of innovation. Innovation refers to the ability of individuals and organizations to embrace and engage in change. If conditions are changing or expected to change, innovators will transform their methods of operation and activities in which they engage to meet the challenges and opportunities that changing conditions can produce. Otherwise, they risk becoming irrelevant at best and an impediment to progress at worst. Individual and organizational strengths in prior situations can become rigidities and weaknesses in future situations; the key is continuous evaluation and evolution in light of new conditions (Seelos and Mair, 2012). Preparing for disasters, given the changing nature of the climate and distribution of population in hurricane prone areas, requires emergency management and others to find new ways of addressing disaster needs. For example, flood zone boundaries are changing because of global warming and rising sea levels. This requires modification of storm evacuation plans, to remove people out of harm's way who were in the past safe from flood waters and provide protection for property (Shaw, Meyer, and Thompson, 2013). This would also include students, education personnel, and educational facilities and their resources.

Third, social learning is promoted the by the presence of an active community of practitioners (CoP). A community of practitioners is a collection of individuals coming together to discuss and gain insights from one another to address issues encountered. This type of collaborative learning has been found to be especially useful in addressing similar disaster situations that have a frequent rate of occurrence. Communities of practice can be composed of a variety of persons, including emergency management experts, business leaders, educators, and local residents, who each have unique knowledge and perspectives to share with the others in the group. These different perspectives are incorporated in disaster preparedness and mitigation plans for organizations and communities, with the goal of comprehensively and successfully addressing future disaster events (Yamori, 2009).

Moreover, communities of practice can also transcend geographical distance. Individuals from one disaster impacted area (i.e., New Orleans) can communicate with individuals in other disaster vulnerable areas (i.e., New York City) about their experiences. This can be accomplished through a variety of means, such as conferences, workshops (Natural Hazards Center, n.d.), and publications (Volunteers of America—Greater New Orleans, n.d.).

After examining the role and importance of social learning (as a component of adaptation) in disaster recovery and mitigation, we turn towards examining the impacts and adaptations which educational institutions pursued after Hurricanes Katrina and Sandy. Through a comparison and contrast of impacts and adaptations for each storm, we illustrate that social learning did likely occur between Katrina and Sandy. However, in several instances the application of knowledge learned in Katrina did not successfully transfer to Sandy.

DATA AND METHODS

This chapter provides a comparison of two cases, Hurricanes Katrina and Sandy, and their impacts on education. We examine the resulting adaptations that the educational system made in response to those impacts. We discuss changes that occurred in primary, secondary, colleges and universities, and related educational facilities. Our information is based on a variety of media sources and reports, published after each disaster.

Disaster Impacts: Hurricanes Katrina and Sandy

When Hurricane Katrina came ashore August 29, 2005, the academic year was just beginning or about to start for many Gulf Coast teachers and students. In the hours prior to the storm, many residents had evacuated from the region, thinking that the storm would have short-term impacts and that they would be able to return home and return to campuses soon. However, the days following Katrina's landfall, images of a demolished Mississippi coastline and a deeply flooded New Orleans nixed those ambitions (Bush, 2005). Residents of the Mississippi coast had in many cases returned to find everything swept to sea by storm surge. Familiar landmarks, signs, and other items previously used to identify and navigate within places were gone or demolished (Holder, 2013).

In New Orleans, the constant pounding of Lake Pontchartrain's waters toppled the levee system, allowing water to surge into the city to depths in some areas of over 20 feet. It took months to remove flood waters completely out of New Orleans (Smith, 2005) and permit residents to return (Bourne, 2007). When they did return, what they found was a foul and toxic combination of sewage and chemical contamination, an explosive infestation of mold, and wrecked landscape (Reible, Haas, Pardue, and Walsh, 2006). Extensive clean-up efforts, including some demolitions, involving a relatively long period of time were required to return some parts of New Orleans back to normal functioning (Bowser, 2008; News Desk, 2010).

As Hurricane Sandy came ashore in the mid-Atlantic coast on October 28, 2012, the academic year was already well underway for educational institutions. In its wake, Hurricane Sandy's storm surge damaged and flooded coastal residences, businesses, and infrastructure (Toro, 2013). Torrential rains flooded inland streets and buildings, and toppled waterways' dams (Porter, 2012). Images from the New Jersey shore showed giant sand dunes dumped into homes and highways away from the shore. High winds toppled trees and power lines onto buildings and streets. In the New York City area, the underground subway system and buildings near the waterfront were flooded, the train system's tracks into areas such as the Rockaways were demolished, trees and power lines were toppled (New York Daily News, 2013), and fires consumed whole communities in Queens (Jennings, 2013).

Disaster Adaptations: Similarities and Differences Between Katrina and Sandy

There were numerous adaptations to the impacts that Hurricane Katrina had on New Orleans' area secondary schools, colleges, and universities. There were changes in the number and types of students enrolled; changes in the number of faculty and staff employed by these institutions; changes in where educational activities took place; changes in the courses and curriculum offered; changes in teaching methods used by instructors and learning outcomes for students; changes in the source of educational institutions funding; changes in governmental policies towards educational institutions and students; and emerging controversies and educational opportunities. Some of these changes, such as the expansion of online education and community service as degree requirements, are still in place after Katrina; other changes, such as the decline in enrollments and use of alternative facilities, were temporary (Eargle, Esmail and Das, 2010).

When Hurricane Sandy rushed ashore in late October 2012, comparisons between that storm and Katrina were readily made. Both produced lots of storm surge, flooding, and damage to their respective strike areas (Kaleem and Wallace, 2012). But, in terms of adaptations to the impacts on education, how do the two storms compare? A review of the literature and published media reports show both similarities and differences in how educational institutions adapted to the impacts of these storms. In the following paragraphs, we highlight some of these similarities and differences.

Hurricane Sandy also provided an opportunity for educational institutions to practice social learning. Did the educational institutions in the mid-Atlantic region apply any potential lessons learned from the Hurricane Katrina disaster? Given the similarity of impacts between the two storms and the widely publicized short-comings during Katrina, one would hope that a better response would occur during Sandy. We investigate this issue as well in the following pages.

Adaptation Similarities

One similarity is how students and/or staff worked together to repair and reopen facilities. After Katrina, Tulane University involved students in community service by having them repair facilities in exchange for credit hours. This allowed Tulane to recover faster from Katrina's destruction than if they had hired outside contractors to do all of the repairs. It also gave the students a sense of responsibility for their community's well-being (Schlueter, 2008). After Hurricane Sandy, many schools within the New York City-New Jersey area were damaged. However, at Liberation Diploma Plus, an alternative school in NYC, staff and volunteers cleaned up the flooded first floor, allowing students to return to their school within ten days after the storm (Garland, 2012). Students also volunteered, did fundraising, and assisted local residents, in both Katrina and Sandy.

Another similarity was the relocation of students to other facilities after the storm. After Katrina, some schools held classes in hotels, another on a cruise ship (Fogg, 2006a), others relocated to sister institutions (American Federation of Teachers, 2005), and some brought in portable trailers to serve as make-shift classrooms (Southern University at New Orleans, 2006). After Sandy, Rutgers University Newark and New Brunswick campuses relocated students to their Piscataway campus. Other institutions waited until the subway system or electric service was restored to reopen (Kingkade, 2012a). Others looked to churches and synagogues and community centers as locations for educational activities (Schneider, 2012).

After Katrina, many low-income students were adversely affected as they had to relocate to other cities and could not return home for months. This meant school districts in other places had to handle a quick influx of students who would be temporarily enrolled, many without their transcripts (Casserly, 2006). After Hurricane Sandy, many low-income students did not have to relocate, but they did have their education interrupted for a week or more and many went without free/reduced meals during those days. Others required the relocation of students to other schools, creating a space and service burden on those institutions and a travel burden on faculty and students from the closed institutions. Attendance at these reopened and relocated schools was down remarkably in some cases, due to the transportation issues, and due to the damage to the neighborhoods like the Rockaways and Coney Island (Chakrabarti and Livingston, 2012). In some school districts in West Virginia (where there was a Sandy-related blizzard), where there is emphasis on group work, students could not move forward on their school work until everyone was back at school (Boucher, 2012).

Another similarity was the extensive damage caused by flooding and the cost to repair facilities. Katrina damaged multiple universities and colleges (Eargle, Esmail, and Das, 2010), as well as many public schools (Casserly, 2006). In New York City alone, 1750 schools were closed for at least a week, with some not slated to reopen until January 2013–two months after the storm (Chakrabarti and Livingston, 2012). After Hurricane Katrina, students' educations were disrupted and many worried about the long-term impacts on learning outcomes (Casserly, 2006; Eargle, Esmail and Das, 2010). After Hurricane Sandy, students' educations were disrupted to a lesser extent than after Katrina, with some school days being lost. However, many still worry about the long term impacts on student learning outcomes. They also worry about how the trauma experienced during Sandy and the hardships faced at home (no electricity, food shortages, etc.) might affect students' ability to concentrate upon their return to the classroom (Chakrabarti and Livingston, 2012).

Also, after Hurricane Katrina, new research initiatives were funded to better understand disaster impacts on communities and individuals. For example, Tulane University established a disaster Management Leadership Academy on its campus, to offer the PhD in international disaster management (Hobgood, 2009). Scholars from Mississippi State University developed disaster research guidelines after the storm (Social Science Research Center, 2006). After Hurricane Sandy, new initiatives were undertaken to better understand the impact of storms like Sandy, as well as how climate change can be expected to impact cities. Many of these initiatives are being undertaken through the Institute for Public Knowledge at New York University. One initiative is conducting a social impact analysis of Sandy, to see what types of people in what neighborhoods were most negatively impacted by Sandy. This initiative also will match up previous prediction plans to what actually occurred in order to see how those plans need to be revised. Another initiative examines community sustainability and resilience as part of the rebuilding of the Rockaways (Institute for Public Knowledge, 2013). Little Bits, a Manhattan based open source library, hosted a workshop for children called "Why Did the Lights Go

Out?" to better understand how and why Sandy had the impacts that it did (Walters, 2012).

After Katrina, many public schools in New Orleans were converted into charter schools—using the disaster as a way to restructure an unsatisfactory education system where students routinely performed below state and national standards, and violence and truancy were common (Casserly, 2006). After Hurricane Sandy, many in New Jersey were seeing the storm as an opportunity to consolidate a bloated school system with too many districts (over 600, more than any state). They argue instead of repairing every school, even those with less than 100 students, perhaps money would be wiser spent constructing newer and larger school facilities (Waters, 2012).

Another similarity is the fund raising efforts. After Katrina, Delgado Community College created a relief fund to help its students get back on their feet (Delgado Community College, 2006). Historically black colleges and universities received an infusion of funds from a fundraiser held by the United Negro College Fund (Managan, 2006). Others received emergency funding from the Congress to initiate facility repairs (Field, 2006).

After Hurricane Sandy, people in other parts of the nation sought to "adopt a school," to raise funds and acquire educational supplies for the school. Businesses such as Prudential Insurance donated millions to the New Jersey School Board to distribute to schools (Schneider, 2012). American Association of School Administrators created a web page to accept donations and provide suggestions on how to help school districts, schools, communities, and children and their families recover from Sandy. In particular, they listed what specific needs that specific schools had after Sandy. They also offered mini-grants to schools to help them with urgent needs (American Association of School Administrators, n.d.). U.S. General Services Administration also gave Sandy impacted schools in New York City excess federal computers. The government routinely replaces older computers with new ones, so instead of just storing them, they gave them to needy schools (General Services Administration, 2013). The New Jersey Department of Education used funds from the Emergency Response to violence program to fund services that would restore safe learning environments for students. Some of the services funded include overtime pay for teachers and other staff, emergency transportation, temporary security measures, and mental health assessments (Drewniak, 2013).

Another similar impact was the closing of University-affiliated hospitals. Often University affiliated hospitals provide health care to low income families or provide cutting-edge treatments to patients with extraordinary medical needs. They are also institutions which provide medical students with hands-on training. Before Katrina hit, Charity Hospital (affiliated with Louisiana State University) was a major health care provider for low income families in the New Orleans area. After Katrina hit, the levees failed, and large sections of the city were flooded, including Charity Hospital's facilities. All patients had to be evacuated (Kutner, 2010). Given the extent of the flood damage and subsequent proliferation of mold, the hospital has remained closed and was eventually abandoned (Rainey, 2014).

When Hurricane Sandy hit, parts of New York University's Tisch Hospital flooded and the back-up generators failed. Hundreds of critical patients, including newborns, had to be evacuated to other medical facilities with electrical service. Patients with less serious health issues were allowed to remain at the hospital in its upper floors. A phased-in reopening of the facility occurred, with complete normal operations resuming about two to three months after the storm (NY1 News, 2012).

During Katrina, student housing at colleges and universities used had to be vacated because of storm damage. Some students were relocated to hotels; others to a cruise ship; still others to rooms within academic buildings (Bonvissuto, n.d.) After Hurricane Sandy, students at various institutions (such as Old Dominion in Norfolk, Virginia and Fairfield University in Connecticut) had to be relocated due to storm surge flooding (McClure, 2012).

University libraries were also impacted. During Katrina, Tulane University's library was flooded and restoration specialists had to be hired to recover/salvage some of the holdings; however, some holdings were lost despite heroic efforts. Before Katrina, library directors considered developing disaster plans a "bother", just more work to do. After Katrina, disaster plans' utility was recognized. This situation replayed itself out with Hurricane Sandy. New York University library realized that it needed to be prepared for more than just minor flood issues, such as those created by broken water pipes (Howard, 2012).

Adaptation Differences

There are several major differences in how Hurricanes Katrina and Sandy affected education in their respective locations. One of those major differences is how long it took for education institutions to fully recover from the disasters. After Hurricane Katrina, some institutions such as Tulane University had the resources to recover within 6 months of the storm (Cowen, 2007). Others such as Southern University at New Orleans were not able to fully replace damaged buildings until 2014 (Southern University at New Orleans, 2014). Among public schools in the New Orleans area, over time they have been either abandoned by families or closed through educational restructuring, so that the New Orleans School District will be the first in the nation to be composed solely of charter schools (Mullins, 2014).

After Hurricane Sandy, colleges and universities in the mid-Atlantic region briefly closed operations for a few days, perhaps a few weeks at most, and resumed normal operations as quickly as possible (Kingkade, 2012b). One of the hardest hit institutions, Kingsborough Community College, opened a week after Sandy hit, but the school was still completing repairs one year later (Clark, 2013). Public schools in the hardest hit areas took longer to recover. For example, in Union Beach, students did not return to their normal school assignments until June 2013, six months after the storm. During the months between Hurricane Sandy's landfall and June, students were completing their studies at other schools in the state (Wanko, 2013).

Another notable difference is the creation of new degree programs. After Hurricane Katrina, Delgado Community College changed the focus of its offerings from liberal arts to more vocational (Evelyn, 2005). Tulane University instituted a new community service requirement for graduation (NBC Nightly News, 2005). It also created a new PhD program of Disaster Management (Hobgood, 2009). Duplichain University was founded to meet the growing needs of on-line graduate education in the Gulf Coast region (Duplichain, 2009). After Hurricane Sandy, the Stevens Institute of Technology in Hoboken, NJ created a new interdisciplinary disaster course called "Sandy Studies" (Stevens Institute of Technology, n.d.). If there were additional new courses or degree programs created, they have not been publicized in the media or made readily known to the public.

A third difference is the methods used for instruction. After Hurricane Katrina devastated the Gulf Coast in 2005, many institutions considering on-line instruction or were providing it on a limited basis shifted to more widespread use of web-based instruction (Eargle, Esmail and Das, 2010). By 2012, when Hurricane Sandy hit, on-line courses have become a common feature at many institutions, without the presence of disastrous storms. The challenge became how to quickly restore electrical and communication services damaged by Sandy (Garbitelli, 2013), not so much how to find alternatives to traditional face-to-face instruction.

A fourth difference is student enrollments. After Hurricane Katrina, many colleges and universities in the Gulf Coast region suffered major declines in enrollments for several subsequent semesters. Tulane was one of the schools to quickly recover its enrollments, within one year of the storm. Dillard University, Delgado Community College, University of New Orleans did not start to fully recover their enrollments until years later (Eargle, Esmail and Das, 2010). After Hurricane Sandy, there have been no reports of declines in student enrollments at mid-Atlantic area institutions of higher education, no doubt due in part to the quick recovery of campuses and efforts to assist students affected personally by Sandy (Rutgers University, 2013; Nealon, 2012).

A fifth major adaptation difference is faculty and staff retention. After Hurricane Katrina, many educational institutions activated faculty and staff layoffs and reassignments. This created a firestorm of controversy, which resulted in investigations by the American Association of University Professors (Fogg, 2006b), teachers unions, and lawsuits (Democracy Now, 2006). Tulane University was unsuccessfully sued by the heirs of Josephine Louise Newcomb to prevent the merger of the Newcomb School with Tulane University. The plaintiffs argued that Newcomb should be a women's only institution, as intended by its original bene-factor. A judge ruled that Tulane should be allowed to incorporate Newcomb as a co-educational institute within the University (Inside Higher Education, 2009). An internet search by the authors for similar stories in education after Hurricane Sandy proved to be unproductive.

In general, there seems to be less discussion of education impacts and adaptations, beyond physical infrastructure damage, for Hurricane Sandy than there was for Hurricane Katrina. Of the thousands of articles found during the authors'

search of the Huffington Post archives for articles Hurricane Sandy's impact on and
adaptation by education institutions, many articles were found that repeated the
same material. Even the Chronicle of Higher Education had fewer stories on
Hurricane Sandy than it did on Hurricane Katrina. In some ways, it feels as though
Hurricane Sandy, its impacts, and resulting adaptations are being quickly forgotten
(O' Neill, 2013). However, as we and others would argue, the education system is
critical – as an important community institution impacted by disasters, as well as
an information provider for the community to prepare for future disasters (Greubel
et. al, 2012).

CONCLUSION

In conclusion, this chapter examined the impacts and adaptations which educational
institutions pursued after Hurricanes Katrina and Sandy. Through a comparison and
contrast of impacts and adaptations for each storm, we illustrate that social learning
did likely occur between Katrina and Sandy. We found the impacts of the two
hurricanes on educational institutions were very similar, with flooding and wind
damage being major problems. Moreover, we found numerous similarities in the
ways which educational institutions responded and adapted to these impacts in both
cases. However, educational institutions seemed to recover much faster and
experienced lesser disruption from Hurricane Sandy than from Hurricane Katrina.
     Future research into social learning and adaptation to disasters should
investigate several issues. First, which methods or mechanisms of social learning
seem to be the most effective in disaster mitigation? As suggested by the blended
instruction literature (O' Reilly and Bradenburg, 2006) and researchers at the
Brookings Institute, the use of multiple approaches might offer the best approach
to disaster mitigation (Greubel et. al, 2012).
     Second, by directly interviewing education officials, we might discover if
previous disaster cases had any influence on the development of their disaster plans.
In other words, by being aware of the problems encountered by educators, schools
and students after Katrina (or later disasters), were there any particular issues that
were given additional attention when creating disaster plans for their schools? Or
was Katrina's problems viewed only as a Gulf Coast issue and not the kinds of
problems that could be experienced by educational institutions in other parts of the
nation? In this chapter, we find information that suggests that educational
institutions in the mid-Atlantic may have learned from Katrina (as well as
Hurricanes Irene, Gustav and other storms), but none of the media accounts directly
cite Katrina or other events as being the influence on how they responded.
     Third, we briefly discuss factors contributing to social learning, such as self-
efficacy, innovation, and community of practitioners. Future research into disaster
mitigation by educational institutions could examine these factors in-depth, to see
to what degree does their presence facilitate social learning and adaptation.
Moreover, research could also investigate the impediments to social learning from

disasters, such as culture (Pahl-Wostl et. al, 2007), technology, and social networks (Levy and Yupangco, 2008), that have occurred.

The authors would like to thank Dr. Nwamaka Anaza for her comments on earlier drafts of this chapter.

REFERENCES

American Association of School Administrators. (N.d). AASA's Hurricane Sandy relief efforts to help schools ravaged by storm. http://www.aasa.org/sandyrelief.aspx. Accessed September 9, 2013.

American Federation of Teachers. (2005). In the wake of Katrina, higher education steps forward. http://www.aft.org/higher_ed/news/2005/katrina.htm

Azad, S. (2014). Parents protest closure of five HISD schools. ABC13 Eyewitness News, February 13. http://abc13.com/archive/9431705

Bandura, A. (1971). Social Learning theory. New York: General Learning Press.

Benight, C. C. and Bandura, A. (2004). Social cognitive theory of posttraumatic recovery: the role of perceived self-efficacy. *Behaviour Research and Therapy*, 42: 1129–1148.

Bonvissuto, K. (n.d.) Hurricane Katrina: Two years later. Minority Nurse, accessed July 14, 2014. http://www.minoritynurse.com/article/hurricane-katrina-two-years-later

Boucher, D. (2012). Superstorm Sandy's snows put school systems behind schedule. Huffington Post, November 5.

Bourne, J.K. Jr. (2007). New Orleans: a perilous future. *National Geographic Magazine*, August. http://ngm.nationalgeographic.com/print/2007/08/new-orleans/new-orleans-text

Bowser, B. A. (2008). Three years on, New Orleans still struggles with hurricane debris. PBS Newshour, June 19. http://www.pbs.org/newshour/bb/weather-jan-june08-nolatoxic_06-19/

Bush, G. W. (2005). Chapter four: A week of crisis. White House Archives, September 15. http://georgewbush-whitehouse.archives.gov/reports/katrina-lessons-learned/chapter4.html

Campbell, D. (1963). Social attitudes and other acquired behavioral dispositions. pp. 94–172 in S. Koch, Psychology: A Study of Science Volume 6. New York: McGraw-Hill.

Casserly, M. (2006). Double Jeopardy: Public education in New Orleans before and after the storm. pp. 197–214 in C. Hartman and G.D. Squires, There Is No Such Thing As A Natural Disaster. New York: Routledge

Chkrabarti, R. & Livingston, M. (2012). The impact of Superstorm Sandy on New York City school closures and attendance. Liberty Street Economics, reprint in Huffington Post on December 24.

Clark, R. 2013. Community college by the bays still shoring up a year after Sandy. Time Warner Cable News, NY1. October 17. http://www.ny1.com/content/news/190602/community-college-by-the-bays-still-shoring-up-a-year-after-sandy

Cowen, S. 2007. Tulane University: From recovery to renewal. *Liberal Education*, Summer issue.

Delgado Community College. (2006). Hurricane Katrina Chronicles. Accessed April 1, 2007. http://www.dcc.edu/katrina_chronicles/overview.htm

Democracy Now. 2006. All New Orleans public school teachers fired, millions in federal aid channeled to private charter schools. http://www.democracynow.org/2006/all_new_orleans_public_schools

Drewniak, M. (2013). Christie Administration announces $1.25 million recover grant awards for 26 Superstorm Sandy-impacted school districts. Office of the Governor. Press Release, April 30. http://www.state.nj.us/governor/news/552013/approved20130 Dupli chain University. 2009. http://www.duplichain.org

Eargle, L. A., Esmail, A. & Das, S. 2010. Disaster Impacts on Education: Hurricane Katrina and the Adaptation and Recovery of New Orleans Area Colleges and Universities" pp. 227–250 in The Sociology of Katrina: Perspectives on a Modern Catastrophe, second edition by D. Brunsma, D. Overfelt, and J. S. Picou (Eds). Landham, MD: Rowman and Littlefield.

Erikson, K. (2010). Foreword. Pp. xvii –xx in D.L. Brunsma, D. Overfelt and J.S. Picou (Eds), The Sociology of Katrina, Second Edition. Lanham, MD: Rowman and Littlefield.

Evelyn, J. 2005. Retooling after the storm: Delgado Community College will focus more on job training as New Orleans rebuilds. Chronicle of Higher Education, December 9.

Field, K. (2006). Damaged colleges get $50 million. *Chronicle of Higher Education*, September 29.

Fogg, P. (2006a). New Orleans Homecoming: At Tulane, living on a cruise ship is no luxury vacation. *Chronicle of Higher Education*, January 20

———. (2006b). New Orleans college presidents decline to meet with AAUP over layoffs. *Chronicle of Higher Education*, September 1.

Garbitelli, B. 2013. Rebuilding NYC's infrastructure after Sandy. *Metrofocus*, May 8. http://www.thirteen.org/metrofocus/2013/05/rebuilding-nyc%E2%80%99s-infrastructure-after-sandy/

General Services Administration. (2013). Local schools impacted by Super Storm Sandy receive excess federal computers. http://www.gsa.gov/portal/content/171103

Greubel, L., Ackerman, X. and Winthrop, R. (2012). Prioritizing education in the face of natural disasters. Brookings Institution, October 31. http://www.brookings.edu/blog/up-front/posts/2012/10/31-natural-disasters-winthrop

Hobgood, K. (2009). Tulane University establishes disaster management leadership academy. http://tulane.edu/news/pr_060409.cfm

Holder, B. B. (2013). Aftermath of Katrina on the Mississippi Gulf Coast. http://www.photosfromkatrina.com/default.htm

Howard, J. (2012). What Katrina Can Teach Libraries About Sandy and Other Disasters. Chronicle of Higher Education, July 15. http://chronicle.com/blogs/wiredcampus/what-katrina-can-teach-libraries-about-sandy-and-other-disasters/40986

Inside Higher Education. 2009. Judge rejects suit on Tulane reorganization. Inside Higher Education, September 1. http://www.insidehighereducation.com/news/2009/09/01/qt#207084

Institute for Public Knowledge. (2013). Superstorm Sandy research initiative. Accessed September 6. http://ipk.nyu.edu/initiatives/superstorm-sandy-research-initiative

Jennings, C. R. (2013). Fires during the 2012 Hurricane Sandy in Queens, New York: A first report. *Fire Safety Science News*, 34: 26-28.

Kaleem, J. & Wallace, T. (2012). Hurricane Sandy vs. Katrina: Infographic examines destruction from both storms. Huffington Post, November 4. http://www.huffingtonpost. com/2012/11/04/hurricane-sandy-vs-katrina-infographic_n_2072432.html

Kingkade, T. 2012a. Superstorm Sandy leaves many colleges on East Coast with clean up job. Huffington Post, October 31.

Kingkade, T. 2012b. Colleges Resume Classes Post-Hurricane Sandy, Attempt To Get Back To Normal. Huffington Post, November 5. http://www.huffingtonpost.com/ 2012/11 /05/colleges-resume-classes-hurricane-sandy_n_2079023.html

Kutner, N. (2010). Health needs, health care, and Katrina. pp. 251–264 in The Sociology of Katrina, (eds.) D.L. Brunsma, D. Overfelt, and J.S. Picou. Lanham, MD: Rowman and Littlefield.

Levy, S. and Yupangco, J. (2008). Overcoming the challenges of social learning in the workplace. *Learning Solutions Magazine*, August 11. http://www. learningsolutions mag.com/articles/85/overcoming-the-challenges-of-social-learning-in-the-workplace

Managan, K. (2006). Ex-presidents join UNCF Katrina fund. *Chronicle of Higher Education*, September 1, A46.

McClure, A. 2012. Hurricane Sandy response and recovery. University Business, December 2012. http://www.universitybusiness.com/article/hurricane-sandy-response-and-recovery

Mullins, D. 2014. New Orleans to be home to nation's first all-charter school district. *Al Jazeera America*, April 4. http://america.aljazeera.com/articles/2014/4/4/new-orleans-charterschoolseducationreformracesegregation.html

National Staff Development Council. (2005). Revised standards for staff development. Retrieved December 15, 2005, from http://www.nsdc.org/standards/index.cfm

Natural Hazards Center. (N.d.) Annual natural hazards research and applications workshop. http://www.colorado.edu/hazards/workshop/

NBC Nightly News. 2005. November 12 broadcast.

Nealon, C. 2012. UB helping students and families impacted by Hurricane Sandy. *UB Reporter*, November 1. http://www.buffalo.edu/ubreporter/archive/2012_11_01/ sandy_response

New York Daily News. (2013). Hurricane Sandy one year later. *New York Daily News*, October. http://www.nydailynews.com/new-york/hurricane-sandy/nyc-hurricane-sandy-stunning-photos-story-article-1.1495544

News Desk. (2010). Katrina 5 years later: the monumental tasks of clean-up and recovery. PBS Newshour, August 3. http://www.pbs.org/newshour/rundown/katrina-5-years-later-the-monumental-tasks-of-clean-up-and-recovery/

NY1 News. (2012). NYU Langone Medical Center hopes to reopen Tisch Hospital by year's end. December 3. http://www.ny1.com/content/news/173295/nyu-langone-medical-center-hopes-to-reopen-tisch-hospital-by-year-s-end

O' Neill, E. (2013). Hurricane Sandy victims feel forgotten in state's recovery efforts, new poll says. *The Star-Ledger*, October 29. http://www.nj.com/news/index.ssf/2013/10/ sandy_monmouth_county_poll.html

O'Reilly, D. J. and Brandenburg, D. C. (2006). Simulation and learning in disaster preparedness: A research and theory review. http://www.files.eric.ed/gov/fulltext/ ED492750.pdf

Pahl-Wostl, C., Tabara, D., Bouwen, R., Craps, M., Dewulf, A., Mostert, E., Ridder, D., and Taillieu, T. (2007). The importance of social learning and culture for sustainable water management. Ecological Economics, doi:10.1016/j.ecolecon.2007.08.007

Porter, D. (2012). New Jersey's Hurricane Sandy-flooded inland towns see no solutions. Huffington Post, December 26. http://www.huffingtonpost.com/2012/12/26/new-jerseys-sandy-flooded_n_2365554.html

Rainey, R. (2014). Charity Hospital's building uncertain future worries many in New Orleans. *The Times Picayune*, June 12. http://www.nola.com/politics/index.ssf/ 2014/06/charity_hospitals_uncertain_fu.html

Reible, D. D., Haas, C. N., Pardue, J. H., and Walsh, W. J. (2006). Toxic and contaminated concerns generated by Hurricane Katrina. The Bridge, Spring. https://www.nae.edu/ Publications/Bridge/TheAftermathofKatrina/ToxicandContaminantConcernsGenerat edbyHurricane Katrina.aspx

Rutgers University. 2013. Students affected by Hurricane Sandy—click here. http:// www.ncas.rutgers.edu/students-affected-hurricane-sandy-click-here

Schlueter, C.J. (2008). Teaming up for post storm progress. New Wave, June 3. http://tulane.edu/news/newwave/060308_chase.cfm

Schneider, M. (2012). New Jersey education has a 'new normal' after Hurricane Sandy. *NJ Today*, November 26. http://www.njtvonline.njtoday/video/new-jersey-has-a-new-normal-after-hurricane-sandy

Seelos, C. and Mair, J. (2012). What determines the capacity for continuous innovation in social sector organizations? Stanford PACS, January 31.

Shaw, A., Meyer, T. and Thompson, C. (2013). Federal flood maps left New York unprepared for Sandy—and FEMA knew it. *ProPublica*, December 6. http://www. propublica.org/article/federal-flood-maps-left-new-york-unprepared-for-sandy-and-fema-knew-it

Smith, J. (2005.) Pumps slowly drying out city. *Sun Sentinel*, September 14. http:// articles.sun-sentinel.com/2005-09-14/news/0509130444_1_pumps-lake-pontchartrain-drain

Social Science Research Center. (2006). Post-Katrina guiding principles of disaster social science research. http://www.ssrc.msstate.edu/Katrina/Publications/Guiding%20Princi ples.pdf

Southern University at New Orleans. (2006). http://www.suno.edu/faq.htm.

———. (2014). SUNO celebrates as last FEMA trailer leaves. June 2 press release. http://suno.edu/suno-celebrates-as-the-last-fema-trailer-leaves-campus/

Stevens Institute of Technology. (N.d.) Stevens research, courses and programming inform storm preparedness, recovery and policy. Accessed July 14, 2014. http://www.stevens.edu/news/sandy

Toro, R. (2013). Hurricane Sandy's impact (infographic). Live Science, October 29. http://www.livescience.com/40774-hurricane-sandy-s-impact-infographic.html

Volunteers of America—Greater New Orleans. (N.d.) Disaster Related Volunteerism: Best practices Based on Lessons Learned from Hurricanes Katrina and Rita. Accessed 2014. http://www.handsonnetwork.org/files/best_practices_manual__disaster _related_volunteerism-1.pdf

Wanko, L. 2013. Union Beach school reopens after Hurricane Sandy. NJTV News, June 3. http://www.njtvonline.org/news/video/union-beach-school-reopens-after-hurricane-sandy/

Walters, H. (2012). The Kit-ifying education of Superstorm Sandy. Wired Opinion, November. http://www.wired.com/opinion/2012/11/the-kit-ifying-education-of-superstrom-sandy

Waters, L. (2012). Superstorm Sandy illustrates why having too many school districts can be a problem. November 22. http://www.newsworks.org/index.php/local/new-jersey/47359-superstorm-sandy-illustrates-why-having-too-many-school-districts-can-be-a-problem

Yamori, K. (2009). Action research on disaster reduction education: Building a `community of practice' through a gaming approach. *Journal of Natural Disaster Science*, 30 92): 83–96.

CHAPTER EIGHT
HURRICANE SANDY AS COMPARED TO HURRICANE KATRINA: POLITICS OF ACCESS TO FEDERAL RELIEF

Jimmy D. McCamey, Jr. and Komanduri S. Murty

ABSTRACT

When it comes to addressing Federal Relief for disaster victims, politics of access seem to be inevitable. The victims' racial and economic background, the disaster region's economic impact on the national economy, local political leaders' influence on federal government, federal political leaders' anticipated returns (also known as dividends on their investment) in terms of popularity, media attention, higher poll ratings, and increase in number of votes that contribute to their success in next elections—all play a role at various degrees.

The purpose of Federal Emergency Management Agency (FFEMA) is to focus on disaster mitigation, preparedness, response, recovery, education, and relief. Emergency responders intervene before and during disasters to save lives, property and to restore disaster riddled communities to their previous functions. Understandably, the uncertainty of disasters makes it increasingly difficult for FEMA to respond timely and accurately to such events. FEMA has been put to the test in the past decade. Many wondered how FEMA was implemented through legislative channels and began questioning whether the leadership of the Oval Office may have dictated (or in some way was responsible) for the outcome of its efforts. In 2005, Hurricane Katrina marked a time in history that mortified the American people due to the lack of efforts and appropriate response time to the human suffering that was witnessed in the national media. Many believe Hurricane Katrina was the most notorious natural disaster of the twenty-first century that posed challenges as well as provided lessons to learn through both prevention-intervention and post-intervention strategies in a time of a natural disaster. Nonetheless, questions remain in the minds of many Americans: what did we learn from Hurricane Katrina, and how did we apply these takeaways during Hurricane Sandy in 2012?

Hurricane Katrina polarized the nation due to the unsatisfactory response efforts lead by then-President, George W. Bush. Remnants of Katrina efforts are still felt by the city of New Orleans and its citizens, who were displaced and never managed to return to the place they called home due to the failed efforts of FEMA and President George W. Bush, in terms of response and recovery of New Orleans, Louisiana. President Obama's response to Hurricane Sandy was different from that of President Bush during the Katrina disaster. The joint efforts of President Obama and New Jersey Governor Chris Christy helped FEMA moved with urgency, sensitivity, and immediate action to provide relief to disaster victims—including basic food and shelter, monetary relief, infrastructure repairs, revitalization, construction and community and neighborhood rebuilding for the affected region. Yet, the Republican dominated House began pressurizing President Obama to identify budget cuts to offset the funds for relief before they could approve relief funds for victims. Was it true that President Bush was slow in responding because the victims were largely black and poor, who lived in the ninth ward of New Orleans? Did President Obama act so fast to score some political points as he was on the brim of re-election for second term? Was it because the New Jersey governor has more influence in the Republican Party as well as on federal government, than Louisiana Governor Kathleen Blanco? Was it because democrats receive more minority votes than republicans? Should FEMA be subjected to ruling party priorities and political ideologies? This paper attempts to seek answers to these and other relevant questions.

INTRODUCTION

The issues of natural disasters have become a national and international reality that has been observed from various view points. More specifically, hurricanes have been a source of natural disaster that has had a profound impact on the lives, the conscious and communities throughout America and abroad. Although the aforementioned notorious disasters are acts of "mother nature," the overwhelming reality (ies) is profound and debilitating to mankind, especially minorities and poor communities. When such storms as Hurricanes Katrina and Sandy hit the shores of Louisiana and New Jersey, the true element of the "has and has not" where made more apparently clear. Such storms clearly showed the vast inequalities, injustices and patters on corruption that poor communities and its citizens experiences (David Brooks, *New York Times*).

Hurricane Katrina, though not an act of terror, took the lives of hundreds and thousands of American people, as America was planning to celebrate the fourth anniversary of 911, which many coined as the worse loss of life in domestic history. Hurricane Katrina further revealed the class divides in the American culture and reopened wounds of an American history of inequality. According to Elliott and Ionescul (2003), Louisiana, Mississippi and Alabama have been and continue to be demographically and economically subordinate to other regions of the country, which may suggest many of its citizens are disenfranchised. The same could be said about the Shores of New Jersey, but one would see a very different social and political response to the citizens of New Jersey. New Jersey Governor Chris Christy seized the moment to work in collaboration with President Obama to implement immediate relief for the citizens throughout the entire city. There were no major lags in a timely response or negative debates and push and pull conflict between Local, State and Federal Government, which proved to demonstrate positive outcome for all citizens in New Jersey and the surrounding municipalities. Geographical locations throughout the South, especially concentrations of poor cities are located along shore lines, which are the first to be hit by Hurricanes.

POVERTY AND LOW SOCIOECONOMICAL STATUS

Hurricanes are notorious and devastating occurrences that leave months, years, and decades of its resemblance long after the storm has departed inlands. Hurricane Katrina is being felt today many years after it approached the shores of Louisiana. The economic impact will be felt for many years to come. However, the loss of life will never be recovered as well as the tens of thousands of New Orleans who have been displaced as a result of the loss of their homes in the third ward. The age old debate of "does race matter or does economic status matter" has a profound impact on the recovery and cleaning efforts both during the Hurricane Katrina and Sandy. The impact of the storm is always secondary to recovery efforts. One can say "economic status" may dictate not only the level of speed of response to citizens, but realistically the citizen's ability to return to life pre-Hurricane status, which has been a daunting task for many residents who have yet to return to the Louisiana. Subsequently, one's economic status has implications of your ability for self help which is interchangeable to public and federal help. Many of the citizens in New Orleans were socially dependent on government assistance and lack solid economic stability during a time in which the devastating Katrina storm hit Louisiana. Whereas New Jersey citizens although ravaged by the storm that cased billions in damage and tremendous loss of life, the response from the local, state and Federal Government was much quicker, precise and calculated that transcended into immediate relief.

As it pertains to Hurricane Katrina, it was recorded as the most devastating storms in the U.S. history, taking the lives of more than one thousand eight hundred (1,800) people leaving millions homeless. According to news, reports, eighty (80 percent) of the entire city of New Orleans was under water, causing nearly eight (80) million dollars in property damage for its residents. The aforementioned figures do not include an estimated sixty (60) to eighty (80) million dollars loss in the local economy due to closure of the business districts and tourism, as well as the loss of jobs to its citizens. Given the above analysis of the economic impact of Hurricane

Katrina, poor citizens are hit the hardest and have less financial capital to recover from such devastation, thus having a more sustained and prolong period of suffering.

New Orleans' poor and migrant population has historically managed to survive through tourism and entertainment opportunities for the citizens. Hurricane Katrina's impact is prevalent nearly eight years later resulting in a sluggish economy and limited jobs and tourism. The demographics of the citizens of New Orleans presents a straggling number of poor citizens, single women with children, and a disproportionate number of individuals living in poverty which is often seen as individuals who concentrate the socioeconomically disadvantage or disenfranchised. As the news media narrated the Katrina story, it must be taken into account the reality of the harsh conditions this disenfranchised group of citizens had to navigate to get to safety.

Many of the citizens of New Orleans relied heavily on public transportation and had limited mobility and access to the escape routes to safety resulting in them having to get on top of the homes until boats and helicopters could remove them to safety. Unlike citizens in New Jersey who had immediate access to escape routes, transportation and resources to quickly recover from Sandy, New Orleans citizens were helpless at a time that contributed to a tremendous death tool that reach nearly 2,000 with hundreds unaccounted for. Although thousands died in this natural disaster, nearly eight hundred(800) are still unaccounted for. Not only does New Orleans have high populations of poor families and women with children, there are a disproportionate number of African-American people who were residing in New Orleans at the time of the storm. According to the U.S. Census, at the time of Hurricane Katrina, 67 percent of its citizens were African-American with 28 percent of the African-American living in poverty. As one authored suggested, the demographics of New Orleans have been well documented throughout history, there are no secrets that New Orleans has a high concentration of African-American citizens with many of them living in grave poverty conditions. New Jersey citizens on the other hand were much more multicultural and economically prepared for the aftermath of Sandy then the citizens of New Orleans

Unfortunately, the debate about poverty conditions becomes political rhetoric common buzz terms, and platforms to attract minority and poor voter's attention during local, state, and national elections. One must question the true intentions of the political goals as it pertains to the War on Poverty. Millions and trillions of dollars are spent annually on defense funds for third world countries and political campaigns with a fraction of the cost to aid the poor, elderly and children in America. New Orleans catastrophic Hurricane Katrina reminded American of the disproportionate number of people who continue to live in poverty conditions.

Hurricane Katrina not only demonstrated the failed political culture as it pertains to poverty, it reviewed a number of social ills that the media was able to exploit such as a weakened government that had limited power to intervene during a natural disaster on American soil. More concerning, the America Federal Government displayed tremendous weakness in intergovernmental communication that not only cost massive destruction to personal property, buildings, businesses but the over (1,800) lives lost due to poor prevention, intervention, and post-tension efforts.

GOVERNOR(S) KATHLEEN BLANCO AND CHRIS CHRISTY

It has been determined that most natural disasters are expected to be addressed by state and local governments giving the Federal Government an option to respond. Given the chain of command of the natural disaster process in America, it is important to focus on elected leaders at the local level and state level, such as councilmen, commissioners, mayors, senators and governors. In doing so, who should take the brunt of responsibility for the prevention, intervention and postvention at the time of a natural disaster? According to critics, Gov. Kathleen Blanco and Mayor Ray Nagin cannot claim they were surprised by the extent of the damage and the need to evacuate so many people.

Detailed written plans were already in place to evacuate more than a million people. The plans projected that 300,000 people would need transportation in the event of a hurricane like Katrina. If the plans had been implemented, numerous lives would likely have been saved. In addition to the evacuation plans, local, state, and federal officials held a simulated hurricane drill 13 months prior to Hurricane Katrina, in which flooding supposedly trapped 300,000 people inside New Orleans. The exercise simulated the evacuation of more than a million residents. The problems identified in the simulation apparently were not solved where also documented and a plan of action was to be completed and implemented to make the necessary adjustments to meet the needs of a successful evacuation of New Orleans citizens.

When Hurricane Ivan approached, New Orleans ordered an evacuation but reportedly did not use city or school buses to help people evacuate, which was a fundamental strategy that planning and zoning of the city had suggested to the Mayor of New Orleans and the Governor of Louisiana that reportedly was ignored. As a result, many of the poorest citizens were unable to evacuate from the city, placing them in great danger and potential loss of life. Fortunately, the hurricane changed course and did not hit New Orleans, but both Gov. Blanco and Mayor Nagin acknowledged the need for a better evacuation plan. Again, however, the leadership in place failed to take make the necessary adjustments to protect the lives of its citizens.

In New Orleans news brief, an article cited in 1998, during a threat by Hurricane George, 14,000 people were sent to the Superdome, and theft and vandalism were rampant because of inadequate security to protect the elderly, children and other citizens. These problems were systematically ignored and a corrective action plan was never devised to address the aforementioned issues, which carried over and contributed to the chaos of Hurricane Katrina, when citizens were placed in the Superdome. The New Orleans contingency plan, even after Hurricane Katrina devastated the shores of New Orleans, states, "The safe evacuation of threatened populations is one of the principle [sic] reasons for developing a Comprehensive

Emergency Management Plan." But the plan was apparently ignored as Katrina headed toward the city. The federal government does not have the authority to intervene in a state emergency without the request of the state's governor. President Bush declared an emergency prior to Katrina hitting New Orleans, so the only action required for federal assistance to be sent was for Gov. Blanco to request the specific type of assistance she needed. Unfortunately, Blanco failed to send a timely request for specific aid resulting in catastrophic death and loss.

In addition, unlike the governors of New York, Oklahoma, California, New Jersey in past disasters, Gov. Blanco failed to take charge of the situation and ensure that the state emergency operation facility was in constant contact with Mayor Nagin and FEMA. It is likely that numerous people died because of the failure of Governor. Blanco to implement the state plan, which mentions the possible need to evacuate up to one million people just months prior to Hurricane Katrina natural disaster. The state plan clearly gives the governor the authority to declare an emergency, send in state resources to the disaster area, and request necessary federal assistance, which Governor Blanco did not follow through with. State legislators and governor's nationwide need to update their contingency plans and the operation procedures for state emergency centers to ensure the citizens are provided the necessary resources and assistance to prevent a loss of life during natural disaster situations.

Hurricane Katrina had been forecast for days and preparations and planning had taken place for years for such a storm, but that will not always be the case with a disaster (terrorist attacks, for example) and still many loss their lives and were viewed by the world as helpless as they sat a top of their roof as they waved shirts and towels as signals of help. It must be made clear that the governor and locally elected officials are in charge of the "first response" which may be the most crucial response to having an effective and successful evaluation plan during the time of a natural disaster. Hundreds of thousands of people were displaced by the flooding —250,000 were absorbed by Texas alone, and local radio reported that Baton Rouge doubled in population as citizens migrated away from the storm and high tides of New Orleans. Federal officials said they have begun to collect corpses but could not guess the total toll because the bodies were being taken to the morgue as rapid numbers and the emergency support stations and communication in New Orleans were chaotic, unorganized and ineffective resulting in additional loss of life. Behind the scenes, a power struggle emerged, as federal officials tried to wrest authority from Louisiana Gov. Kathleen Babineaux Blanco (D), who many suggest was incompetent and lack adequate leadership during the time of storm Hurricane Katrina, contributing to the chaos that took so many innocent lives of the poor, children and elderly. Shortly before midnight the day prior to the storm, the Bush administration sent her a proposed legal memorandum asking her to request a federal takeover of the evacuation of New Orleans, a source within the state's emergency operations center reported, but Blanco failed to respond in a timely manner.

The state government administration sought unified control over all local police and state National Guard units reporting to the governor but much time had passed and the city of New Orleans were reportedly out of control with violence crimes such as robbery, stealing and even murder. Louisiana officials rejected the request after talks throughout the night, concerned that such a move would be comparable to a federal declaration of martial law. Some officials in the state suspected a political motive behind the request. One news review stated "Quite frankly, if they'd been able to pull off taking it away from the locals, they then could have blamed everything on the locals."

A senior administration official said that Bush cleared legal authority to federalize National Guard units to quell civil disturbances under the Insurrection Act and continued to try to unify the chains of command that are split among the president, the Louisiana governor and the New Orleans mayor. Louisiana did not reach out to a multi-state mutual aid compact for assistance until long after the storm had devastated the city. According to New Orleans Mayor Ray Nagin, "80 percent" of the city was evacuated before the storm hit, but Bob Williams, a FEMA expert, was quoted as saying "that's not good enough." Williams dealt with emergency response issues as a state representative in Washington when his district was forced to deal with the eruption of Mount St. Helens in 1980. According to Williams, "If the plan were implemented, lives would have been saved and New Orleans leadership may have been regarded as the most talented group of leaders of their time." Unfortunately, the leadership in New Orleans and the Governor's office took grave criticism as result of their efforts or lack thereof.

There's no question the federal government plays a major role in disaster relief. But federal officials say in order to get involved, they must first be asked to do so by state officials.

As one FEMA official told ABC News, Louisiana Gov. Kathleen Blanco failed to submit a request for help in a timely manner. Shortly before Katrina hit, she sent President Bush a request asking for shelter and provisions, but did not specifically ask for help with evacuations, which has proven to be the worst mistake she could have made, given the contingency plan she had in placed required heavy evacuation measures. One aide to the governor told ABC News Blanco thought city officials were taking care of the evacuation—which turned out to be a detrimental assumption that caused a tremendous loss of life.

Some experts argue that the federal government should have been more pro-active and used executive order to take over the state of Louisiana if the Governor's office was acting in an incompetent manner or performing poorly in meeting the needs of its citizens. While attention has focused on the performance of former Federal Emergency Management Agency director Michael D. Brown, and communications breakdowns that kept Washington from recognizing for 12 to 16 hours the scope of flooding that would drive the storm's death toll above 1,200, the clash over military control highlights government officials' lack of familiarity with the levers of emergency powers.

Blanco's top aides relied on ad hoc tutorials from the National Guard about who would be in charge and how to call in federal help, which is common in the chain of command. The tragedy is that Blanco had little to no checks and balances to ensure the job was being carried out with efficiency to protect and save the lives of the citizens. But in the chaos of fast-moving events, partisan differences and federal/state divisions prevented top leaders from working in collaboration to meet the need of its citizens; politics trumped the safety of the citizens. Many critics said the people around Bush were trying to maneuver the governor into an unnecessary change intended to make Bush look presidential.

The federal government has an agency that exists for purposes of coming to the rescue of localities in a natural disaster, and that organization did not live up to what it was designed for or promised to and failed at all levels to include local, state and federal governments. According to documents and aides, her team was not familiar with relevant laws and procedures, believed the change would have disrupted Guard law enforcement operations in New Orleans and mistrusted the Bush team, which they saw as preoccupied with its own public relations problems and blame shifting.

REFERENCES

Anjaria, Jonathan Shapiro. 2006. "Urban Calamities: A view from Mumbai." *Space and Culture* 9(1): 80–82.

Avdeyeva, Tatyana V., Kristina Burgetova, and David I. Welch. 2006. "To Help or not to help?factors that determined helping responses to katrina victims." *Analyses of Social Issues and Public Policy* 6(1): 159–173.

Banipal, Kulwinder. 2006. "Strategic Approach to Disaster Management: Lessons Learned From hurricane Katrina." *Disaster Prevention and Management* 15(3): 484–94.

Bartling, Hugh. 2006. "Suburbia, mobility, and urban calamities." *Space and Culture* 9(1): 60–62.

Bier, Vicki. 2006. "Hurricane Katrina as a bureaucratic nightmare." pp. 243–254 in On Risk andDisaster: Lessons from Hurricane Katrina, edited by R. J. Daniels, D. F. Kettl, and H. Kunreuther. Philadelphia: University of Pennsylvania Press.

Brown, Christia Spears, Rashmita S. Mistry, and Rebecca S. Bigler. 2007. "Hurricane Katrina: african american children's perceptions of race, class, and government involve mentamid a national crisis." *Analyses of Social Issues and Public Policy* 7(1): 191–208.

American Association of University Professors. 2007. Report of an AAUP special committee:hurricane Katrina and New Orleans universities. Washington, DC: American Association of University Professors. http://www.aaup.org/AAUP/protect/ academic freedom/investrep/2007/katrina.htm

Bureau of Labor Statistics. 2006. "The labor market impact of hurricane Katrina: An overview." *Monthly Labor Review*, August: 3–10.

Button, Gregory and Anthony Oliver-Smith. 2008. "Disaster, displacement, and employment: distortion of labor markets during post-Katrina reconstruction." pp. 123–145 in Capitalizing on catastrophe: neoliberal strategies in disaster reconstruction, edited by N. Gunewardena and M. Schuller. Lanham, MD: AltaMira Press.

Cahoon, Lawrence S., Diane E. Herz, Richard C. Ning, Anne E. Polivka, Maria E. Reed, EdwinL. Robinson, and Gregory D. Weyland. 2006. "The current population survey response to hurricane Katrina." *Monthly Labor Review*, August: 40–51.

Godfrey, Nessa P. Hurricane Katrina: Impact, Recovery and lessons learned. New York, NY: Nova Science Publishers, 2009.

Davis, L. E. (2007). Hurricane Katrina : lessons for army planning and operations. Santa Monica, CA: RAND.

HayesJr., Vernon R. :Falling to establish a unified command in Louisiana during hurricane Katrina." *Journal of Homeland Security & Emergency Management* 9.1 (2012): 1–11. Criminal Justice.

Herron, Jason1, and Michael W.1 Smith. "The Disaster of hurricane Katrina: malfeasance, official deviance and the failure to serve and protect a community." *International Journal of Interdisciplinary Social Sciences* 6.5 (2011): 127–139. OmniFile Full Text Mega (H.W. Wilson). Web. 2 Sept. 2013.

Thomas, Lynell. 2008. "'The city I used to . . . visit': tourist New Orleans and the racialized response to hurricane Katrina." pp. 255–270 in Seeking higher ground: the hurricaneKatrina crisis, Race, and public policy reader, edited by M. Marable and K. Clarke.New York: Palgrave Macmillan.

Whelan, Robert K. 2006. "An old economy for the 'new' New Orleans? Post-hurricane Katrina economic development efforts." pp. 215–232 in There is No such thing as a natural disaster: race, class, and hurricane Katrina, edited by C. Hartman and G. D. Squires. New York: Routledge.

Whitaker, Matthew C., and Jeremy I. Levitt. Hurricane Katrina: America's unnatural disaster. Lincoln: University of Nebraska Press, 2009.

Wilson, Nancy. 2006. "Hurricane Katrina: unequal opportunity disaster." *Public Policy and Aging Report* 16(2): 8–13.

Wright, Beverly, and Robert D. Bullard. Race, place, and environmental justice after hurricane Katrina: struggles to reclaim, rebuild, and revitalize New Orleans and the Gulf Coast. Boulder, CO: Westview Press 2009

Zottarelli, Lisa K. 2008. "Post-hurricane Katrina employment recovery: the interaction of race and place." *Social Science Quarterly* 89(3): 592–607.

CHAPTER NINE
PUTTING HURRICANE SANDY IN CONTEXT: COMPARING SANDY, KATRINA, AND GUSTAV

Kelly Frailing and Dee Wood Harper, Jr.

INTRODUCTION

The ubiquitous media coverage of modern day disasters in the United States seems to encourage comparisons between the most disruptive of these events. We believe these comparisons are warranted when they help us to understand the effects of disasters on the physical and social environments. Utilizing Killian's (2002) phase model as an organizing framework, this chapter compares Hurricane Sandy, which hit the northeast coast of the United States in October of 2012 to Hurricane Katrina, which hit the Gulf Coast in August of 2005, on a number of different dimensions, including meteorological details, physical destruction and social disruption. Our comparison of the social disruption includes a discussion of crime in the wake of each storm as well as in the wake of Hurricane Gustav, which hit the Gulf Coast in September of 2008. This comparison gives us the opportunity to observe the different types of destruction caused by each storm as well as to test theoretical propositions that incorporate pre-disaster social conditions, the presence or absence of capable guardianship and the consequent level of antisocial behavior.

THE PHASE MODEL OF DISASTERS

Before proceeding to a discussion of Hurricanes Sandy and Katrina, it behooves us to discuss Lewis Killian's (2002) phase model of disasters. Killian's (2002) four phase model is commonly employed in disaster research and consists of the warning, impact, emergency and recovery phases. The warning phase is the period in which information about a highly likely disastrous event is available "but before the danger has become immediate, personal and physically perceivable." The impact phase is the "period where the destructive agent is actually at work." The emergency phase "is the post impact period during which rescue, first aid, emergency medical care, and other emergency tasks are performed." The recovery phase is "the period, which begins roughly as the emergency crisis passes and during which the longer-term activities of reconstruction, rehabilitation and recovery proceed" (Killian, 2002, p. 51).

Though this phase model is designed to apply a timeline to disasters, it is not without its critics. Some charge that though Killian's (2002) phase model takes time into account, it does not consider the differential impact of disaster depending on location. Within a geographic location impacted by disaster, certain areas that take a direct hit may move through the phases differently and at a different pace than more distant areas that are not directly struck but are nevertheless impacted by disaster. Moreover, even when the warning, impact and emergency phases are relatively obvious, the pace of recovery is often nonlinear and can be difficult to predict. The degree to which the infrastructure was affected, the socioeconomic makeup of the impacted area and the political will to commit money and other resources to the impacted area are among the important factors in determining how, when and if the disaster-stricken area will recover (Thornton and Voigt, 2012). Perhaps the most serious criticism of this phase model and others like it (i.e., Carr, 1932; NGA, 1979; Drabek, 1986; Neal, 1997) is that it assumes a single impact disaster with relatively distinctive phases. Obviously, not every disaster is going to fit neatly into this model and whether Killian's (2002) phase model is useful across disasters of different types remains a debatable issue.

The mention of types of disasters brings us to another opportunity for clarification. Gill, Picou and Ritchie (2012) identify four types of disasters, natural, technological, natech and terrorism. A natural disaster is "triggered by natural processes and hazards that threaten human life and damage the "built" and "modified" environments" (p. 74). Built environments include homes and businesses and modified environments include roads, highways, bridges and utilities. Examples of natural disasters include earthquakes, hurricanes and floods. It is common for a therapeutic community to emerge in the wake of a natural disaster in which survivors come together to support one another and affirm social networks (Barton, 1969). A technological disaster involves "irresponsible and reckless behavior on the part of individuals, groups, corporations or institutions, which result in the failure of technology and subsequent breakdown in organizations designed to control technological processes" (Gill, Picou and Ritchie, 2012, p. 74). Technological disasters damage bioregions, which are those regions established by natural rather than manmade boundaries; different bioregions contain different vegetation, animal life, climate, soil, water and landforms (Sale, 1991). Well-known examples of technological disasters include the Union Carbide plant gas leak in India in 1986 and the Chernobyl disaster in Ukraine, also in 1986. Technological disasters damage bioregions through toxic contamination and loss of resources; this damage is often invisible. The invisibility of the damage in combination with denial of culpability on the part of the individuals, groups or corporations responsible for the disaster leads to the formation of a corrosive rather than a therapeutic community. A corrosive community is one characterized by conflict, diminished social capital and ongoing trauma, both individual and social.

These classic disaster categories do not adequately capture some recent disasters including Hurricane Katrina and 9/11. Katrina has been called a natural technological or natech disaster because although it was caused by a hurricane, it also involved the breakdown of the modified environment (i.e., the levees, as seen below) and the release of toxins into the natural environment. The term natech was first introduced by Erickson (1994) and Showalter and Myers (1994) and natech disasters involve both certainty about the causes of damage, similar to natural disasters, as well as uncertainty about the invisible damage and long term effects, similar to technological disasters. Survivors may therefore experience both therapeutic and corrosive communities, with acute and long term trauma characteristic of the latter (Gill, Picou and Ritchie, 2012). Finally, 9/11 is a clear example of a terrorism disaster. Terrorism disasters damage the natural, built, modified and engineered environments, including crucial infrastructure such as power grids, telecommunications and computer networks. They often occur with very little warning and hence very little opportunity to mitigate damage. Like natech disasters, both therapeutic and corrosive communities emerge after terrorism disasters. The formation of therapeutic communities results in part from the outpouring of support from people all over the affected country. The formation of corrosive communities results from feelings that officials did not do enough to thwart the disaster or mitigate its impact; Freudenburg (2000) coined the term recreancy to describe the failure of officials or experts to carry out the duties with which society has entrusted them (Gill, Picou and Ritchie, 2012).

The disasters under consideration in this chapter clearly fall into one of these four categories. As mentioned, Hurricane Katrina is an example of a natech disaster. It damaged the built, modified and natural environments, part of the damage was due to natural forces and part to human irresponsibility and survivors experienced both therapeutic and corrosive communities. But what about Hurricane Sandy? In our estimation, Hurricane Sandy is natural disaster. It was triggered by a natural process, it damaged only the built and modified environments and survivors experienced a therapeutic community. Because we make reference to Hurricane Gustav below, we should also mention that it too qualifies as a natural disaster.

Astute readers may be asking themselves if it is appropriate to compare a natech disaster such as Katrina to a natural disaster such as Sandy. Is this a valid comparison, or are we deep into apples and oranges territory? While we do not wish to engage in the same careless and dismissive comparisons that some politicians have (e.g., Alpert, 2013), we believe that a comparison between Hurricanes Katrina and Sandy is valid and we think of it as thoroughly comparing different types of apples rather than apples to oranges. The comparison that follows allows us to put each disaster in context and to think critically about successful and unsuccessful efforts to mitigate the effects of disaster. Our use of Killian's (2002) phase model is especially helpful in the latter effort. Though it is subject to the criticisms noted above, the four phase model allows us to observe how both Katrina and Sandy progressed, the most and least useful attempts to ameliorate these disasters' impacts through the various phases and what can be done differently and more effectively in the future when disasters strike anew. The remainder of this chapter compares and contrast Hurricanes Katrina and Sandy in the warning, impact, emergency[1] and recovery phases and concludes with observations on effective ways to handle antisocial behavior in the wake of disasters as well as on longer term rehabilitation.

The Warning Phase

As mentioned, the warning phase is the period in which information about a highly likely disastrous event is available "but before the danger has become immediate, personal and physically perceivable" (Killian, 2002, p. 51). Here we consider the warning phase of Hurricanes Katrina and Sandy in turn.

Hurricane Katrina

As is widely known, Hurricane Katrina made landfall in southeastern Louisiana on August 29, 2005. The warning phase of this disaster began six days earlier on August 23, when the National Hurricane Center in Miami, FL issued its first warning about the tropical storm that would eventually become Hurricane Katrina. The tropical storm had formed over the Bahamas and at that time, was about 350 miles east of Miami. On August 24, the tropical storm was named Katrina and had moved 120 miles closer to Miami (Drye, 2005). On August 25, Katrina had strengthened to a Category 1 hurricane with maximum winds of 75 miles per hour and while many remember the devastation Katrina visited on Mississippi, Alabama and especially on Louisiana, it is likely fewer remember that Katrina first made landfall as a Category 1 storm in Florida on August 25, near North Miami Beach on the state's southeastern coast. On August 26, Katrina moved across Florida and into the Gulf of Mexico as a tropical storm, but intensified immediately upon contact with the warm water; its winds increased to almost 100 miles per hour in just a few hours after entering the Gulf. Both Governor Kathleen Blanco of Louisiana and Governor Haley Barbour of Mississippi declared a state of emergency in their respective states (Drye, 2005). By August 27, Katrina's circulation covered the entire Gulf of Mexico and its winds had increased to 115 miles an hour, making it a Category 3 hurricane; it would become a Category 5 hurricane with maximum winds of 175 miles an hour by mid-morning on August 28. August 28 was also the day on which then New Orleans, LA. Mayor Ray Nagin issued a mandatory evacuation order for the city. Tens of thousands people fled the city,[2] but many were unable or unwilling to go. Many of those who were unable to leave or who chose to stay in New Orleans took shelter in the Superdome later that night. Hurricane

Katrina made landfall in Plaquemines Parish, just south of New Orleans on August 29 (Drye, 2005).

Hurricane Sandy

Hurricane Sandy made landfall in eastern New Jersey on October 29, 2012. The warning phase of this disaster began seven days earlier on October 22, when Tropical Storm Sandy formed in the southern Caribbean Sea off the coast of Nicaragua with maximum winds of 40 miles per hour. By October 24, Sandy had strengthened into a Category 1 hurricane with maximum winds of 80 miles per hour. It struck Jamaica on its way northward through the Caribbean and dumped 20 inches of rain on Haiti and the Dominican Republic to the east. Sandy strengthened as it moved away from Jamaica and toward Cuba; its winds were just one mile an hour below Category 3 hurricane status as it struck Cuba and the Bahamas on October 26 (Drye, 2012). On October 27, Sandy turned toward the northeast off the eastern coast of Florida. It weakened briefly into a tropical storm but intensified into a Category 1 hurricane as it moved northeast along the coasts of Georgia and the Carolinas on October 28. On that day, meteorologists started to warn that a high pressure cold front north of Sandy would force the storm to turn toward some of the biggest cities on the East Coast, including Baltimore, Washington, Philadelphia and New York. That in combination with the expected full moon would increase the storm surge to over 12 feet in some places (Drye, 2012). New Jersey Governor Chris Christie declared a state of emergency on October 27 and ordered a mandatory evacuation for the Barrier Islands, Atlantic City casinos and all national parks (CBS, 2012). New York mayor Michael Bloomberg issued a mandatory evacuation for the low lying areas of the city, including Battery Park and the financial district in Manhattan, parts of Brooklyn and Staten Island and the Rockaway Peninsula in Queens on October 28 (Peltz, 2012). On October 29, Sandy made its predicted sharp turn toward the coast of New Jersey and by then, had moved 300 miles over open water which allowed it to strengthen. It had also begun to interact with the cold front to the north, creating a hybrid snowstorm hurricane (Drye, 2012).

Impact Phase

As mentioned, the impact phase is the "period where the destructive agent is actually at work" (Killian, 2002, p. 51). Here we consider the impact phase of Hurricanes Katrina and Sandy in turn.

Hurricane Katrina

Hurricane Katrina came ashore in Buras, LA in the early morning of August 29, 2005 as a strong Category 3 hurricane. Though Katrina went on to devastate Biloxi and Gulfport, MS that morning, many Louisiana residents, especially those who had remained in the city, believed the worst to be over as the sun rose on August 29.

However, as is widely known, the impact phase of Katrina involved much more than the arrival of the storm. The Industrial Canal levee on the east side of New Orleans breached at 8:14am and less than five hours later, 40,000 homes in the Ninth Ward and St. Bernard Parish, adjacent to New Orleans, had flooded with at least eight feet of water. By 2pm, the 17th Street Canal levee on the northwest side of New Orleans failed and at 4pm, two levees along the London Avenue Canal failed; 12 hours later, 80 percent of the city was underwater and would remain so for two weeks (Thornton and Voigt, 2012a; Time, 2005).

As Thornton and Voigt (2012a) point out, what we refer to as Hurricane Katrina was actually a multi-impact disaster in which any of the impacts would constitute a disaster in its own right. Of course, there was Katrina itself and the levee breaches, but there were three other impacts that followed Katrina within less than a month. A chemical storage facility near the Mississippi River east of the French Quarter exploded in the early morning hours of September 2. On September 4, Murphy Oil USA in St. Bernard Parish adjacent to New Orleans reported that one of its above ground storage tanks had been damaged by Katrina's floodwaters and leaked over a million gallons of oil into a residential area. Finally, Hurricane Rita struck southwest Louisiana near the Texas border on September 24 as a strong Category 3 storm. Though its landfall was hundreds of miles from New Orleans, its rainfall breached the Industrial Canal levee in the city a second time.

Hurricane Sandy

Hurricane Sandy came ashore in Brigantine, NJ just north of Atlantic City at 8p.m. on October 29, 2012, downgraded from a hurricane to a post-tropical nor'easter. The storm surge was worst for New York and New Jersey because of their position relative to Sandy's strongest winds. Sandy arrived at high tide and with the aforementioned effect of the full moon, the storm surge was nearly 14 feet in New York Harbor. The storm surge topped the seawall in the Battery in lower Manhattan and flooded part of the subway system, as well as the tunnel connecting lower Manhattan and Brooklyn. Staten Island was particularly hard hit; half of the deaths in New York due to Sandy occurred there. New York and New Jersey were subject to punishing rains and flooding through the next day and a half (Drye, 2012).

Table 9.1 provides a by the numbers comparison of Hurricanes Katrina and Sandy that helps to put both storms in context. As Table 9.1 reveals, Katrina was a stronger storm than Sandy in terms of its category, its wind speed, its barometric pressure, its storm surge and its rainfall and it was a more destructive storm in terms of number of people displaced, its death toll and its monetary cost. Sandy was a physically bigger storm than Katrina, affected a greater population, delivered more snow and left many more without power. The two were fairly equal in terms of length of warning phase, time over land and number of states affected by winds.

Table 9.1. Hurricanes Katrina and Sandy by the Numbers

	Hurricane Katrina	Hurricane Sandy
Type of disaster	Natech	Natural
Category upon landfall	3	Similar to but less than 1
Length of warning phase	6 days	7 days
Maximum winds	125 mph in LA	94 mph in NJ
Maximum landfall winds	120 mph in LA	80 mph in NJ
Time over land	33 hours	32 hours
Maximum diameter (extent of high winds)	415 miles	1,000 miles
Barometric pressure (lower is stronger)	920mb	948mb
Storm Surge	14 feet (28 feet in NO)	13 feet
Rainfall	15 inches	13 inches
Snowfall	0 inches	34 inches
People evacuated before storm	1,000,000	850,078
States in disaster area	4 (AL, FL, LA, MS)	3 (CT, NJ, NY)
Number of states affected by winds	16	17
Population in affected areas	15,000,000	17,500,000
Peak power outages	3 million in 8 states	8.51 million in 16 states and Washington, D.C.
Buildings damaged or destroyed	1.2 million	380,000
Insured losses	$48.7 billion (in 2012 dollars)	$16-$22 billion
FEMA assistance	738,318 approved applications	465,000 applications filed by late November, 2012
People displaced	1,000,000	More than 100,000
Death toll	1,833	132
Days until presidential visit	4	2
Total monetary cost	$148 billion (in 2012 dollars)	$72 billion

Sources: Wallace and Kaleem, 2012; Fischetti, 2012; Newman, 2012.

Emergency Phase

As mentioned, the emergency phase "is the post impact period during which rescue, first aid, emergency medical care, and other emergency tasks are performed"

(Killian, 2002, p. 51). Here we consider the emergency phase of Hurricanes Katrina and Sandy in turn, as well as examine Hurricane Gustav, which helps to put the lessons learned from Katrina in a meaningful context.

Hurricane Katrina

The most banal way to accurately describe the emergency phase of Hurricane Katrina is complete and utter chaos. Because the city flooded so quickly and so many people were unable or unwilling to leave in advance of the storm, thousands of people were left to the mercy of the fetid water, many scrambling into their attics and through to their roofs. The Coast Guard in helicopters and ordinary citizens who commandeered boats engaged in innumerable rooftop rescues, but of course there were few options for shelter once residents were rescued. Many were taken to the Superdome, which was not designed to be a long term shelter or to the Morial Convention Center, which became a makeshift shelter for approximately 15,000 once the situation at the Superdome became untenable. Those at both locations in the first days after Katrina made landfall on August 29 found themselves without food, water, medicine or supplies and no idea when more would be available, nor was it clear when and how they would be able to leave the city.[3] On September 1, then Mayor Nagin went on local radio and delivered a now famous tirade against both the state and federal level responses. He begged for buses to evacuate the stranded and troops to control looters and the addicts searching for drugs; he also lambasted both then Governor Blanco and President Bush, calling on both state and federal officials to "get off your asses and do something, and let's fix the biggest goddamn crisis in the history of this country" (CNN, 2005). Though small scale evacuations began on September 1 and troops arrived at the Convention Center on September 2, thousands remained stranded there, at the Superdome or on one of the Interstate 10 overpasses; the most infirm and in need of medical care awaited evacuation at the Louis Armstrong International Airport, about 15 miles away from downtown New Orleans and were still waiting on September 4 (NOLA, n.d.).

As Thornton and Voigt (2012) note, each phase of disaster has characteristics that are conducive to certain types of crime and the emergency phase is certainly no exception. The type of criminal activity most closely associated with the emergency phase of disasters generally and certainly with the emergency phase of Katrina specifically is looting and here, we turn our attention to the factors that facilitate this crime in the wake of disaster.

It is a long held notion in disaster research that looting is common during riots and other civil disturbances and rare during natural disasters. During civil disturbances, looting is done by locals in full view of others and functions as a way to send a message about the conditions that initially set the civil disturbance in motion. The small amount of verified looting that occurs in the wake of natural disasters is done by outsiders clandestinely and is strongly condemned by locals, in large part because property becomes collective during the formation of a therapeutic community (e.g., Dynes and Quarantelli, 1968; Quarantelli and Dynes, 1970).

However, the extent of verified looting after Hurricane Hugo devastated St. Croix in 1989 caused eminent disaster researcher Quarantelli (1994, 2007) to soften his position on the issue; he noted that the socioeconomic conditions in St. Croix before Hugo struck facilitated the widespread looting that occurred there.

Quarantelli (2008) now believes that the study of looting and other antisocial behavior in the wake of natural and other disasters should remain a part of the research agenda. We concur and have extensively documented the large scale looting in New Orleans in the wake of Hurricane Katrina (i.e., Frailing and Harper, 2012; Frailing and Harper, 2010; Frailing and Harper, 2010a; Frailing and Harper, 2007). Throughout these publications, we claim there are two key factors that affect looting. The first of these is the socioeconomic conditions in the affected area. Simply put, the worse the socioeconomic conditions of the area, the more likely looting is to occur in the wake of disaster. New Orleans' history with hurricanes and looting supports this contention. In the 1940s, 1950s and 1960s, New Orleans was a city on the rise. The population was growing, the unemployment rate was falling and the median family income was increasing. However, in the late 1960s, New Orleans began a slow descent that was fueled by the departure of high wage manufacturing jobs and their replacement with low wage food and hotel service jobs, a botched school desegregation effort, the exodus of population, both white and African American, and the movement of most oil industry jobs to Houston. All these factors helped create a permanent, primarily African American underclass with very limited opportunities for quality education or for lucrative employment (Frailing and Harper, 2012). Table 9.2 reveals the socioeconomic state of New Orleans in the lead up to Hurricane Katrina.

With the socioeconomic conditions in New Orleans in recent decades established, we turn to looting rates after three major storms to hit the city up to and including Katrina. In measuring looting in the wake of a disaster, it is important to point out several caveats, the first of which is the use of burglary as a proxy for looting. We have used burglary as a proxy for looting because no looting statute existed in Louisiana prior to 1993 and more importantly, because we believe burglary more accurately captures the kind of looting we are concerned with. That is, we believe it is likely that a homeowner or a business owner would be much more likely to report high value electronics, jewelry, clothing, shoes, other personal and household items and merchandise as stolen than they would water, food, diapers and medicine, items necessary for survival in the chaos of Katrina. Table 9.3 reveals burglary rates in the wake of the unnamed storm of 1947, Hurricane Betsy in 1965 and Hurricane Katrina in 2005.

When we consider Tables 9.2 and 9.3 in conjunction, it is clear that the socioeconomic conditions in New Orleans are correlated with post-storm burglary rates, with better conditions associated with lower increases in burglary rates after each hurricane. Socioeconomic conditions are also correlated with pre-storm burglary rates, with better conditions associated with lower burglary rates prior to disaster.

Table 9.2. The Socioeconomic State of New Orleans in the Decades Prior to Katrina

	1950	1960	1970	1980	1990	2000
Population	570,445	627,525	593,471	557,515	496,938	484,674
White population	387,814 (68%)	392,594 (63%)	323,420 (54%)	238,192 (43%)	173,305 (35%)	136,241 (28%)
Black population	182,631 (32%)	234,931 (27%)	267,308 (46%)	308,039 (57%)	308,364 (65%)	325,216 (72%)
Percent female head household	N/A	16.2	21.6	29.8	38.4	41
White unem-ployment rate	4.9	3.9	4.1	4.0	3.0	3.6
Black unem-ployment rate	8.6	8.7	8.3	10.1	17.8	13.1
White median family income*	3,143	4,394	6,961	6,241	7,472	8,829
Black median family income*	1,391	2,018	2,392	3,046	2,868	3,594

* In 1950 constant dollars
Source: Frailing and Harper, 2012.

Table 9.3. Burglary Rates per 100,000 in the Month Before and Month After Three New Orleans Hurricanes

	Burglary rate in the month before	Burglary rate in the month after	Percent increase
Unnamed 1947 hurricane	13.9	27.0	94.2
Hurricane Betsy, 1965	7.8	9.0	15.4
Hurricane Katrina, 2005	82.3	245.9	198.8

Source: Frailing and Harper, 2012.

Hurricane Gustav

Hurricane Gustav was a Category 2 hurricane that hit the coast of Louisiana on September 1, 2008, nearly three years to the day after Katrina did. We do not tend to remember Gustav as being on par with either Katrina or Sandy, but we describe it here because it was the first major storm to threaten New Orleans after Katrina and it permits us to observe the lessons learned from Katrina. Gustav began as a tropical depression on August 25 in the eastern Caribbean Sea. It hit Hispaniola as a Category 1 hurricane on August 26; making landfall on the island weakened Gustav to a tropical storm, but it as it moved back into the Caribbean Sea, it strengthened again and by August 29, was a Category 1 hurricane with maximum winds of 75 miles per hour when it passed over Jamaica and the Cayman Islands

(Drye, 2008). As it headed toward Cuba, Gustav rapidly gained strength and struck the western tip of Cuba on August 30 as a Category 4 hurricane with maximum winds of 145 miles per hour. Gustav headed into the Gulf of Mexico on August 31 as a Category 3 storm with maximum winds of 125 miles per hour and appeared to be headed directly toward New Orleans; forecasters feared Gustav would gain strength on its way through the Gulf. An evacuation order was issued for New Orleans and much of the Gulf Coast and approximately two million people fled inland (Drye, 2008).[4] Now a strong Category 2 hurricane with 110 mile per hour winds, Gustav came ashore on the morning of September 1, 2008 in Cocodrie, LA, which is about 70 miles southwest of New Orleans. As the storm moved along the Louisiana coast, its 12-foot storm surge pushed water into the Industrial Canal, which had infamously failed during Katrina. This time, though, the levee held and the city was spared a flood (Drye, 2008), though it was not unscathed. Gustav killed 48 people in Louisiana, most as a result of falling debris caused by the storm's strong winds. Gustav is estimated to have caused $15 billion in property damage and $5 billion in lost business activity. Over two thirds of customers in Louisiana, approximately 1.3 million, lost power due to Gustav, with 88 percent having power returned after nine days (LPB, 2008).

Always quick to investigate crime in the wake of disaster, Frailing and Harper (2010) documented the burglaries that occurred in the month before and the month after Gustav. Table 9.4 reveals burglary rates in the wake of the unnamed storm of 1947, Hurricane Betsy in 1965, Hurricane Katrina in 2005 and Hurricane Gustav in 2008.

It is clear from Table 9.4 that the percent increase in the burglary rate after Gustav is about equal to the percent increase after the unnamed storm of 1947 and about half of the percent increase after Katrina. Remember the first of Frailing and Harper's (2012, 2010, 2010a, 2007) key contentions about looting in the wake of disaster, the worse the socioeconomic conditions, the greater the likelihood that looting will occur in the wake of disaster. This begs the question of whether the lower burglary rate after Gustav is due to an improvement in socioeconomic conditions in the city of New Orleans from 2005 to 2008. Table 9.5 presents data on the socioeconomic conditions of New Orleans in those three years.

It is clear from Table 9.5 that the socioeconomic conditions in New Orleans in the years leading up to Gustav were similar to those in the last few decades leading up to Katrina as seen in Table 9.2. The majority African American population was unemployed at much higher rates than whites, African Americans earned about half of what whites did and many more African Americans were in poverty than whites.

It appears, then, that the socioeconomic conditions of New Orleans cannot explain the decrease in looting rates after Gustav as compared to Katrina, which brings us to Frailing and Harper's (2012, 2010, 2010a, 2007) second key factor that affects looting in the wake of disaster: guardianship. The notion of guardianship is consistent with Cohen and Felson's (1979) routine activity theory of crime. This theory holds that three things need to converge in time and space for crime to occur, motivated offenders, suitable targets and the absence of capable guardianship. The theory takes motivated offenders as a given and focuses on the suitability of targets and the absence of guardianship as the most important factors in producing crime. Simply put, Cohen and Felson (1979) believe that suitable targets that lack capable guardians are more likely to be victimized by crime.

Table 9.4. Burglary Rates per 100,000 in the Month Before and Month After Four New Orleans Hurricanes

	Burglary rate in the month before	Burglary rate in the month after	Percent increase
Unnamed 1947 hurricane	13.9	27.0	94.2
Hurricane Betsy, 1965	7.8	9.0	15.4
Hurricane Katrina, 2005	82.3	245.9	198.8
Hurricane Gustav, 2008	68	130.4	91.8

Sources: Frailing and Harper, 2012, 2010.

Table 9.5. The Socioeconomic State of New Orleans in the Years Between Katrina and Gustav

	2005 (before Katrina)	2006	2007	2008
Population	437,186	223,388	230,709	311,853
White population	122,262 (28%)	82,107 (37%)	77,973 (34%)	108,598 (35%)
Black population	295,259 (68%)	131,441 (59%)	139,820 (61%)	191,628 (61%)
White unemployment rate	0.86	1.3	0.77	2.9
Black unemployment rate	7.4	5.6	5.7	6.7
White median household income	48,137	56,048	55,103	58,924
Black median household income	23,394	26,639	27,460	27,021
Percent white in poverty	3	3.2	4	4.4
Percent Black in poverty	20.2	17.5	15.2	16.5

Source: Frailing and Harper, 2010.

As seen above, then New Orleans Mayor Nagin alluded to the lawlessness that reigned in the wake of Katrina, with sick, starving and stranded residents alongside predatory looters and desperate drug addicts. As Harper (2012) details, local law enforcement were exclusively engaged in search and rescue because of the extent of Katrina's damage and the number of people who remained in the city. There were simply no local law enforcement personnel to quell the looting that was taking place. The first soldiers arrived in the city on September 2 and by September 5, 16,000 National Guard troops were patrolling the city, some engaged in search and rescue, some engaged in more traditional law enforcement activities, including looting prevention (NOLA, n.d.). Put in terms of routine activity theory, there was a complete absence of capable guardianship in New Orleans for nearly a week after Katrina struck.

Gustav gave New Orleans the opportunity to correct some of the many things that went wrong during Katrina. In advance of Gustav, evacuation buses were placed on standby in the New Orleans area, the State Emergency Operations Center was activated, shelters were prepared across the state and food and water were amassed in staging areas (LBP, 2008). Guardianship was also greatly improved as the threat of Gustav increased. Louisiana Governor Bobby Jindal declared a state of emergency several days before Gustav hit and mobilized the 7,000 member state National Guard; 1,500 additional troops were requested from nearby states. Approximately 500 troops assisted with evacuation in advance of the storm and the day before Gustav made landfall in Louisiana, 1,800 soldiers were patrolling the city. Jindal made the impetus for this early patrol clear—he wanted residents to feel that their homes and their contents were safe and that they should not stay and put themselves in physical danger to protect their belongings (Frailing and Harper, 2012). This form of guardianship helped to reduce looting, as it permitted local law enforcement to make 119 arrests of people entering or leaving properties in the week after Gustav; we believe it also served as a deterrent. For example, two National Guard troops were stationed at each pharmacy and drug store in the city to minimize burglaries of those locations (Frailing and Harper, 2012). We contend that improved guardianship in the wake of Gustav is an important reason burglary rates were lower in the month after that storm than they were in the month after Katrina. Other disaster research bears out the importance of capable guardianship in post-disaster crime prevention (i.e., Cromwell, Dunham, Akers and Lanza-Kaduce, 1995; Zahran, Shelley, Peek and Brody, 2009).

Hurricane Sandy

Sandy's wider effects were easily observed in the days after it made impact. The airports serving New York and New Jersey were shut down and remained closed for two days. More than 12,000 flights were cancelled and the New York subway system sustained the worst damage in its century of existence. Trading was suspended on Wall Street for two days. Three nuclear reactors experienced shut-downs (CNN, 2013). On October 30, an estimated eight million people in 15 states and Washington, D.C. were without power. By November 1, the number without power was approximately 4.8 million, by November 4, it was 2.2 million and by November 7, it was approximately 600,000.[5] The availability of gasoline at gas stations is predicated on electricity, so power outages were the principal reasons for the infamous gas shortages in the wake of Sandy. On November 2, nearly 70 percent of gas stations in metropolitan New York had no gas for sale, down to 38 percent by November 3 (CNN, 2013). The power outages and gas shortages may have been the most devastating effects of Sandy, though there were reports of residents of Staten Island trapped on their roofs by rising waters and needing rescue by helicopter. More than 725 patients in New York's Bellevue Hospital were evacuated on October 31 after extensive damage to the structure was discovered (CNN, 2013).

As seen above, looting was extensive in New Orleans in the wake of Katrina, but what about Sandy? To answer this question, we examined available information on burglaries before and after Sandy in New York, as well as the socioeconomic conditions of the places where looting was reported to police and recorded in Compstat reports, which each police precinct in New York City generates on a weekly basis. We used burglary as a proxy for looting once again for the reasons detailed above.

It is clear from Table 9.6 that socioeconomic conditions in the areas of New York hard hit by Sandy were associated with burglary rates, supporting Frailing and Harper's (2012, 2010, 2010a, 2007) contention on this point. While Staten Island's precincts had the highest percent increase in burglary rates, this is very likely due to the low numbers of burglaries in those precincts in the month preceding Sandy. Compared to the other boroughs, to New York City as a whole and to New York state as a whole, Staten Island had better socioeconomic conditions as determined by many of the same measures used in the previous research detailed above on Hurricane Katrina. Queens and especially Brooklyn had worse socioeconomic conditions—more people in poverty, more people unemployed, a lower household income—compared to Staten Island, New York City as a whole and New York state as a whole and they experienced notable increases in burglary in the month after Sandy as compared to the month before.[6]

A number of anecdotal reports of looting in the wake of Sandy surfaced shortly after the storm. Many of these reports note that in New York City, there was a drop in various types of crime, with the notable exception of burglary. Murders were down 86 percent as compared to the same time the previous year, rapes were down 41–44 percent, robberies were down 21–30 percent, assaults were down 19–31 percent, larceny was down 47–48 percent and car thefts were down 20-24 percent for an overall decrease in crime of 32 percent (Reuters, 2012, 2012a; Parascandola and Jacobs, 2012).[7] However, the overall burglary rate for New York City increased from 3–6 percent in the wake of Sandy, with officers across the city making 54 arrests for burglary in the days following Sandy's landfall (Reuters, 2012a; Parascandola and Jacobs, 2012).[8] A number of areas that were hard hit by the storm experienced even greater increases in burglary. The Rockaway Peninsula area of Queens experienced anywhere from a 350–500 percent increase in burglaries in the week after Sandy as compared to that same week the previous year (DeStefano, 2012; Dejohn, 2012);[9] as seen above, the increase in post-storm burglaries in this part of the city is consistent with our contention that socioeconomic conditions are associated with looting.

Table 9.6. Burglary Rate Change After Sandy and Socioeconomic Conditions for New York City Precincts and Boroughs

Location	Burglary rate per 100K in the month before (# of burglaries)	Burglary rate per 100K in the month after (number of burglaries)	Percent Increase	Population**	Percent Black**	Unemploy- ment rate**	Percent in Poverty**	Median household income**
Brooklyn (60th*)	32.4 (32)	68.9 (68)	112.7%	2,565,635	35.8%	9.4	22.1%	$44,593
Brooklyn (61st*)	12.2 (12)	56.8(56)	365.6%	2,565,635	35.8%	9.4	22.1%	$44,593
Queens (100th*)	26.8(32)	56.8 (68)	111.9%	2,272,771	20.9%	9.0	13.7%	$56,406
Staten Island (122nd*)	6.8(8)	30.6 (36)	350%	470,728	11.6%	6.8	11%	$72,752
Staten Island (123rd*)	3.4 (4)	27.2 (32)	700%	470,728	11.6%	6.8	11%	$72,752
New York City	—	—	—	8,336,697	25.5%	9.5	19.4%	$51,270
New York State	—	—	—	19,570,261	15.9%	8.1	14.5%	$56,971

*These are the precinct numbers; each borough in New York City has a number of police precincts. The burglary rates were determined using the populations for the precincts instead of the boroughs as whole entities.
**These data are for the boroughs as whole entities in 2012 and thus explain the repetition in the table; disaggregation by police precinct proved impossible.
Sources: Berke, 2012, 2012a; U.S. Census, 2012.

Anecdotal reports of looting in New Jersey also surfaced in the wake of Sandy. There were six arrests for looting and 19 reports of burglaries in Atlantic City, just south of where Sandy made landfall, in the days following impact. Police in Ventnor City, just southwest of Atlantic City on New Jersey's Atlantic shore, reported four instances of looting of both residences and businesses (Lemongello, 2012). There were also up to 20 homes looted in Seaside Heights on the New Jersey shore, 13 businesses looted in the inland town of Green Brook, seven burglaries of homes and businesses in Carteret, just across the Hudson River from Staten Island, nine burglaries from homes and cars in the inland town of Glen Ridge and 46 burglaries, including 41 incidents of looting of businesses, in Jersey City, just east of Manhattan across the Hudson River; there are ten other cities in New Jersey that experienced unspecified amounts of looting (Queally, 2012). We can see in Table 9.7 that looting in these cities, again as measured by burglary, likely contributed to an increase in burglary of various classifications for the entire year of 2012. It is also clear from Table 9.7 that the same patterns with regard to socioeconomic conditions and looting in the wake of disaster that were evident in New Orleans after Katrina and in New York after Sandy were evident in New Jersey after Sandy as well; high rates of unemployment and of poverty and low household incomes are associated with increased burglary in the wake of disaster. This is most obvious in the cases of Perth Amboy, Ventnor, Keansburg, Long Branch, Carteret, Jersey City and especially Atlantic City.

We have established the occurrence of looting during the emergency phase of Hurricane Sandy and connected it to the socioeconomic conditions of the impacted areas. But what about guardianship? Remember that formal guardianship was completely absent in New Orleans in the wake of Katrina, but that the city learned the lesson of the importance of guardianship and applied it during Gustav. Similarly, formal guardianship was in place in New York and New Jersey when Sandy made landfall. On October 28, New York governor Andrew Cuomo mobilized the Army and Air National Guard and on October 29, 6,700 National Guard members went on active duty to support the states impacted by Sandy (CNN, 2013). On November 1, both National Guardsmen and New Jersey state troopers, about 600 in total, were deployed to the hardest hit counties in New Jersey to minimize looting in the wake of Sandy (Queally, 2012; Drewniak and Roberts, 2012). In New York, approximately 500 police officers went on patrol in the Rockaway Peninsula area of Queens; many of these officers reported in from other precincts. In addition, police established checkpoints at three bridges leading out of the Rockaway Peninsula area in order to stop the removal of disabled cars (Dejohn, 2012). Thousands of New York City police officers patrolled areas of the city without power in the week after the storm to minimize looting and they monitored open gas stations in order to minimize disputes over limited gasoline (Reuters, 2012a). It is clear that in the case of Hurricane Sandy, officials in what were predicted to be the hardest hit areas took action before the storm made landfall to ensure that sufficient formal guardianship was in place and we believe these actions likely limited the amount of looting that occurred in the wake of that storm. Again,

Table 9.7[10] Socioeconomic Conditions, Looting Incidents and Burglary Increase from 2011 to 2012 in NJ Cities with Reported Looting in the Wake of Sandy (See Note 10 for Sources)

Location	Population	Percent Black	Unemploy-ment rate	% in Poverty	Median household income	No. of Looting Incidents Report-ed (where known)	Increase in Burglary Rate from 2011 to 2012?*
Atlantic City	39,504	38.3	16.7	29.3	$28,526	19	Yes, 272 to 330 (FE)
Beach Haven**	—	—	—	—	—	Unknown	Yes, 4 to 5 (FE), 8 to 12 (UE) and 0 to 2 (AFE)
Carteret	24,062	14.9	12.5	12.7	$63,633	7	Yes, 3 to 10 (AFE)
Glen Ridge	7,594	5%	4.9	2.7	$162,908	9	Yes, 12 to 24 (FE) and 22 to 34 (UE)
Green Brook**	—	—	—	—	—	13	Yes, 20 to 29 (FE)
Jersey City	254,441	25.8	10.3	16.4	$57,520	46	Yes, 723 to 871 (FE) and 73 to 86 (AFE)
Keansburg	10,013	6.6	10.6	15.1	$46,458	Unknown	Yes, 30 to 31 (UE) and 6 to 7 (AFE)
Lavallette**	—	—	—	—	—	Unknown	Yes, 4 to 11 (FE)
Long Branch	30,646	14.2	9.3	14.4	$52,266	Unknown	Yes, 84 to 100 (FE) and 1 to 7 (AFE)
Perth Amboy	51,744	10.5	6.8	19.9	$45,369	7	Yes, 225 to 226 (FE) and 27 to 38 (AFE)
Seaside Heights**	—	—	—	—	—	20	Yes, 23 to 25 (UE) and 0 to 2 (AFE)
Ship Bottom**	—	—	—	—	—	Unknown	Yes, 3 to 4 (FE) and 0 to 1 (AFE)
Surf City**	—	—	—	—	—	Unknown	Yes, 1 to 5 (UE)
Toms River	88,937	2.8	8.6	6.2	$73,796	Unknown	Yes, 285 to 304 (FE), 222 to 247 (UE) and 82 to 89 (AFE)
Ventnor	10,615	4.3	8.6	11.3	$53,918	4	Yes, 26 to 27 (FE)
New Jersey State	8,864,590	13.7	8.7	9.4	$71,180	—	—

what looting did occur can be explained by the socioeconomic conditions of the areas in which it occurred.

RECOVERY PHASE

As mentioned, the recovery phase is "the period, which begins roughly as the emergency crisis passes and during which the longer-term activities of reconstruction, rehabilitation and recovery proceed" (Killian, 2002, p. 51). Here we consider the recovery phase of Hurricanes Katrina and Sandy in turn.

Hurricane Katrina

At the time of this writing, it has been eight years since Hurricane Katrina devastated New Orleans and the wider Gulf Coast and the recovery process has been closely tracked across that time. As seen above in Table 9.5, the population of New Orleans in 2006, a year after Katrina made landfall, was about half of what it was in 2005. At that time, flooded homes were still being demolished and with less housing in the city, rents were on the rise. The number of temporary trailer homes distributed by the Federal Emergency Management Agency (FEMA) had risen to 114,000, with the greatest increase between February and August of 2006. Only half of the buses and streetcars were operating. Just 41 percent of homes with gas service and 60 percent of homes with electricity service prior to Katrina had those services restored one year later. With the loss of 190,000 workers, the labor force remained 30 percent smaller than it was when Katrina hit and unemployment was higher than before the storm. Less than a third of schools and only 11 hospitals had reopened. However, tourism in the city had rebounded to 80 percent of pre-Katrina levels, though only a third of restaurants had reopened (Liu, Fellowes and Mabanta, 2006).

By 2010, five years after Katrina's impact, New Orleans had sustained the impact of not just Katrina, but also the Great Recession of 2008 and the BP oil spill of early 2010. Nevertheless, New Orleans had recovered 78 percent of its pre-storm population and 85 percent of its pre-storm jobs by 2010. There was a four percent increase in household income and a 14 percent increase in wages, which coincided with an increase in knowledge-based (rather than low wage food and hotel service-based) jobs, such as those in higher education, insurance and legal services. Twenty three percent of New Orleanians were in poverty in 2010, higher than the national average of 13 percent, but the lowest in the city since 1979. Fifty nine percent of public schools met state standards in 2010, up from 28 percent in 2003. The number of vacant and blighted homes had dropped 35 percent by 2010. A master plan to streamline and improve recovery in the city had been approved by residents, as had a master plan for coastal and wetland restoration. All of these positive changes are rooted in New Orleans' resiliency (Liu and Plyer, 2010).

However, New Orleans continued to struggle in some areas five years after Katrina. The economy remained sluggish and sometimes stagnant because of its heavy reliance on tourism, oil and gas and shipping industries as economic drivers.

As detailed elsewhere (Frailing and Harper, 2010a; Frailing and Harper, 2010), the exodus of high wage oil and gas as well as shipping jobs left a static economy built mostly around low wage food and hotel service jobs. Though there were increases in wages and household income between 2005 and 2010, the majority African American population did not enjoy these increases to the degree that whites did; African Americans' household incomes were 44 percent lower than those of whites. The cost of owning and especially renting a home was high, with New Orleanians spending upwards of 35 percent of their pre-tax income on housing. And by 2010, both violent and property crime were on the rise in New Orleans (Liu and Plyer, 2010).

By 2013, as New Orleans continued its recovery from Katrina, the Great Recession and the BP oil spill, the city had recovered 84 percent of its pre-storm population and had one percent more jobs than it did in 2008; the United States as a whole experienced a two percent loss in jobs during that time. The city continued its efforts to diversify its economy with more knowledge-based jobs[11] and productivity was 14 percent higher than the national average, but the average wage of $47,295 was six percent lower than the national average and the median household income of $44,044 was 13 percent lower than the national average. Importantly, the median household income for the majority African American population, $28,265, remained much lower than both the city and national averages and just 53 percent of working age African American men were employed. Violent and property crime were down in 2011 as compared to pre-Katrina levels, but were still much higher than national averages. Similarly, the jail incarceration rate declined from 1,251 per 100,000 in 2004 to 912 per 100,000 in 2011, but this rate was still about four times higher than the national rate. Fifty four percent of New Orleanians were still spending more than 35 percent of their pre-tax income on housing in 2011, up from 43 percent in 2004. Over $10 million was spent on youth recreational programs, which increased in number by 18 percent between 2004 and 2011. By 2013, 68 percent of New Orleans' public school students were attending schools that met state standards, up from 30 percent of students before Katrina (Plyer, Ortiz, Horwitz and Hobor, 2013). The recovery from Katrina and subsequent disasters in New Orleans has been slow, uneven and imperfect, but there is reason for optimism for the coming years.

Hurricane Sandy

At the time of this writing, it has been less than a year since Hurricane Sandy struck New York, New Jersey and the wider northeastern coast. The recovery to date appears to be speedier and more thorough than the recovery from Katrina was at the one year anniversary of that storm. In fact, progress from the emergency to the recovery phase after Sandy was quite quick by some measures. By October 31, two days after the storm made impact, the New York Stock Exchange had reopened, local airports had resumed partial service and many public schools in New York were able to reopen on November 5 (CNN, 2013). Electricity was back in lower Manhattan within a week of Sandy's landfall and most buildings with basement flooding were reopened and operational or livable by January of 2013. In Staten Island, tons of debris were cleared in the first three months after the storm and most buildings that sustained damage were made livable or operational again (NYT, 2013). President Obama and New Jersey Governor Chris Christie presided over a ceremony reopening Jersey Shore attractions six months after Sandy, just in time for the Memorial Day weekend; this was an important milestone for both residents' morale and the $40 billion tourist industry (Gonzalez, 2013).

However, there are indications of a slower paced, more uneven recovery from Sandy. In Staten Island, approximately 300 buildings were still without electricity and 200 were rendered uninhabitable by damage a full three months after Sandy made landfall. The population of Long Beach, NY was still down by 40 percent in January of 2013, where many homes and businesses were still waterlogged and moldy. New York City's public housing residents were still dealing with unpleasant and potentially hazardous effects of Sandy three months after its impact, including generator-powered boilers that only sporadically produced hot water, infestation by various types of vermin and mold from flooding of lower floors; it bears mentioning that many public housing residents did not have the means to evacuate and used what little money they had to replace food that spoiled during the power outage (NYT, 2013). Six months after Sandy made landfall, many New Jersey residents were still in the process of rebuilding their storm-damaged homes (Gonzalez, 2013). Local officials across New York and New Jersey acknowledged that a full recovery from the storm would likely take over a year (O'Regan, 2013); remember that New Orleans is still recovering from Katrina eight years after it made landfall and the deputy mayor of the city, Cedric Grant, estimates a full recovery will not be complete until 2018 (O'Regan, 2013).

There are likely two important reasons for the relative speed and thoroughness of the recovery from Sandy, the working relationship among federal, state and local levels of government and FEMA's response to the disaster. The first reason, the fruitful working relationship across levels of government, was well illustrated by Republican Chris Christie's high praise for Democrat President Obama's response to Sandy (Newton-Small, 2012). President Obama showed real commitment to recovery when he created the Hurricane Sandy Rebuilding Taskforce in December of 2012. The Task Force was designed to help homeowners and businesses rebuild quickly, to strengthen local economies and importantly, to ensure even better disaster preparation, mitigation and response capabilities for the future. In other words, the plan is focused on short term recovery and long term resilience[12] (Puentes and Katz, 2013; Jacobs, 2013). The second reason, FEMA's response to the disaster, stands in the starkest contrast to the Agency's response to Katrina. Due in large part to the nepotism-driven appointment of the woefully inexperienced Michael Brown as FEMA director before Katrina, the federal response to that storm was horribly botched, both in the short and longer term.[13] The FEMA response to Sandy was coordinated and effective, due in large part to Agency director Craig Fugate and his years of experience with emergency response and management. FEMA's response to Sandy earned praise from Governor Christie as well as from those directly impacted by the storm (Newton-Small, 2012; Simon, 2012). By April of 2013, FEMA had paid out $3.3 billion to National Flood Insurance Program policyholders. It had also approved $821 million in housing assistance to individuals, nearly $1.4 billion for Small Business Administration (SBA) disaster loans to individuals and businesses and nearly $847 million in public assistance grants to communities and public service agencies, all this in New York alone (FEMA, 2013).

CONCLUSION

In this chapter, we have compared Hurricanes Katrina and Sandy using Killian's (2002) phase model as an organizing framework. We identified the similarities and differences between these storms, we described and provided evidence from New Orleans to support our contention that poor socioeconomic conditions and the absence of capable guardianship facilitate looting in the wake of disaster and we found support for these contentions upon an examination of data from those places impacted by Hurricane Sandy.

We close with two points, the first of which is the need for more research on crime and disaster. This scholarship is evolving (e.g., see Harper and Frailing, 2012a as a definitive source), but more in depth investigations into American and international disasters of various types, longitudinal examinations of those areas hit by disasters and explorations of the factors that facilitate other types of crime in the wake of disasters is crucial to better understand how these phenomena interact and what we can do to prevent criminal activity in the wake of disaster.

The second point is the applicability of these findings. This scholarship in this chapter is interesting in and of itself, but it also has obvious policy implications—as Frailing (2007) has pointed out and we reiterate here, potential looting must be part of disaster response planning. Increased criminal penalties and prosecution after the fact may have some utility for punishing those who would take advantage of widespread physical, economic and social devastation,[14] but they do little to stop looting in the wake of disasters. Communities must build capable guardianship into their disaster response plans and do what they can now to ameliorate poor socioeconomic conditions. To fail on this is to practically guarantee revictimization of those hardest hit by disasters.

NOTES

1. As mentioned, Hurricane Gustav will also be discussed in the context of the emergency phase, as it reveals how lessons learned from Katrina were taken into account in New Orleans when the city was visited with its next hurricane.
2. The first author evacuated New Orleans in the early morning hours of Sunday, August 28 in advance of the order from the mayor. She packed enough clothes, toiletries and various supplies for four days away from the city and proceeded with a friend to another friend's house in Birmingham, AL. The highways were set up for contraflow, with both sides headed in the same direction and on the way, the first author and her friend joked about receiving an unexpected hurricane vacation (or "hurrication") thanks

to Katrina. Ultimately, they would not return to the city until late September during the earliest part of the recovery phase.

3. Adding to the misery of those trapped in New Orleans in the day after Katrina was the weather. Of course, Katrina knocked out all power in the city, which meant no climate control was available for those indoors. Typical late August and early September weather in New Orleans is hot and humid, with temperatures in the 90s and dew points in the 60–70 percent range.

4. The second author evacuated to Birmingham, AL in advance of Gustav. Because of the hundreds of thousands of other evacuees, what is normally a five hour drive turned into a 19 hour, bumper to bumper drive.

5. Note that the many without power in the area impacted by Sandy were experiencing temperatures in the 1940s and 1950s.

6. Astute readers may be wondering why we did not take a longitudinal look at New York City to better inform on socioeconomic conditions over time, similar to what we did with New Orleans. We determined that doing so made little sense in the case of New York, as the city has not been impacted repeatedly by the same type of disaster as New Orleans has.

7. These accounts report slightly different drops in these varieties of crime, hence the ranges of percent drops for most of these crimes.

8. The range of percent increase in burglary is again due to slightly different reports. A third source reports an 11 percent increase in burglary across the city in the week after Sandy; for astute readers, these discrepancies should highlight the inherent difficulty in accurately measuring crime in the wake of disaster.

9. Dejohn (2012) reports that a small part of the increase in burglaries reported to the police may be due to people filing false reports, wittingly or unwittingly, for items that were destroyed by the storm and not stolen.

10. Table 9.7 Notes. * FE=forcible entry, UE=unlawful entry and AFE=attempted forcible entry. ** No Census data available for these cities. Sources: NJSP, 2012; U.S. Census, 2012a.

11. See page 17 of Plyer, Ortiz, Horwitz and Hobor (2013) for a graphic depiction of the dominance of tourism industry jobs in the New Orleans economy.

12. For an enlightening discussion of the importance of resilience in recovering from disaster, see Harper and Frailing (2012).

13. The first author's husband had myriad problems with FEMA in the wake of Katrina, not the least of which was Agency staff confusing his and his father's applications for assistance. Suspecting fraud, FEMA denied both applications despite the fact that both their homes had flooded.

14. See Vargas (2013) and Simerman (2013) on the ineffectiveness of criminal prosecutions for looting.

REFERENCES

Alpert, B. (2013). Reid says Hurricane Katrina was "nothing in comparison" to Sandy. *Times Picayune*. Retrieved from: http://www.nola.com/politics/index.ssf/ 2013/01/ reid_says_hurricane_katrina_wa.html.

Barton, A. (1969). Communities in disaster: A sociological analysis of collective stress situations. Garden City, NJ: Doubleday.

Berke, N. (2012). Contrary to initial reports, looting stats skyrocketed in communities hit by Sandy. Sheepshead Bites. Retrieved from: http://www.sheepsheadbites.

com/2012/11/despite-initial-reports-looting-stats-skyrocketed-in-communities-hit-by-sandy/.

Berke, N. (2012a). 61st precinct crime statistics: 10/29-11/4/12. Sheepshead Bites. Retrieved from: http://www.sheepsheadbites.com/2012/11/61st-precinct-crime-statistics-1029-1142012/.

Carr, L. (1932). Disaster and the sequence-pattern concept of social change. *American Journal of Sociology*, 38, 207–218.

CBS. (2012). Christie declares state of emergency; Orders evacuations in some parts of N.J. CBS New York. Retrieved from: http://newyork.cbslocal.com/2012/10/27/evacuations-begin-in-some-areas-of-new-jersey-for-hurricane-sandy/.

CNN. (2005). Mayor to feds: "Get off your asses." CNN. Retrieved from: http://edition.cnn.com/2005/US/09/02/nagin.transcript/.

CNN. (2013). Hurricane Sandy fast facts. CNN. Retrieved from: http:// www.cnn.com /2013/07/13/world/americas/hurricane-sandy-fast-facts/ index.html?iref=allsearch.

Cohen, L. and M. Felson. (1979). Social change and crime rate trends: A routine activity approach. American Sociological Review, 44, 588–608.

Cromwell, P. R. Dunham, R. Akers and L. Lanza-Kaduce. (1995). Routine activities and social control in the aftermath of a natural catastrophe. European Journal on Criminal Policy and Research, 3, 56–69.

Dejohn, I. (2012). Burglary is crime du jour post-Sandy, stats show. New York Daily News. Retrieved from: http://www.nydailynews.com/new-york/queens/spike-burglaries-rockaways-article-1.1205331.

DeStefano, A. (2012). Rockaways burglary reports surge 500 percent as Hurricane Sandy victims return to homes. Huffington Post. Retrieved from: http://www.huffingtonpost.com/2013/01/29/rockaways-burglary-surge-500-percent-hurricane-sandy-_n_2572167.html.

Drabek, T. (1986). Human system responses to disaster. New York, NY: Springer-Verlag.

Drewinak, M. and K. Roberts. (2012). New Jersey State Troopers deployed at shore to provide enhanced security in the wake of storm. State of New Jersey Office of the Governor. Retrieved from: http://www.nj.gov/oag/newsreleases12/pr20121101b.pdf.

Drye, W. (2005). Hurricane Katrina: The essential timeline. National Geographic. Retrieved from: http://news.nationalgeographic.com/news/2005/09/0914_050914_katrina_timeline_2.html.

———. (2008). Hurricane Gustav: The essential timeline. National Geographic. Retrieved from: http://news.nationalgeographic.com/news/2008/09/080902-gustav-timeline.html.

———. (2012). A timeline of Hurricane Sandy's path of destruction. National Geographic. Retrieved from: http://newswatch.nationalgeographic.com/2012/11/02/a-timeline-of-hurricane-sandys-path-of-destruction/.

Dynes, R. and E. Quarantelli. (1968). What looting in civil disturbances really means. Trans-action, 5, 71–73.

Erickson, K. (1994). A new species of trouble: Explorations in disaster, trauma, and community. New York, NY: W.W. Norton.

FEMA. (2013). Disaster assistance to New York survivors of Hurricane Sandy. Federal Emergency Management Agency. Retrieved from: http://www.fema.gov/news-release/2013/04/19/new-york-recovery-hurricane-sandy-numbers.

Fischetti, M. (2012). Sandy versus Katrina, and Irene: Monster hurricanes by the numbers. Scientific American. Retrieved from: http://www.scientificamerican.com/article.cfm?id=sandy-vs-katrina-and-irene.

Frailing, K. (2007). The myth of a disaster myth: Potential looting should be part of disaster plans. Natural Hazards Observer, 31, 3–4.

―――― and D. W. Harper. (2007). Crime and hurricanes in New Orleans. In D. Brunsma, D. Overfelt and J. Picou (Eds.), The sociology of Katrina: Perspectives on a modern catastrophe, pp. 51–68. Lanham, MD: Rowman & Littlefield.

――――. (2010). Crime and hurricanes in New Orleans. In D. Brunsma, D. Overfelt and J. Picou (Eds.), The sociology of Katrina: Perspectives on a modern catastrophe, 2nd edition, pp. 55–76. Lanham, MD: Rowman & Littlefield.

――――. (2010a). School kids and oil rigs: Two more pieces of the post-Katrina puzzle in New Orleans. *American Journal of Economics and Sociology*, 69, 1–19.

――――. (2012). Fear, prosocial behavior and looting: The Katrina experience. In D. W. Harper and K. Frailing (Eds.), Crime and Criminal Justice in Disaster, second edition, pp. 101–121. Durham, NC: Carolina Academic Press.

Freudenbrug, W. (2000). The "risk society" reconsidered: Recreancy, the division of labor, and risks to the social fabric. In M. Cohen (Ed.), Risk in the modern age: Social theory, science and environmental decision-making, pp. 107–122. New York, NY: St. Martin's Press.

Gill, D., J. Picou and L. Ritchie. (2012). When the disaster is a crime: Legal issues and the Exxon Valdez oil spill. In D. W. Harper and K. Frailing (Eds.), Crime and Criminal Justice in Disaster, second edition, pp. 73–96. Durham, NC: Carolina Academic Press.

Gonzalez, J. (2013). President Obama, Chris Christie address Sandy recovery. WJLA. Retrieved from: http://www.wjla.com/articles/2013/05/president-obama-chris-christie-address-hurricane-sandy-recovery-89324.html.

Harper, D. W. (2012). The New Orleans Police Department during and after Hurricane Katrina—Lessons learned. In D. W. Harper and K. Frailing (Eds.), Crime and Criminal Justice in Disaster, second edition, pp. 285–312. Durham, NC: Carolina Academic Press.

―――― and K. Frailing. (2012). The heavy lifting—Local emergency response planning and preparedness: An interview with Colonel Terry Ebbert. In D. W. Harper and K. Frailing (Eds.), Crime and Criminal Justice in Disaster, second edition, pp. 313–338. Durham, NC: Carolina Academic Press.

―――― (Eds.). (2012a). Crime and Criminal Justice in Disaster, second edition. Durham, NC: Carolina Academic Press.

Jacobs, A. (2013). Hurricane Sandy Rebuilding Task Force releases rebuilding strategy. U.S. Department of Housing and Urban Development. Retrieved from: http://portal.hud.gov/hudportal/HUD?src=/press/press_releases_media_advisories/2013/HUDNo.13–125.

Killian, L. (2002). An introduction to methodological problems of field studies in disasters. In R. A. Stallings (Ed.), Methods of Disaster Research. Bloomington, IN: Xlibris Corporation, 49–93.

Lemongello, S. (2012). Atlantic City, Ventnor police report looting; Margate mayor says there was none there. Press of Atlantic City. Retrieved from: http://www.presso fatlanticcity.com/news/press/atlantic/atlantic-city-ventnor-police-report-looting-margate-mayor-says-there/article_5ace74fc-23c2-11e2-8c12-001a4bcf887a.html.

Liu, A., M. Fellowes and M. Mabanta. (2006). Special edition of the Katrina index: A one-year review of key indicators of recovery in post-storm New Orleans. Brookings Institution. Retrieved from: http://www.brookings.edu/metro/pubs/2006_katrina index.pdf.

Liu, A. and A. Plyer. (2010). The New Orleans index at five: An overview of greater New Orleans, from recovery to transformation. Brookings Institution. Retrieved from: http://www.brookings.edu/~/media/research/files/reports/2011/8/29%20new%20orle ans%20index/08neworleansindex.pdf.

LPB. (2008). Hurricane Gustav: Aftermath and recovery. Louisiana Public Broadcasting. Retrieved from: http://beta.lpb.org/index.php/publicsquare/topic/09_08_-_hurricane _gustav_aftermath_and_recovery/.

Neal, D. (1997). Reconsidering the phases of disasters. *International Journal of Mass Emergencies and Disasters*, 15, 239–264.

Newman, A. (2012). Hurricane Sandy vs. Hurricane Katrina. New York Times. Retrieved from: http://cityroom.blogs.nytimes.com/2012/11/27/hurricane-sandy-vs-hurricane-katrina/.

Newton-Small, J. (2012). As government reacts to Sandy, lessons from Katrina and other natural disasters. *Time*. Retrieved from: http://swampland.time.com/2012/10/30/lessons-from-katrina-and-other-natural-disasters/.

NGA (National Governors Association). (1979). Emergency preparedness project final report. Washington, D.C.: U.S. Government Printing Office.

NJSP. (2013). State of New Jersey Department of Law and Public Safety Division of State Police Uniform Crime Reporting Unit Crime Trend Feedback. Retrieved from: http://www.njsp.org/info/pdf/ucr/current/081613_ucr_2012stats.pdf.

NOLA. (n.d.). The Katrina files: Timeline. Times Picayune. Retrieved from: http://www.nola.com/katrina/timeline/

NYT. (2013). Recovery remains spotty three months after hurricane. *New York Times*. Retrieved from: http://www.nytimes.com/2013/01/22/nyregion/recovery-remains-spotty-3-months-after-hurricane-sandy.html?pagewanted=all&_r=0

O'Regan, D. (2013). Looking to Katrina for perspective on Sandy recovery timeline. Long Island Press. Retrieved from: http://www.longislandpress.com/2013/01/02/looking-to-katrina-for-perspective-on-sandy-recovery-timeline/.

Parascandola, R. and S. Jacobs. (2012). Hurricane Sandy drives down major crimes in New York City—but burglaries surge. *New York Daily News*. Retrieved from: http://www.nydailynews.com/new-york/burglaries-surge-hurricane-sandy-article-1.1196245.

Peltz, J. (2012). NYC evacuations begin over Hurricane Sandy; Public schools closed. Huffington Post. Retrieved from: http://www.huffingtonpost.com/2012/10/28/nyc-evacuations-hurricane-sandy-public-schools-closed_n_2034613.html.

Plyer, A., E. Ortiz, B. Horwitz and G. Hobor. (2013). The New Orleans index at eight: Measuring greater New Orleans' progress toward prosperity. Greater New Orleans Community Data Center. Retrieved from: https://gnocdc.s3.amazonaws.com/reports /GNOCDC_NewOrleansIndexAtEight.pdf.

Puentes, R. and B. Katz. (2013). A statement on the Hurricane Sandy Rebuilding Task Force Report. Brookings Institution. Retrieved from: http://www.brookings.edu/blogs/the-avenue/posts/2013/08/19-hurricane-sandy-puentes-katz.

Quarantelli, E. (1994). Looting and antisocial behavior in disasters. University of Delaware Disaster Research Center Preliminary Paper #205.

———. (2007). The myth and the realities: Keeping the "looting" myth in perspective. *Natural Hazards Observer*, 31, 2–3.

———. (2008). Conventional beliefs and counterintuitive realities. *Social Research: An International Quarterly of the Social Sciences*, 75, 873–904.

———. and R. Dynes. (1970). Property norms and looting: Their patterns in community crises. Phylon: The Atlanta University Review of Race and Culture, 31, 168–182.

Queally, J. (2012). Hurricane Sandy looters took from those who lost everything. *New Jersey Star-Ledger*. Retrieved from: http://www.nj.com/news/index.ssf/2012/11/hurricane_sandy_looters_took_f.html.

Reuters. (2012). New York City crime down by a third in wake of superstorm. Reuters. Retrieved from: http://www.reuters.com/article/2012/11/04/us-storm-sandy-newyork-crime-idUSBRE8A301T20121104.

———. (2012a). New York City crime is down after Sandy, but worry remains. Reuters. Retrieved from: http://www.reuters.com/article/2012/11/06/us-storm-sandy-crime-idUSBRE8A504W20121106.

Sale, K. (1991). Bioregionalism. In A. Dobson (Ed.), The green reader: Essays toward a sustainable society, pp. 77–83. San Francisco, CA: Mercury House, Inc.

Showalter, P. and M. Myers. (1994). Natural disasters in the United States as release agents of oil, chemical, or radiological materials between 1980–1989: Analysis and Recommendations. *Risk Analysis*, 14, 169–182.

Simerman, J. (2013). Looting prosecutions yield mixed results. The Advocate, pp. 1A, 4A.

Simon, S. (2012). Lessons from Katrina boost FEMA's Sandy response. National Public Radio. Retrieved from: http://www.npr.org/2012/11/03/164224394/lessons-from-katrina-boost-femas-sandy-response.

Thornton, W. and L. Voigt. (2012). Disaster phase analysis and crime facilitation patterns. In D. W. Harper and K. Frailing (Eds.), Crime and Criminal Justice in Disaster, 2nd edition, pp. 37–72. Durham, NC: Carolina Academic Press.

———. (2012a). Disaster rape: Vulnerability of women to sexual assaults during Hurricane Katrina. In D. W. Harper and K. Frailing (Eds.), Crime and Criminal Justice in Disaster, 2nd edition, pp. 123–156. Durham, NC: Carolina Academic Press.

Time. (2005). Hurricane Katrina: The storm that changed America. New York, NY: Time Books.

U.S. Census. (2012). New York State and County Quick Facts. Retrieved from: http://quickfacts.census.gov/qfd/states/36000.html.

U.S. Census. (2012a). New Jersey State and County Quick Facts. Retrieved from: http://quickfacts.census.gov/qfd/states/34000.html.

Vargas, R. (2013). Isaac looting cases hitting courts. *Times-Picayune*, pp A1, A11.

Wallace, T. and J. Kaleem. Comparing disasters: Sandy vs. Katrina. Huffington Post. Retrieved from: http://www.huffingtonpost.com/2012/11/04/hurricane-sandy-vs-katrina-infographic_n_2072432.html.

Zahran, S. T. Shelly, L. Peek and S. Brody. (2009). Natural disasters and social order: Modeling crime outcomes in Florida. *International Journal of Mass Emergencies and Disasters*, 27, 26–52.

EDITORS

LISA A. EARGLE

Lisa A. Eargle, PhD, is a Board of Trustees' Research Scholar, Professor and Chair of the Department of Sociology at Francis Marion University (FMU). Dr. Eargle is also the co-coordinator of the Criminal Justice Program at FMU. Her research focuses on a variety of issues, including development, environment, disasters, and social justice. She is the co-editor of the volume, *Black Beaches and Bayous: The BP Deepwater Horizon Oil Spill Disaster* (University Press of America, 2012), *Gun Violence in American Society: Crime, Justice and Public Policy, and Terrorism Inside America's Borders* (forthcoming, University Press of America).

Dr. Eargle has numerous book chapter and journal article publications. These include Hurricane Katrina's impacts on education (in the first and second editions of The Sociology of Katrina), "The Impact of Culture on Crime" (in the *Journal of Race, Class and Gender*), "Traditional Bullying to Cyber Bullying: A Criminal Pathology" (in *Alleviating Bullying: Conquering the Challenge of Violent Crimes*), "Corporate Deviance" (in The Encyclopedia of Social Deviance), "The Roles of Family Structure, Family Interactions and Gender on African American Delinquency" (in the *Journal of Education and Social Justice*), "Economic Reforms, Values, and Politics as Determinants of Cross-National Sex Trafficking Network in Developing Countries: A Theoretical Overture Using Global Commodity Chain Approach" (in the *Journal of Race, Class And Gender*), and "Incorporating Peace Education Strategies in University Classroom: Approaches Used in Sociology Courses" (in *Youth Violence in American Schools: How It Can Be Alleviated*).

She has conducted workshops at professional conferences on integrating environmental issues into the Sociology curriculum (for the American Sociological Association and South Carolina Sociological Association), using Geographic Information Systems in teaching and research (South Carolina Sociological Association), and approaches to teaching theory to undergraduates (American Sociological Association and Southern Sociological Society). Papers presented at professional conferences include "Disaster Preparedness Planning for Disabled

176

Populations: The View through Marketing's Lens" (for Marketing and Public Policy), "Applying the Disaster Resilience of Place Model to the BP Oil Spill" (for Mid-South Sociological Association), "The Influence of Infrastructure Type and Prevalence on Crime Rates" (for Southern Criminal Justice Association), "Abolishing or Limiting Parole: Potential Benefits and Costs" (for South Carolina Sociological Association) and "Arizona SB 1070 'Paper Please' And Similar Laws' Impact on Whites in the U.S." (American Society of Criminology). Dr. Eargle teaches a variety of sociology and criminal justice courses, including Population in Society, Environmental Sociology, Urban Sociology, Crime & Organizations, Alcohol, Drugs & Society, and Social Problems. Dr. Eargle has also created a course on Disasters and Extreme Events that she will teach in the Spring 2016 semester.

ASHRAF M. ESMAIL

Ashraf M. Esmail, PhD, is the Coordinator of the Criminal Justice Program at Dillard University in New Orleans, LA. His research interests include criminology, social problems, deviance, urban, multicultural, and peace education, family, cultural diversity, and political sociology. He has co-edited numerous volumes, including the books *Youth Violence in American Schools: How Can it Be Alleviated* and *Black Beaches and Bayous: The BP Deepwater Horizon Oil Spill Disaster, Alleviating Bullying: Conquering the Challenge of Violent Crimes and Qualitative Study of Job Satisfaction Experiences of Forensic Scientists*. Dr. Esmail recently published articles entitled A Brief History of Social Justice Among Juveniles and Teaching Social Justice to Urban Students, Cross-National Sex Trafficking Network in Developing Countries: A Theoretical Overture Using Global Commodity Chain Approach, Learning to Change: Does Life Skills Training Lead to Reduced Incident Reports Among Inmates in a Medium/Minimum Correctional Facility and The Roles of Family Structure, Family Interactions and Gender on African American Delinquency, and Impact of Culture on Crime. Dr. Esmail has also examined the effects of race, gender, and victim blame on date rape and examined juvenile homicide and perceptions of violence in Chicago.

He currently serves as the senior editor of the *Journal of Education and Social Justice*. He served as the conference chair for the National Association of Multi-cultural Education 22nd Annual International Conference in 2012. He also was elected as President of the National Association for Peace Education in 2010. He is the Proposal Review Lead for the National Association for Multicultural Education and serves on the Board of Directors for the National Association for Peace Education.

CONTRIBUTORS

NWAMAKA A. ANAZA

Nwamaka A. Anaza, PhD, is an Assistant Professor of Marketing in the School of Business at Francis Marion University. She received her PhD in Consumer Behavior from Purdue University, West Lafayette, Indiana and her MBA from Southern Illinois University Carbondale. Her areas of expertise include service marketing management, social marketing management, and sales management. As part of her research, she focuses on the development and management of disaster preparedness plans for the disabled population. She is a frequent contributing author for a number of leading academic journals including the *Journal of Service Management, Psychology & Marketing*, among many others. She has received numerous research awards and has been invited as a visiting professor at respected institutions around the world, including Wuhan University. She remains active in different professional associations including the American Marketing Association, Society of Marketing Advances, Academy of Marketing Science, and International Academy of African Business and Development.

ELIZABETH BORLAND

Elizabeth Borland, PhD, is an Associate Professor of Sociology at The College of New Jersey. Her scholarly and teaching interests include social movements, gender, organizations, and applied sociology. She has published work on women's movements in Argentina in Mobilization, Feminist Studies, Gender and Society, Research in Social Movements, Conflicts and Change, and several edited volumes.

KELLY FRAILING

Kelly Frailing, PhD, is an Assistant Professor of Criminal Justice at Texas A&M International University in Laredo, TX. Her primary research interests are offenders with mental illness and disaster crime. Her research has appeared in the *International Journal of Forensic Mental Health, International Journal of Law and Psychiatry, American Journal of Economics and Sociology, Deviant Behavior, CIP Report* and *Natural Hazards Observer*. In addition, she is the co-author/co-editor of three books with Dee Wood Harper, most recently the second edition of *Crime and Criminal Justice in Disasters and Fundamentals of Criminology: New Dimensions*.

DANA GREENE

Dana Greene, PhD, is a Research Fellow in the Institute for the Environment at the University of North Carolina, Chapel Hill. Dr. Greene earned her masters and doctorate degrees in Sociology from the University of Michigan, Ann Arbor. She also earned a certificate in Core Concepts in Public Health from the Gillings School of Public Health at the University of North Carolina, Chapel Hill. Dr. Greene is an active member of several professional organizations including the American Sociological Association, National Hazard Mitigation Association, Southern Sociological Society, Midwest Sociological Society, Eastern Sociological Society, among many others.

In the "disaster world," Dr. Greene often volunteers with relief agencies to assist with rebuilding post-disaster, while concurrently engaging in field work to learn more about the social, political, and economic impacts of disasters on vulnerable populations. An accomplished teacher-scholar, Dr. Greene enjoys integrating her research interests in the sociology of disasters into her teaching. She is a frequent peer reviewer for academic journals, and is presently working on two book contracts (in addition to her other academic journal article writing).

TANYA GULLIVER-GARCIA

Tanya Gulliver-Garcia is the Research Coordinator at the Canadian Observatory on Homelessness/Homeless Hub. She is also contract faculty teaching Environmental Disasters and a PhD student studying Community Resiliency and Recovery After Catastrophic Disasters, both in the Faculty of Environmental Studies at York University. Her Masters work developed North America's first risk-based heat registry for low-income and homeless people. Tanya is a trained disaster responder both in Canada and the US with a large international, disaster relief organization. She splits her time between Toronto and New Orleans.

DEE WOOD HARPER, JR.

Dee Wood Harper, Jr., PhD, is Professor Emeritus of Sociology and Criminology at Loyola University New Orleans. His scholarly research, spanning over 45 years, has been wide ranging, but focuses currently on violence, violent crime and disaster crime. His research has appeared in the *American Journal of Sociology*,

Sociological Spectrum, Annals of Tourism Research, International Journal of Law and Information Technology, Artificial Intelligence and Applications, Criminal Justice Review, American Journal of Criminal Justice, Homicide Studies, Deviant Behavior and the *American Journal of Economics and Sociology*. In addition, he is author, co-author/editor of five books, most recently (with Kelly Frailing) *Fundamentals of Criminology: New Dimensions*.

JIMMY D. MCCAMEY, JR.

Jimmy D. McCamey, Jr., PhD, Associate Professor of Graduate Counseling Program at Fort Valley State University, has twenty years of experience in clinical practice, mental health counseling, clinical social work services, assessment and treatment of children, adolescents and adults. He has over a decade of leadership and management experience in residential treatment, psychiatric and community base treatment facilities; and taught courses at both the undergraduate and graduate levels. A former faculty member at the University of North Carolina at Wilmington, Dr. McCamey was a part of developing and implementing a new CSWE approved MSW program. As a License Clinical Social Worker (LCSW), License Professional Counselor (LPC) and a Diplomate in Clinical Social Work (DCSW), he has supervised over 50 MSW and MS clinicians for Georgia state licensure for LCSW or LPC.

Dr. McCamey's published manuscripts focused on issues such as adolescent sexual offenders, diversity, and African-American Males. His research interests include mental health assessment, adolescent sexual offenders, adult mental illness, , criminal justice, poverty and African-American male issues. He received his PhD in Social Work from Clark Atlanta University.

KOMANDURI S. MURTY

Komanduri S. Murty, PhD, Professor and Coordinator of Sociology Program at Fort Valley State University, is the author or co-author of five books including the recent *Poison Ivy: A Social Psychological Typology of Deviant Professors and Administrators in Higher Education* (2010); more than 60 book chapters and articles which have appeared in numerous books and journals, including the *Crime and Criminal Justice in Disaster, Black America: A State-by-State Encyclopedia, Encyclopedia of American Prisons, Encyclopedia of Anthropology, Encyclopedia of Great Black Migration, Intimate Violence; Journal of Race, Gender and Class; Criminal Justice Review, The Status of Black Atlanta, Studies in Symbolic Interactionism, Deviant Behavior, International Journal of Comparative and Applied Criminal Justice, Journal of Police Science Administration, Journal of Social and Behavioral Sciences*, and *Victimology*, etc.; and, presented more than 90 articles at professional meetings—nationally and internationally. He served as professor and chairman of criminal justice and sociology for 25 years at Clark Atlanta University, where he received the 2005 Aldridge McMillan award for Outstanding Overall Achievement. He was the Visiting Fellow of the United Negro

College Fund Special Programs (UNCFSP) in 2005; and the University Grants Commission (UGC) Visiting Professor of Criminal Justice at Andhra University, India, in 1996, where he earned his M.A. in Sociology in 1977. He also holds a two-year Diploma in Population Studies from the International Institute for Population Studies (sponsored by the United Nations) in 1979; and PhD in Sociology (with a minor in Economics) from Mississippi State University in 1984.

JESSICA M. SCARDINO

Jessica M. Scardino was an undergraduate student at The College of New Jersey. She graduated in 2014 with a major in sociology and minors in religious studies and women's and gender studies. Her scholarly interests include social and feminist theory, gender, and the philosophy of religion.

STAN WEEBER

Stan Weeber is Professor of Sociology. He earned his Ph.D in Sociology at the University of North Texas. In 2010, he received a Certificate in Social Justice Studies from the Oxford Roundtable at Oxford University.

His interests in sociology include political sociology, collective behavior, and sociology of technology. The author or editor of 21 books, his work has appeared in American Sociologist, Sociological Quarterly, the Journal of Public Management and Social Policy, the International Review of Modern Sociology, and several other journals. Dr. Weeber serves on the editorial board of numerous sociology journals. He teaches Introductory Sociology, Sociological Theory, Social Stratification, U.S. and World Extremism, Collective Behavior and Social Movements, and Science, Technology and Society at McNeese State University.

CPSIA information can be obtained
at www.ICGtesting.com
Printed in the USA
BVHW051943020619
549946BV00016B/310/P